with Excel

MONEYMATICS

Where Money and Mathematics Meet

Kendall Hunt
publishing company

BERNARD L. DILLARD

Cover image © Shutterstock.com

Kendall Hunt
publishing company

www.kendallhunt.com
Send all inquiries to:
4050 Westmark Drive
Dubuque, IA 52004-1840

ISBN 978-1-5249-4982-2

Published in the United States of America

To Genevee, my first finance instructor and
the first entrepreneur that I ever knew,
who is also my mother

Table of Contents

Preface

Finance textbooks in general possess a uniqueness all their own, especially given recent developments on the global economic landscape. Textbooks on personal finance, though, have lagged behind considerably from their traditional finance counterparts. The meltdown of 2008 shined the light on the greed of crooked executives on Wall Street for sure; however, very little has been discussed concerning the general public's role in the fiasco: a basic lack of financial literacy. Granted, a detailed understanding of securities and derivatives is not expected of the average citizen or college student, but basic knowledge concerning home ownership, mortgage types, and budgeting is. Sensing this lack, I sought out to do what I could within the confines of my own world of mathematics. On my campus, I developed two courses, one titled **The Mathematics of Personal Finance** and the other titled **The Mathematics of Financial Life Management**. Whereas the first course is a mathematically based honors course in personal finance, the second one is a similar version available to all students.

On one hand, what motivated the textbook is simple. While developing the courses, I struggled to find a book whose content matched exactly what I wanted to cover in the classroom. After perusing for months, I finally settled on one and had students purchase it. When the semester began, students faithfully brought the text to class, but I rarely ever used it. I generally posted my own notes online to which students referred. At almost every class meeting, I began by apologizing for not using the text for the current class session and began flipping through my trusted set of notes. After about my fourth apology, a student finally inquired, "Professor, why don't you just write your own book for the course? You already have all the notes for it." I must have stopped writing on the board mid-equation because her suggestion hit me like a ton of bricks. I stared at her and responded, "You know, you're absolutely right! Why don't I?" So I did. Thanks, Annie Jaffrey!

On a deeper level, this text emanates from the same source of origination as the course itself: my sincere concern for the level of basic financial illiteracy among college students. After watching Ferguson's *Inside Job*, I was discouraged by how the common person bore the brunt of fund mishandling. After I saw the documentary *Maxed Out*, I realized how shackled many people feel with respect to consumer credit and its effect on one's lifestyle. Finally, as I pass through campus on a daily basis, I notice very few mechanisms in place to educate the next generation about money management and its role in fostering a healthy spending and saving diet. This issue surely is not confined to the walls of my institution. Banks continue to seek college students at an alarming rate in an effort to make good on new prospects in the dash to award fresh credit. Students across the country and beyond have to use loans to finance their education and then learn how to balance their own personal finances once they graduate. It becomes an egregious disservice to them if academe drops the ball by not empowering them in some way to strengthen their financial selves in addition to preparing them in their more traditional academic majors. This textbook aims at fulfilling that vision of empowering students through basic financial knowledge.

To play on the whole financial theme throughout the text, "Chapters" are referred to as "Assets," which is a key term in finance that means anything owned having positive economic value. By no means is this another one of those *Personal Finance for Dummies* texts. It assumes a basic understanding of algebra. In fact, Asset One provides a quick review of algebraic fundamentals that are key to grasping basic ideas in personal finance. In Asset Two, the notion of interest is discussed and the many different ways it rears its head in the world of personal finance through several basic savings strategies.

Asset Three discusses the mathematics behind credit cards and owning a home. We address credit scores as well as paying back student loans. This is a particularly interesting topic for college students, as many of them have at least one credit card that they are learning to incorporate into their financial lives. We discuss benefits and challenges related to owning a home versus renting an apartment and the benefits and challenges of both.

Asset Four addresses the ideas behind investing for retirement. We distinguish between savings in this regard as opposed to the type of savings in Asset Two. We also address how significant it becomes for college students to start saving for retirement in their twenties as opposed to waiting until later.

Taxation and budgeting are key topics in Asset Five. How much of a budget should go toward housing? transportation? food? We challenge college students to learn how to perfect budgeting before landing that dream job. We also help students understand tax brackets and offer suggestions for putting themselves in the best position when tax time comes.

Assets Six and Seven shift to discussing personal finance within the context of statistics. Fortunately, this topic may be navigated without a deep understanding of algebra, but it has its own set of challenges and subtleties. Asset Six helps convey finance through the eyes of simple and multiple linear regressions, with special emphasis on the idea of correlation. Asset Seven discusses the notion of stocks and their relation to time series.

I intersperse some lessons in Excel to help students understand the benefits of using software to reinforce the theory they have learned. Being familiar with Excel poises college students to be a cut above their competition as they pursue careers and become entrepreneurs in their own right.

Finally, for those who wish to appreciate this textbook without subjecting themselves to the mathematics presented, we have placed articles on select financial topics at the end of each asset; each article is entitled *MoneyTalk*. One may read these articles without feeling any mathematical anxiety. There are no equations, no mathematics, and no stress. These articles simply provide a break from the academic slant of the text and allow for a bit of casual financial reading. Such topics explored in these articles include combatting identity theft, the plight of social security, and why having a will is a must.

My hope is that this textbook would serve as a spark in the lives of college students and pique their interest to pursue an understanding of the presented concepts even more. Through a deliberate and joint effort, students can be equipped with the weapons they need to combine their love for money with their passion for mathematics or what I call *Moneymatics*.

Disclaimer

No material in this textbook is interpreted as the author's providing financial, investment, legal, accounting, or any related type of advice. The author does not hold degrees or certification in finance. Information included in the textbook are for general purposes and may not be appropriate for your particular financial situation. There is no expectation that results discussed herein, good or bad, will be duplicated in your financial state of affairs. If expert advice is required, you should consult with a financial expert or certified public accountant. Although the author and publisher have done their best to prepare this textbook, they disclaim any liability concerning accuracy or entirety of included information.

Developing a Mathematically Based Course in Financial Literacy at the College Level

Several curricular innovations focus on financial literacy and personal finance for grades K-12. The Jump$tart Coalition for Personal Financial Literacy is among the leaders on the educational scene that promote the National Standards for Financial Literacy. Some curriculum on financial literacy exists for college students; however, the number of financial-literacy courses in departments on college campuses across America remains depressingly low.

Following is a guide for developing such a course in financial literacy on the college level. Mathematics departments or economics departments may offer it. Consistent with an understanding of this textbook, the course assumes sufficient proficiency in algebra. Units are based on material presented in this textbook, but instructors may tweak according to their liking. The course assumes a 15-week semester, in which four hours per week are dedicated for the course (ideally two hours per meeting, two days a week). Two exams and a cumulative final exam are suggested. A more advanced course may incorporate course projects, in which students research a topic in finance and present findings via PowerPoint or Prezi to the class. For a course project also, students may read separate books on a topic in finance and write a response paper, analyzing the book's strengths and shortcomings.

A Course Proposal

Suggested Course Title	The Mathematics of Personal Finance
Prerequisite	Algebra proficiency
Suggested Course Credits	4 hours per week; 3 credits (2 hours lecture, 2 hours lab)

Course Rationale

Basic literacy in personal finance remains a constant challenge for today's college student. Without adequate knowledge in this respect, students run the risk of damaging their financial well-being and destroying their financial health. This could haunt them long after graduating from college. Recent assessment conducted by the Organization for Economic Cooperation and Development revealed that students in the United States scored below the average of the 18 countries evaluated; results also exposed below-average rankings for the United States as they relate to the percentage of students who have a baseline level of competence regarding personal finances. All relevant disciplines, including mathematics, have a role and responsibility to address this dire reality in their own unique style.

Course Description

Primarily, this course is designed to strengthen students' mathematical core using algebraically based techniques associated with topics in personal finance. Further, students use computer software to make practical sense of financially based mathematical formulas and to analyze related results visually through graphs and charts. Finally, the aim of the course is to increase students' baseline competence in select areas of personal finance. Although some of the topics in the course have been on the financial scene for a long time (e.g., interest, annuities, budgeting), other areas of exploration serve as fairly new developments on the financial landscape (e.g., PEG ratios, forecasting methods for time series). Using advanced topics in mathematics and statistics, students gain primary insight into select topics in personal finance by performing comparative analyses and by scrutinizing software results. Several of these mathematical topics include annuity analysis, regression analysis, and time series. Through discussing articles, watching relevant videos, and listening to guest speakers, students are additionally exposed to particulars that fortify their understanding of salient topics in personal finance.

Catalog Description

Uses advanced mathematical and statistical techniques to analyze select topics in personal finance. Includes exploration into annuity analysis, regression methods, and time series analysis. Application areas involve managing credit cards, paying back student loans, and choosing a stock. Uses computers to analyze and interpret financially based data.

Course Objectives

Upon completion of this course, students will be able to:

- Distinguish between interest types used for various kinds of savings accounts
- Compare the effects of various interest rates on retirement accounts, mortgages, and credit cards

- Complete a budget form based on personal financial situations
- Discuss in writing pros and cons associated with renting versus buying property
- Show savings obtained from different credit scores for the same purchase
- Determine how much in federal and state taxes are owed in simple tax situations
- Demonstrate techniques associated with simple linear regression techniques using personal finance data
- Define what a stock is and master how to choose a stock based on PEG ratios
- Predict stock prices and smooth series using the latest in time series methods

Course Textbook

Dillard, Bernard L. 2018. *Moneymatics: Where Money and Mathematics Meet*. Dubuque, IA: Kendall Hunt.

Suggested Course Assessment

The final course grade may be determined as follows:

1. **Labs and In-Class Assignments** (20%). Excel exercises and basic problem sets are to be turned in during class. No makeup chance is suggested. This serves as basic class participation.
2. **Quizzes** (15%). Four quizzes are suggested with the lowest quiz grade dropped. Quizzes should be no longer than 25 minutes.
3. **Exam 1** (20%). This two-hour exam is based on Unit 1 through Unit 9 (partial). The exam should evaluate mathematical proficiency as well as material discussed in articles and in videos.
4. **Exam 2** (20%). This two-hour exam is based on Unit 9 (partial) through Unit 15. The exam should evaluate mathematical proficiency as well as material discussed in articles and in videos.
5. **Final Exam** (25%). This is an exam that *must* cover material from all Units.

Learning Units of Study

(Note: Instructors are strongly advised to contact financial-literacy foundations to have volunteer guest speakers take the lead on Unit 10. A basic online search should reveal volunteer agencies in your area that provide basic financial-literacy education to colleges and universities.)

Unit 1 Money: Then and Now — 1 hour

This serves as the opening unit for the course. The unit introduces the notion of money and provides a working definition for money. The unit focuses on a brief history of money and how bartering existed before banknotes became the exchange standard. Emphasis is placed on the progression of the currency form from bartering to representative money to metal coins to fiat money. The unit addresses when the first paper money was issued in the United States. Key terms to discuss are as follows: currency, money, barter, and representative money.

- *Recommended Video on the History of Money*
  Outlearn on YouTube. "The History of Money (combined)." YouTube video. YouTube, December 1, 2015. Accessed August 15, 2016. https://goo.gl/Zr4dDl.

Unit 2 Interest and Savings 2 hours

This unit focuses on the basic notion of interest. Instructors should have students read in class an article on interest and three key savings programs. Students are expected to highlight notable differences between the regular savings account, the certificate of deposit (CD), and the money market account (MMA). Instructors should introduce what Federal Deposit Insurance Corporation (FDIC) means and discuss its significance in relation to savings accounts. Instructors should supplement the discussion with a video that summarizes key points. Several articles and videos exist; however, some acceptable suggestions follow:

- *Recommended Article on Interest and the Three Savings Instruments*
  Taylor, Joe. "Compare Savings Accounts, Money Market Accounts, and CDs." *MoneyRates.com*. Accessed August 7, 2016. http://goo.gl/7PmJZJ.
- *Recommended Video on Savings Accounts, CDs, and MMAs*
  Personal Finance in the Elementary Grades. "4.2 Savings Accounts." YouTube video. YouTube, August 15, 2014. Accessed August 7, 2016. https://goo.gl/B3uHlW.

Unit 3 Linear Equations and Exponential Functions 2 hours

This unit introduces linear equations. Students demonstrate how to find the equation of a line, given two points. Only examples within the context of personal finance should be used (e.g., hours worked as x and income received as y). Students master the concept of slope and y-intercept and demonstrate how to graph the line using only those two values. Students work primarily with the slope–intercept form of the line.

The unit transitions to a discussion of exponential equations. Examples to motivate exponential functions is the historic one in which the student saves a penny and then doubles it each day and continues the pattern for 30 days (two cents, four cents, eight cents, etc.), giving note to how much money has been saved by the end of the month. Students write conceptual differences between linear equation and exponential functions. Students master finding the base and the coefficient for exponential functions. Students graph exponential functions and compare to graph of linear equations over time, noting visual differences.

Unit 4 Simple and Compound Interest 4 hours

This unit explores the mathematics behind simple and compound interest. The unit stresses the major difference between simple and compound interest. Students show parallels between the formula for simple interest and linear equations; students also show parallels between the formula for compound interest and exponential equations. Students master how to solve iteratively for each variable in both interest formulas. Students learn how to apply properties of logarithms. Students will be able to define the following key terms: interest, principal, and interest rate.

Students work in Excel to show how money grows over time in simple and compound interest with the same initial deposit, interest rate, and time. When programming, students discover how to exploit absolute and relative cell range references. Students graph these results in Excel, observing which interest type generally outperforms the other over time. Students use Excel to write formulas that solve for each variable in terms of the others for the two interest types.

Unit 5 Credit and the Credit Score — 2 hours

This unit is dedicated to discussing credit and its role in personal finance. Instructors introduce the term *credit* and the idea of the credit score. To motivate the notion, the credit score and one's personal finance history are discussed in relation to a college student's grade point average (GPA) and their academic past. Students research what Fair Isaac Corporation (FICO) stands for. They must be able to state and discuss in writing the five elements of a FICO credit score and what percentage each element contributes to the score. Instructors define what a credit card is and tie to the discussion of interest from the previous unit. Students may read about the five elements in the suggested textbook. Otherwise, instructors find a comprehensive article discussing elements. Students should be encouraged to visit sites like www.creditkarma.com to locate their credit score for free. Students should be advised that they will have to enter their social security number but should not enter any credit card information to secure score. Implications of the credit score will be addressed in a future unit. Key terms to discuss are the following: minimum payment, credit card perk, annual fee, due date, and penalty. A recommended video about credit scores follows.

- *Recommended Video on the Credit Score and Its 5 Elements*
  Federal Reserve Bank of St. Louis. "Understanding How a FICO Credit Score is Determined." YouTube video. YouTube, January 24, 2015. Accessed May 6, 2017. https://goo.gl/tUOjN4.

Unit 6 Present Value of an Annuity: Credit Cards — 5 hours

This unit introduces mathematical content that provides the backdrop for an understanding of credit cards. Instructors define annuity and introduce the formula for the present value of an annuity. Instructors conceptually distinguish between this formula and savings formulas introduced in Unit 4. Using the calculator, students practice solving iteratively for each variable in the equation, especially solving for time using logarithmic properties. Key terms to discuss are the following: annuity, present value of an annuity, and compounding period.

This unit further explores scenarios involving making the minimum monthly payment for credit card bills versus paying more than the minimum per payment. Students use the present value formula to compare how much time is saved in paying off a credit card balance when the same minimum payment is made each month versus when the same more-than-minimum amount is paid per month. Instructors discuss and show examples related to possible traps associated with credit cards. Instructors also discuss how these concepts may be used to the consumer's advantage through discipline. The following key terms are discussed: credit card perk, balance transfer, teaser rate, and deferred interest.

The Excel exercise in this unit should give students practice showing the paying down of a credit card each month making minimum payments. Instructors should also make students use Excel to show how doubling the payment affects time it takes to pay the credit card balance off. Students should also be able to determine in Excel whether it saves them more money to transfer a balance from one card to the next.

- *Recommended Video on Credit Cards*
  Keen, Trevor. "FUNNY MONEY - Get it on Credit." YouTube video. YouTube, May 16, 2013. Accessed May 6, 2017. https://goo.gl/IEXZNl.

Unit 7 Present Value of an Annuity: Student Loans — 3 hours

This unit continues discussion of the present value of an annuity as applied to student loans. This unit is more personalized with students since most will probably have current student loans. Students verbalize the major difference between subsidized/unsubsidized loans and consolidated loans (i.e., interest rate based on credit score or not). If students have student loans, they must research the interest rate. Students calculate interest on subsidized student loans, assuming the six-month grace period has ended after their graduation. Instructors introduce the notion of loan consolidation, discussing pros and cons associated with it. Students determine mathematically whether it makes sense to consolidate several loans into one, given a set time to pay it off, certain interest rates, and origination fees tied to consolidation. That is, students calculate the total interest saved for payoff of a consolidated loan and compare to total interest saved for payoff of separate student and private loans. The unit presents problems for which loan consolidation mathematically makes sense and when it does not. Special emphasis explores situations when the time-to-loan payoff for current separate loans is shorter than the time to payoff for the consolidated loan even though the latter may promise a lower interest rate. Key terms to explore are the following: subsidized loan, unsubsidized loan, loan consolidation, origination fee, and loan default.

- *MANDATORY Video to Watch on Student Loans and Credit*
  iGrad. "Financial Literacy in College | Financial Literacy Video." YouTube video. YouTube, December 16, 2011. Accessed August 14, 2016. https://goo.gl/G93tjN.

Unit 8 Renting versus Buying — 2 hours

This unit explores renting and owning property. The purpose of this model is for students to use class time to research and report to fellow students the pros and cons associated with both ideas. This unit stresses no mathematical techniques proper but is dedicated to strengthening students' ability to work together, gather data, and present results. The instructor does *not* teach this topic in the typical lecture format. Students are expected to take the lead. Students learn how to work in groups within time constraints to locate, synthesize, analyze, and present information without instructors' assistance. In groups, students may use any creative means possible to present findings (e.g., presentation at the board, skits). The unit concludes with a showing of a comprehensive video clip to summarize pros and cons, which may address material that students overlooked. One possible video suggestion follows.

- *Recommended Video on Renting versus Buying*
  Bank of America. "Is Buying a Home Right for You?" Online video clip. *Better Money Habits*. Bank of America Corporation in Partnership with Khan Academy. Accessed August 10, 2016. https://goo.gl/JtJ1rd.

Unit 9 Present Value of an Annuity: Mortgages 6 hours

This unit works through the present value of annuity formula applied to mortgages. One aim of this unit is to use mathematics to show comparatively how much money students save on the purchase of the same home but for different interest rates. The notion of the credit score is reintroduced from a perspective of securing a lower interest rate for a higher score. Students calculate the monthly payments for the higher interest rate (lower credit score) and the lower interest rate (higher credit score). Students show the amount of interest paid back in both scenarios and the total amount of interest saved overall, thus revealing the value of having a high credit score. Another aim of this unit is to use mathematics to show comparatively the value of financing a mortgage for a shorter period of time. Students use the formula to show how much is saved in interest when a mortgage is financed for one time period compared to a shorter period of time. Finding the monthly payments associated with both, students calculate the amount of interest paid in each scenario.

This unit then discusses amortization schedules. Students calculate each of the four columns, showing the paying-down effect of loan repayment. Students also learn how to calculate columns when a down payment is involved. Key terms to address in this unit are: fixed, variable, down payment, and amortization schedule.

In Excel, students practice creating a spreadsheet table solving for monthly mortgage payments when the interest rate and time varies. Students should also create amortization schedules in Excel, showing the remaining mortgage balance as it dwindles to zero.

Unit 10 Budgeting 2 hours

This unit addresses budgeting and managing money. Coverage includes discussion of percentage recommendations for budget components (e.g., 30% for housing), according to the College Board. Students practice completing a budget and applying the recommended percentages, assuming an initial dollar amount. Hence, this unit helps students understand percentages clearer. Students understand budgets from the perspective of the time element and the budget's goal. Instructors develop a list on the board that students construct, which highlights daily steps students may take to decrease spending in a budget (e.g., walk instead of catching a cab for five blocks). Students are exposed to paper-and-pencil budget sheets as well as free, modern-day budget programs found online and on mobile apps. Students are encouraged to use budget sheets on a regular basis. Instructors may assign reading in addition to coverage in textbook and may incorporate the watching of a video clip on budgeting. Key terms in budget discussion include the following: need, want, budget, percent, projected budget, and actual budget.

- *Recommended Article on Budgeting*
  "Budgeting 101." *BestColleges.com*. Accessed August 10, 2016. http://goo.gl/xbM2qE.
- *Recommended Video on Budgeting*
  Mountain America Credit Union. "Budgeting for College and School Activities." YouTube video. YouTube, October 7, 2015. Accessed August 10, 2016. https://goo.gl/7xdk0p.

Unit 11 My Paycheck and Basic Taxes 2 hours

(Instructors should note that **no** information in this unit should be used as tax advice to students. Students should seek a certified public accountant for professional tax advisement.)

Students observe a sample pay stub and notice key deductions on it. Students calculate percentages on a paycheck that are deducted for Medicare benefits and also for social security. Students verify these percentage deductions on a reputable website. Students use mathematics to calculate how much in federal and state taxes is owed when the standard deduction is used. With the calculator, students use current federal schedules and agreed-upon state schedules to accomplish the task.

The unit further discusses taxes owed after basic pretax deductions and basic itemized deductions. Using an online tax calculator (such as http://goo.gl/cfqb2m or any other reputable one), students calculate how much is owed in taxes, given certain basic financial data provided by the instructor. Students observe how much is saved in taxes owed when pretax deductions and/or itemized deductions are considered. Students become familiar with the following terms: taxes, gross pay, net pay, Federal Insurance Contributions Act (FICA), deduction, pretax deduction, and itemized deduction.

Unit 12 Future Value of an Annuity: Retirement — 6 hours

This unit introduces retirement and the future value of an annuity. Instructors begin with a discussion of retirement in general. Instructors revisit the notion of interest and discuss how it can be used positively for consumers as opposed to negatively in the case of credit cards and student loans. Students are introduced to the following key terms: retirement, individual retirement account (IRA), traditional IRA, Roth IRA, and the time value of money.

Students discover the conceptual difference between the future value of an annuity and the present value of an annuity with respect to a "lump sum." The unit introduces the formula used in future-value problems and stresses how to solve for each variable in terms of the other variables. Specific emphasis is placed on algebraic properties, including use of the logarithm. The unit uses mathematics to comparatively show how much is in a retirement account when only the time variable changes and even when the amount invested is considerably less for the longer investment period. Instructors highlight how much more money is in the account when one starts contributing to the account at different ages. Students calculate how much interest accrues to the account in all scenarios. Finally, students use mathematics to calculate the age at which they would need to start investing to reach their financial retirement goals, solving for the time variable in the formula.

The Excel exercise simulates one's retirement account as it is drawn down during retirement. Starting with a lump sum of students' choosing and the amount of yearly income required, the account should be drawn down for 35 years with students making adjustments based on the target retirement period.

Unit 13 Stocks and Shares — 4 hours

This unit discusses stocks, shares, and basic related concepts. Students distinguish between a stock and a share. Students understand the purpose behind stocks and how investment savings can increase (or decrease) at a quicker rate with stocks when compared to other financial savings instruments. Risk tolerance is introduced, along with the concepts of the retirement portfolio and diversification (eggs-in-more-than-one-basket scenario). With respect to diversification, instructors show charts or graphs of historical examples of a portfolio's behavior when only stocks are invested (one basket) versus stocks and mutual funds (two baskets) versus stocks and mutual funds and bonds (three baskets). Students discover how the portfolio's value increases more (generally) in the latter case. To illustrate the idea of stocks' ability to lose money briefly but gain more money over time, instructors may show a zoomed-in decreasing trend of a certain time period of a retirement portfolio but overall increasing trend of the same portfolio when zooming out. The unit introduces Vanguard's suggested asset percentage allocations by age. Using them, students use mathematics to calculate how much of their retirement funds should be invested into separate allocation categories. Key terms to define are as follows: stock, share, ticker symbol (stock symbol), risk tolerance, retirement portfolio, and diversification.

The unit transitions into discussing one method for choosing a stock to invest in. The instructor strategically chooses four stocks to illustrate this method. Instructors motivate the idea by discussing growth capacity. Students are introduced to the PEG ratio as the stock-choosing strategy. The instructor goes through each phase of arriving at the PEG ratio, highlighting which of the four stocks are the "best" to choose at different phases of the process. That is, students observe which stock is the best when only considering price per share (PPS). Students calculate the price-to-earnings (P/E) ratio of chosen stocks, observing which stock now is the "best," discussing earnings per share (EPS) at this phase. Finally, students calculate the PEG ratio and observe which of the stocks is the "best" at this phase. An ideal choice of a stock when teaching this topic is one that has the highest PPS but has a PEG ratio closer to zero. Using this mathematical process, students discover that just because a stock is expensive does not mean it is not the best one to buy. Students discuss in writing the meaning behind different PEG ratio values and their implications for a stock's predicted growth. Key terms are as follows: growth capacity, price per share, earnings per share, P/E ratio, and PEG ratio.

Unit 14 Stocks and Time Series — 5 hours

This unit explores stocks in relation to time series. The concept of time series is defined, along with the four components that comprise a time series. Students demonstrate how to smooth a time series using the simple moving average (SMA) and the exponential weighted moving average (EWMA). They verbalize differences between both conceptually. Students also demonstrate how to predict stock prices one time period outside of the given data range of the stock's prices using EWMA techniques. Students further use Excel regression techniques to predict a stock's value one time period outside of the stock price's data range. Using the *Data Analysis ToolPak*, students show how to adjust the explanatory-variable column to make regression techniques meaningful when using time series. Students write interpretations for the slope and y-intercept within the context of time series. Students forecast a stock's value one time period outside of the data range using the regression line. Students model how to plot time series of original data, SMA values, and EWMA values on the same plot.

Students use Excel to practice smoothing and plotting time series. Students are given an appropriate set of financial data (e.g., closing stock values for the Dow Jones Industrial Average) and comment on trend and seasonal components. They create columns for an SMA and an EWMA and plot original series and the other two on the same plot. They also perform a regression on the original data after adjusting explanatory column and write the equation for the regression line, interpreting meanings of the slope and y-intercept. They predict one time period outside of the given range.

Unit 15 Simple Linear Regression — 5 hours

This unit introduces simple linear regression. Instructors review basic concepts of a line and lead into discussion of the least-squares regression line, highlighting the meaning behind bivariate data. Explanatory (independent) and response (dependent) variables are examined. When applied to a problem, examples of both variables are only discussed within the context of personal finance (e.g., number of credit cards owned as explanatory and credit score as response). Students learn how to construct scatterplots and understand how to find and draw the regression line best fitting the data. In the process, students define slope and y-intercept and solve for both by hand using appropriate formulas. Students must write the interpretation for the meanings of the slope and y-intercept within the context of the financial world of the problem. Students predict the response variable given a value for the explanatory variable. Students also describe why the least-squares regression line is called such. Further, students define correlation coefficient and coefficient of determination; they write the interpretation for the meanings of both within the financial context.

Excel tests students' ability to construct formulas to find the slope and y-intercept in simple linear regression. Students use the formulas for both as starting points and build numerators and denominators through their programming skills. Students also create a scatterplot from the data and superimpose the regression line on the same graph, placing the equation as well as the coefficient of determination on it. Using the *Data Analysis ToolPak*, students show how Excel renders results. Students locate slope, y-intercept, correlation coefficient, and coefficient of determination on Excel results.

Learning Units of Study and Suggested Hours		
Week	**Unit**	**Hours**
1	Course Introduction; Units 1 and 2	4
2	Units 3 and 4	4
3	Units 4 (cont.) and Unit 5	4
4	Unit 6	4
5	Units 6 (cont.) and 7	4
6	Unit 8 and ***Exam 1***	4
7	Unit 9	4
8	Units 9 (cont.) and 10	4
9	Units 11 and 12	4
10	Unit 12 (cont.)	4
11	Unit 13	4
12	Unit 14	4
13	Units 14 (cont.) and 15 and ***Exam 2***	4
14	Unit 15 (cont.)	4
15	Review for Final Exam and ***Final Exam***	4
	Total hours	60

About the Author

BERNARD L. DILLARD is an associate professor of mathematics at Fashion Institute of Technology in New York City. He enjoys teaching a variety of courses, including Statistical Analysis, Data Analysis for Business Applications, and The Mathematics of Personal Finance. He is the coauthor of *Elementary Statistics (4th edition)*, also published by Kendall Hunt. Away from mathematics, Bernard enjoys acting, modeling, traveling, and watching independent films.

Asset One

Algebra in a Flash: A Review

Chapter Outline

Men are liars. We'll lie about lying if we have to.
I'm an algebra liar. I figure two good lies make a positive.

Tim Allen

1.1 Linear Equations

Space in this review chapter does not permit a thorough review of all algebraic concepts. The exercises at the end of the chapter, however, test students' comprehension of general ideas covered in most algebra classes. Students should seek out tutorial assistance for any deficiencies that may exist as they relate to these exercises. This chapter only reinforces certain algebraic concepts that relate specifically to topics explored in later chapters. We only provide a quick review of material related to linear and exponential functions.

Chief to understanding basic notions concerning personal finance is that of the line. Linear equations provide the fundamental framework needed to grasp most things financial. The mathematical model of a line helps to explore the relationship between two variables, which have unique and special properties.

1.1.1 The Slope

Example 1.1 Suppose Cassie is promised by her parents that she will receive $450 for graduating from high school. In addition, she will receive $40 for each acceptance letter she receives from the colleges to which she applies. How much does Cassie receive if she graduates from high school and receives four acceptance letters?

As we explore the earlier example, we note that if she receives no acceptance letters, we intuitively see that Cassie will receive $450 as long as she finishes high school. If she receives one acceptance letter, she will receive $490. And so forth. In table form, it seems as though we have the following, which shows the relationship of college acceptance letters and how much Cassie receives based on her parents' promise:

TABLE 1.1 Cassie's Acceptance Letters vs. Cassie's Money Earned from Parents

Number of Possible College Acceptance Letters Cassie Receives	How Much Cassie Possibly Receives From Parents
0	$450
1	$490
2	$530
3	$570

In other words, in Table 1.1, we can represent Cassie's acceptance letters and money that she receives as (x, y) ordered pairs. In her case, we have four sets of ordered pairs: (0, $450), (1, $490),

(2, \$530), and (3, \$570). In a nutshell, the y variable refers to the variable that is affected by the x variable. Many refer to the y variable as the response variable. Since Cassie's money depends on how many acceptance letters she receives, the y variable is the column referring to how much she receives, while the x variable is the column referring to how many acceptance letters she receives. We can probably guess how much Cassie would receive for four acceptance letters without analyzing the situation too deeply. However, we explore a few ideas before answering.

We note that from no acceptance letters to one acceptance letter, Cassie's reward goes from \$450 to \$490. From one to two, her reward goes from \$490 to \$530. From no acceptance letters to two, her reward goes from \$450 to \$530. When we explore this relationship between acceptance letters and reward received, we have a relationship that is rather peculiar.

When we look at the ratio of the difference in any two of her rewards and the corresponding difference of acceptance letters, we make an interesting observation. We see that for no acceptance letters and one acceptance letter, we use the first two (x, y) points, namely (0, \$450) and (1, \$490) to get:

$$\frac{\$490 - \$450}{1\text{ letter} - 0\text{ letters}} = \frac{\$40}{1\text{ letter}}$$

For two letters and three letters, we use (2, \$530) and (3, \$570) to get:

$$\frac{\$570 - \$530}{3\text{ letters} - 2\text{ letters}} = \frac{\$40}{1\text{ letter}}$$

Even if we observe this same ratio for one letter and three letters, we use (1, \$490) and (3, \$570) to get:

$$\frac{\$570 - \$490}{3\text{ letters} - 1\text{ letter}} = \frac{\$80}{2\text{ letters}} = \frac{\$40}{1\text{ letter}}$$

In each case, we see that the ratio is the same, or $\frac{\$40}{1\text{ letter}}$. When we discuss this ratio of differences between the amount of money Cassie receives and her acceptance letters, we are speaking of the idea of **slope**, which is denoted by $\boldsymbol{m}$.

Definition

The **slope (*m*)** *refers to the change in the y variable divided by the corresponding change in the x variable. Or, we say:*

$$m = \frac{y_2 - y_1}{x_2 - x_1} = \frac{y_1 - y_2}{x_1 - x_2} = \frac{\Delta y}{\Delta x}$$

Hence, we say that the slope exploits the ratio between the change in y values divided by the change in x values. The Greek symbol delta, Δ, simply means change or difference. In the definition, note that it does not matter which y value is subtracted first as long as the corresponding x value is subtracted in the same order. Applying this, for example, the definition shows:

$$m = \frac{\$570 - \$490}{3\text{ letters} - 1\text{ letter}} = \frac{\$490 - \$570}{1\text{ letter} - 3\text{ letters}} = \frac{\$40}{1\text{ letter}}$$

Essentially, $m = \frac{\$40}{1\text{ letter}}$ means that for every one acceptance letter that Cassie receives, the amount she receives from her parents increases by \$40. This notion of slope is key to understanding the basic essence of a line.

Solution 1.1 According to the values in Table 1.1, we can figure out how much Cassie's parents owe her for four acceptance letters. The simple notion of slope just means we can add \$40 to the amount she receives for three letters. Since she receives \$570 for three letters, she would receive \$570 + \$40 for four letters or \$610.

1.1.2 Slope–Intercept Form of the Line

In the previous section, we observe that the slope is the same, regardless of which two pairings we observe. In all three cases, the value of m is the same. Note that for all of these ordered pairs, we have a slope that is the same $\left(m = \frac{\$40}{1\text{ letter}}\right)$. When all of the values of m are the same (or constant) for all the x and y pairings, we say the data represents the model for a **line**.

Definition

A **line** *characterizes a relationship between two variables such that the slope is the same (or constant) for all ordered pairs (x, y). The most common form of a line is the slope-intercept form, whose equation is given by:*

$$y = mx + b, \qquad \textbf{Equation 1.1}$$

where m is the slope and b is the y-intercept.

Visually, we represent Cassie's scenario by simply plotting these four sets of ordered pairs and connecting the dots. We place the number of acceptance letters she receives on the horizontal (x) axis while placing the amount of money she receives on the vertical (y) axis. We then plot the four sets of ordered pairs on the normal Cartesian plane and observe the result, as shown in Figure 1.1.

Notice that the line intersects the y axis at the value of 450. The point at which the line crosses this y axis is logically referred to as the y-intercept and is given by, in this specific case, (0, \$450). In Cassie's scenario, this means that our equation of the line would be given by:

$$y = 40x + 450$$

We simply insert the value of 40 for the slope (m), which we found earlier, and we insert the value of 450 for the value of the y-intercept (b).

This form of the line helps us to determine values of y for given values of x, and vice versa. For example, in the example presented earlier in this chapter, we wanted to know how much money

Cassie would receive for four acceptance letters. We can solve as we did before or simply use our equation to help us find the answer. Placing the value of 4 in place of x, we have:

$$\begin{aligned} y &= 40x + 450 \\ &= 40(4) + 450 \\ &= 160 + 450 \\ &= 610 \end{aligned}$$

So, using the mathematical equation of the line, we get the same results of \$610 that Cassie is due if she receives four acceptance letters.

The line is key to understanding basic concepts concerning personal finance, as we will see later.

1.1.3 The Graph of the Line

Of course, we can translate the mathematics equation of a line to its graph. The visual representation of the line shows that as we go from one x value to the next, the corresponding y value increases at the same rate. For example, according to Figure 1.1, we see that as the x value goes from zero to one, the corresponding y value goes from \$450 to \$490 (increase of \$40). As the x value goes from one to two, the y value goes from \$490 to \$530 (increase of \$40). This is what we mean when we say the value of the slope (m) is constant. In this case of the line, the slope increases in increments of \$40.

To the naked eye, a line may appear straight. However, if one of the slopes between any two of the points differs from any other slope between two of the other points, then the result is no line.

One way to plot the line when we only have the slope-intercept form is pretty simple. We begin by plotting the y-intercept, which is (0, \$450) in this case. Figure 1.1 shows this point clearly. From the y-intercept, we use the value of the slope to determine where the next point should be placed on the graph. From the y-intercept, we move one unit to the right (which represents the denominator of the slope) and then \$40 up. This means that we land at the new point (1, \$490), which is another point we see in Figure 1.1. We can continue this process from each new plotted point, but we realize that one iteration should suffice. From these two points—(0, \$450) and (1, \$490)—we are able to connect the points to draw the line. In this instance, we label each point on the graph, but this is not ordinarily done in practice.

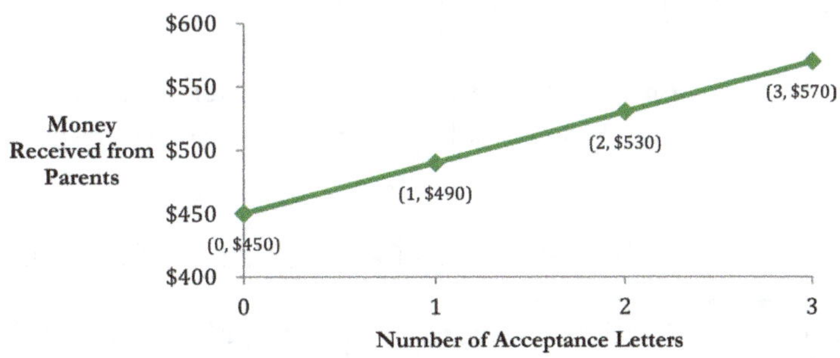

FIGURE 1.1 **Cassie's Acceptance Letters vs. Her Money Earned from Parents**

Example 1.2 Prove that (3, 7), (−2, 2), and (1, 5) are on the same line, and graph the line.

Solution 1.2 We prove this by showing that the slopes are the same for each of the pairs:

$$\text{Pair one, } (3,7) \text{ and } (-2,2)\text{: } m = \frac{2-7}{-2-3} = \frac{-5}{-5} = 1.$$

$$\text{Pair two, } (-2,2) \text{ and } (1,5)\text{: } m = \frac{5-2}{1-(-2)} = \frac{3}{3} = 1.$$

$$\text{Pair three, } (3,7) \text{ and } (1,5)\text{: } m = \frac{5-7}{1-3} = \frac{-2}{-2} = 1.$$

Since the slopes are the same ($m = 1$) for all pairs, then we conclude that all three points are on the same line.

Graph of the Line:

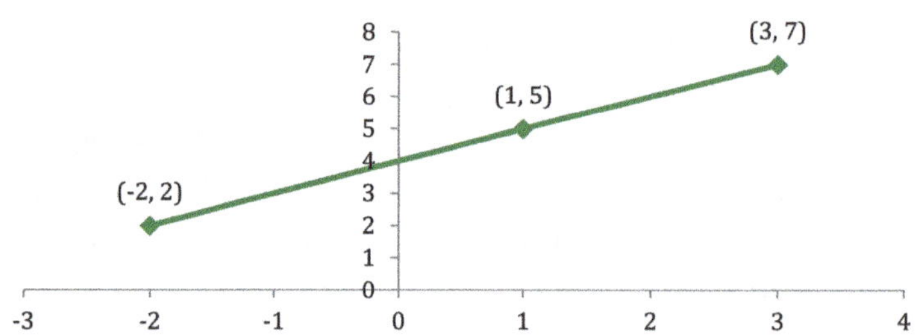

1.2 Exponential Equations

In addition to the idea of the line, the notion of the exponential function is key to grasping certain aspects of personal finance. In the case of the line, we saw that as the value x increases, the value of y increases (or decreases) at a constant rate. With exponential functions, we will see that as x increases, the value of y increases (or decreases) at a rate that is *not* constant.

1.2.1 A New Rewards System

For teaching purposes, we examine a similar example to the earlier one concerning Cassie's acceptance letters and money she earns. We put forth an example and discuss the solution to it in Section 1.2.3.

Example 1.3 Suppose Cassie is promised financial reward by her parents according to the following, as shown in the table. How much does Cassie receives if she receives four acceptance letters?

TABLE 1.2 New Monetary Reward Criteria for Cassie

Number of Possible College Acceptance Letters Cassie Receives	How Much Cassie Possibly Receives From Parents
0	$100
1	$200

Number of Possible College Acceptance Letters Cassie Receives	How Much Cassie Possibly Receives From Parents
2	$400
3	$800

In this case, notice that Cassie's parents reward her more than before for each additional acceptance letter she receives. We witness that, for every additional acceptance letter Cassie receives, her parents seem to double the previous amount. This is, in fact, true. The growth of Cassie's reward does not increase at a constant rate ($100 to $200 to $300). As the number of her acceptance letters increases, her reward seems to increase at a faster rate than in the previous example.

We even see that, in the previous example (Table 1.1), she receives more money for her acceptance letters when she has no letters, one letter, and two letters. When she receives three acceptance letters, however, she begins to receive more money based on figures in the current example (Table 1.2).

1.2.2 The Equation and Some Exponent Properties

The values in Table 1.2 describe a mathematical relationship for an **exponential equation**.

Definition

An **exponential equation** *is an equation in which a variable in the expression occurs in the exponent position. It is generally written in the form of:*

$$y = c \times a^x, \qquad \textbf{Equation 1.2}$$

where c is the coefficient and a is the base.

We recall that the role of an exponential function goes hand in hand with that of multiplication. When we have an expression raised to an exponent (or power), we multiply the base by itself as many times as the power requires. For example, the expression 3^4 does not mean "three times four." Instead, we interpret it as multiplying the value of three by itself four times, or:

$$3^4 = 3 \times 3 \times 3 \times 3 = 81.$$

We will see in future assets ("chapters") just how important the notion of exponential equations is to grasping significant concepts with respect to personal finance. However, it is advisable that students take a moment to refresh their comprehension concerning relevant properties of exponents. We present a few:

Properties of Exponents

Property 1.1 $\quad a^m \times a^n = a^{m+n}$

Property 1.2 $\quad \dfrac{a^m}{a^n} = a^{m-n}$

Property 1.3 $\left(a^m\right)^n = a^{m \cdot n}$

Property 1.4 $(ab)^m = a^m \times b^m$

Property 1.5 $\left(\frac{a}{b}\right)^m = \frac{a^m}{b^m}$

Property 1.6 $a^{-m} = \frac{1}{a^m}$

Property 1.7 $a^0 = 1$

We encourage students to grapple with the problems at the end of the chapter to get more practice and experience working with these properties of exponents. It is not wasted time to review these basics before delving into the deeper realm of select personal finance topics.

1.2.3 A Closer Look at the Equation

We return to the example at the beginning of this section. As we modeled the values in Table 1.1 according to the laws of a linear equation, we see that we can model the values in Table 1.2 according to the laws of an exponential equation. Cassie's reward in this new scenario appears to summarize the mathematical relationship as follows:

$$y = 100 \times 2^x$$

For example, for no acceptance letters (or $x = 0$), we have:

$$\begin{aligned} y &= 100 \times 2^0 \\ &= 100 \times 1 \\ &= 100 \end{aligned}$$

In the case in which Cassie receives one acceptance letter, we have:

$$\begin{aligned} y &= 100 \times 2^1 \\ &= 100 \times 2 \\ &= 200 \end{aligned}$$

Solution 1.3 We can continue in the same pattern to find out how much she makes if she receives four acceptance letters, or:

$$\begin{aligned} y &= 100 \times 2^4 \\ &= 100 \times 16 \\ &= 1600 \end{aligned}$$

Hence, in this mathematical model, Cassie receives \$1600 for four acceptance letters as opposed to only \$610 according to the linear model. Cassie would surely prefer to be rewarded according the exponential equation model.

In this equation, we can easily identify the value for the coefficient (c) and for the base (a). When we compare this equation with that of the general form of the exponential equation provided in the definition, we see that the value for the coefficient (c) must be 100 while the value for the base (a) must be two. We notice that the value of a is only that part of the exponential equation that is raised to the power. We present some problems at the end of the chapter, which give students practice with identifying the values of the coefficients and the base in various exponential equations.

1.2.4 The Slope

As we did with the line, we discover that we can find the different slopes of the values in Table 1.2. For the line, we discovered that all of the slopes (m) were equal, regardless of which two ordered pairs we considered. In the case of exponential equations, we see if the same result is true. We observe the slopes for different ordered pairs from Table 1.2.

We consider the first two ordered pairs and find the slope. These ordered pairs are (0, \$100) and (1, \$200). The slope (here as m_1) using these two points is as follows:

$$m_1 = \frac{200 - 100}{1 - 0} = \frac{100}{1} = 100$$

We consider the last two ordered pairs and find the slope. These ordered pairs are (2, \$400) and (3, \$800). The slope (which we denote as m_2) using these two points is as follows:

$$m_2 = \frac{800 - 400}{3 - 2} = \frac{400}{1} = 400$$

So we note that:

$$m_1 = 100 \neq 400 = m_2$$

In other words, in the case of exponential functions, it is not the case that the slopes are constant for all points.

1.2.5 Graphing Exponential Functions

Using information from Table 1.2, we can construct the corresponding graph. We note how this graph differs from that of the line:

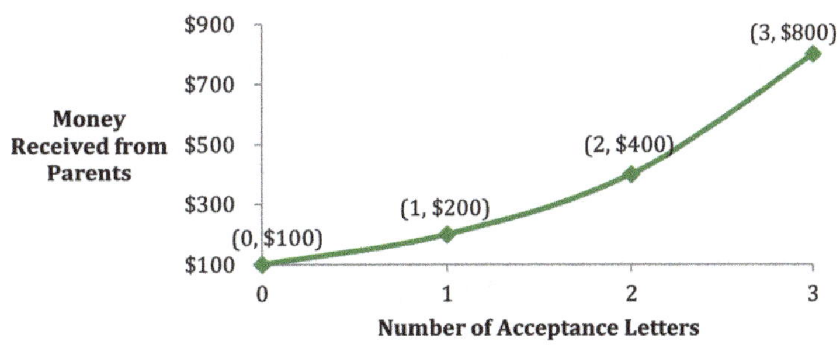

FIGURE 1.2 New Reward Criteria for Cassie (Exponential Growth)

We recall that Figure 1.2 represents the graph of the following equation:

$$y = 100 \times 2^x.$$

To graph, we simply plot each of the four points and connect the dots. We note that this graph of the exponential function shows that as the number of acceptance letters increases, the line becomes more and more steep. Unlike the graph of the line, this exponential graph shows a slightly curvy nature. The graph initially increases at a small rate but climbs rather acutely as it extends to the right. When an exponential function shows this type of pattern, we refer to it as showing *exponential growth*.

When an exponential function shows a reverse pattern, in which the y values decrease at an accelerated rate as the x values increase, we refer to it as showing *exponential decay*. This phenomenon arises in several real-life financial applications, including repayment of interest on a mortgage or on a credit card. Illustrated in Figure 1.3, the notion of exponential decay pervades and continues to show how mathematics becomes a real and touchable aspect of everyday financial life.

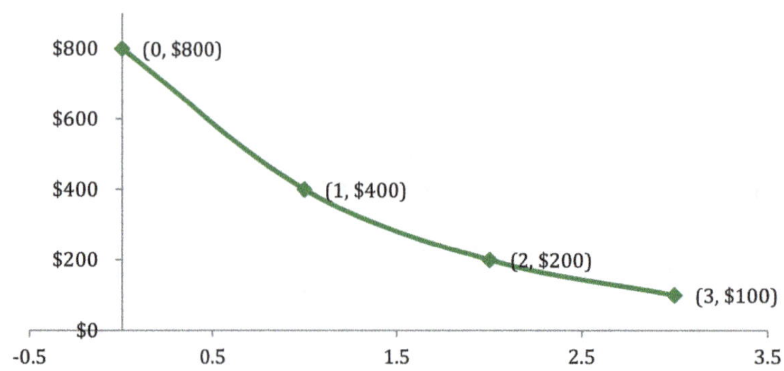

FIGURE 1.3 Example of Exponential Decay

Money: A Brief History

Money as we know it did not start out as money at all. If people wanted to "buy" something, both parties traded or swapped what they knew was valuable to the other. Whether it involved natural resources, food, or livestock, people in the world figured out creative ways to "pay" for the items they wanted. The word for this practice is generally referred to as bartering. Dating back to the beginning of time, bartering was the chief means through which societies made exchanges to get what they wanted.

From bartering, some civilizations used cowry shells as money. Widely used in China and some parts of Africa, these shells have been used the longest in history (Horesh 2012). Subsequently, coins made of precious metals were introduced, which tied their value to their weight and composition. Since these were rather durable and difficult to forge, this form of money maintained a certain intrinsic value and enabled better trade with other communities. Limitations of money in this form were that carrying too many coins proved problematic in terms of weight and that those who made the coins often devalued their worth by mixing cheap metal substitutes into coin composition. In a sense, these money modes fell into the category of commodity money in that the item used in place of money had some sort of intrinsic value.

Making its way from leather money to early forms of paper currency in China to wampum used by North American Indians, the idea of money later transitioned to banknotes, which became officially tied to the value of gold in England in the early 1800s and later in the United States in the early 1900s (Kwarteng 2014). After the Great Depression in the 1930s, the value of gold plummeted, and the linkage between gold and banknotes expired in America. Britain followed suit shortly afterward.

At present, fiat money is the global form of money in operation. This means that paper money and coins are not backed by physical commodities such as gold or silver; their value is supported by good faith and how well countries sense other countries are governing themselves and their own economy (Goldberg 2012). When President Richard Nixon ripped the dollar away from gold backing in the 1970s, he hoped to reduce unemployment in the States; unfortunately, unemployment still rose despite his efforts to combat it via this new mode of money identity.

In addition to the current state of currency as fiat money, a rather new development of money has surfaced in the form of cryptocurrency. First introduced in 2009, this digital mode of currency, which is generally unregulated by banks and the government, is transacted almost entirely online (Vora 2015). Cryptocurrency is a virtual, global, and borderless payment system that many believe will continue to threaten consumer confidence in fiat money. More and more businesses like cafés and Paypal are accepting payment with cryptocurrency (e.g., Bitcoin) in day-to-day payment transactions. Cryptocurrency ATMs have also begun to appear in major cities worldwide like Vienna, Toronto, New York, and Singapore.

Student Exercises: Algebra in a Flash

1.1 a. Add: $-\frac{7}{8}+\frac{5}{6}$

b. Multiply: $-7 \times 9\frac{1}{3}$

c. Subtract: $-3.11-(-4.6)$

d. Divide: $\frac{4}{5} \div \frac{3}{10}$

1.2 Simplify the following expressions:

a. $9-4[-6-4(1-3)]$

b. $-3 \times 4-\frac{5+7}{2+1}$

c. $-2^2-(6 \times 7-10 \div 2)-(-3)^2$

d. $7(-9s+4)-(2s-8)$

1.3 Solve for the indicated variable:

a. For v: $4v-(v-2)=7-2(3v-4)$

b. For j: $5.5-3j=j-3.5$

1.4 Simplify:

a. $(-4k^3)^3$

b. $\frac{25x^2}{35x^3}$

c. $\sqrt{144c^{10}}$

1.5 Prove that these points are not on the same line: (2, 6), (1, 1), (−4, 0). Don't graph.

1.6 Find another point that is on the same line as the following: (5, 3) and (−2, −1). Don't graph.

1.7 In the following exponential functions, identify the value of c and the value of a:

a. $y=5 \times 4^x$

b. $f(t)=\frac{3^t}{2}$

c. $f(m)=\left(\frac{2}{3}\right)^m$

d. $y=4^x \times 6^x$

1.8 Solve the following:

a. $\log_5 125$

b. $\log_4\left(\frac{1}{256}\right)$

c. $\log 10{,}000$

d. $\ln e^{6y}$

1.9 **(Excel)** Graph the following lines: $y=\frac{1}{2}x-4$ and $y=-4x+3$

a. Graph without using Excel.

b. Graph using Excel

1.10 Make a table of values for and graph the exponential function: $y=\left(\frac{1}{3}\right)^x$

References

Goldberg, Dror. 2012. "The Tax-Foundation Theory of Fiat Money." *Economic Theory* 50(2): 489–97.

Horesh, Niv. 2012 "The Great Money Divergence: European and Chinese Coinage before the Age of Steam." *Journal of Chinese Studies*. Accessed August 21, 2016. http://goo.gl/65Glne.

Kwarteng, Kwasi. 2014. "A Chinese Gold Standard?" *The New York Times*. Accessed August 21, 2016. http://goo.gl/FDV15z.

Vora, Gautam. 2015. "Cryptocurrencies: Are Disruptive Financial Innovations Here?" *Modern Economy* 6:816–32.

Asset Two

Interest and Savings

Chapter Outline

Rule No. 1: Never lose money.
Rule No. 2: Never forget Rule No. 1.

Warren Buffet

2.1 The Notion of Interest

Getting control of one's own finances is probably one of the most difficult tasks to accomplish. At any point in time, personal finances can get out of control because of a number of factors. Emergencies happen; spending patterns fluctuate; and saving becomes harder and harder sometimes. Despite these realities, it becomes critical to understand which financial tools have been put into place to assist in helping to fortify one's finances. One of the most prominent tools that is available for those who desire to gain control of their personal finances is that of **interest**.

Definition

The cost of borrowing money is referred to as **interest**.

Interest plays a highly significant role in helping to assist in the accumulation of money. The way most people used to save money was to tuck it under a mattress or keep it in a proverbial piggy bank. Saving money these ways does very little in helping people's money to "work" for them. Of course, the original amount of money deposited remains. However, in these savings strategies, there is no significant reward obtained for the time that the money has sat where it has. This notion of reward or cost becomes key to the understanding of the notion of interest.

Most of the time when we think of interest, we think of the amount of money we have to pay a bank for the privilege of borrowing its money. Thinking of interest only in this vein, though, robs us of the benefit we are able to procure through saving. Just as the bank makes money when people borrow money from it, individuals are able to make money when the bank borrows money from them. And the way that the bank borrows money from people is through different types of savings accounts. It's the bank's way of saying "thank you" for letting it access your funds. Central to the idea of interest is that of the **principal** and the **interest rate**.

Definition

The **principal** *is the initial amount of money invested or saved. The* **interest rate** *is the portion charged on the principal by one who lends to those who borrow. This portion is normally revealed as a percentage of the principal.*

Essentially, the interest rate determines the reward on money that has been invested. This rate fluctuates and is determined, for the most part, by the Federal Reserve Bank (the Fed), whose chief headquarters are in New York City. Various economic factors, such as supply and demand, influence this rate; hence, interest rates can change all the time. For example, if money policy makers desire to increase the supply of money in the economy, they generally decrease the interest rate, which would in turn discourage citizens from making deposits and increase retail bank borrowing from the Fed.

If financial policy makers desire to decrease the supply of money in the economy, they generally increase the interest rate, which would in turn encourage citizens to make deposits and decrease retail bank borrowing from the Fed.

2.2 Simple Interest

In this section (as well as the next two), we deal with investment types in which a customer makes a *one-time* investment or deposit at a specified interest rate agreed upon by the bank or lending institution. In each of these sections, we observe how the interest rate and how frequently the rate are applied to the principal factor into the amount of funds available at the end of a given time span.

2.2.1 The Simple Interest Formula

The first interest plan we explore is the accrual of interest under the **simple interest** strategy.

Definition

In **simple interest,** *interest accrues only on the principal, not on the principal and any earned interest. In simple interest, the amount of interest accumulated is given by:*

$$I = P \cdot r \cdot t, \qquad \textbf{Equation 2.1}$$

where I is the amount of interest received; P is the principal; r is the annual percentage rate (APR); and t is the time expressed in years. At the end of the investment time period, the total amount that is now accessible is given by:

$$A = P + I \ \text{ or } \ A = P + P \cdot r \cdot t, \qquad \textbf{Equation 2.2}$$

where A is the total amount of money accumulated after t years.

In Equation 2.2, the amount A is also referred to as the **maturity value.** This term references the basic notion of growth in children, who eventually become teens. Over time, children eventually grow or mature into young adults. Although they may still seem like they are children (in mind and deed—smile!), their physical state progresses to the point to which they are considered less childish or mature.

Definition

The original loan plus accrued interest is the **maturity value.**

In everyday life, simple interest is not generally used among creditors. Creditors are not interested in having interest accrue only on the original principal at the end of the time frame specified. They are interested in having their loans make money at a quicker rate. We practice our mathematics, however, using this most basic interest plan in the following section. We explore other types of interest strategies in future sections.

2.2.2 Simple Interest as a Linear Equation

Before discussing how to solve simple interest problems, we discover the similarity between the simple interest formula and linear equations in general. An algebraic understanding of linear equations helps us get a better feel for the simple interest formula. We are able, then, to solve for various components of the simple interest formula based on our comprehension of the line.

We recall Equation 1.1, which describes the basic equation of a line:

$$y = mx + b.$$

We observe that we can express this equation in the following manner:

$$y = m(x) + b.$$

Expressing y as $f(x)$, we have:

$$f(x) = m(x) + b. \qquad \textbf{Equation 2.3}$$

Equation 2.3 shows that as the value for x changes, so does the value of $f(x)$. We easily see that this equation mirrors that of Equation 2.2, in which we have the following:

$$A = P + P \cdot r \cdot t.$$

If we restructure this equation, we observe:

$$\begin{aligned} A &= P + P \cdot r \cdot t \\ A &= P \cdot r \cdot t + P \\ A(t) &= (P \cdot r)(t) + P \end{aligned} \qquad \textbf{Equation 2.4}$$

If we notice the formulas for Equations 2.3 and 2.4, we observe similarities in both. Table 2.1 highlights these similar components in both equations:

TABLE 2.1 Components of Linear Equation vs. Simple Interest Formula

Linear Equation	Simple Interest Formula
x	t
$f(x)$	$A(t)$
m	$P \cdot r$
b	P

As one might deduce, as the time (t) changes, so does the amount of money that is accumulated. Indeed, the simple interest formula highlights this relationship (Equation 2.4). In other words, we might anticipate that as the value of time goes from $t = 1$ to $t = 5$, for example, the total amount accumulated would increase as well, assuming that the slope component of the function stays positive. Generally speaking, the longer money stays in an account, the more money tends to accumulate. This essentially says that as t increases, $A(t)$ also increases. We look at a few cases in which we solve a few problems using the simple interest formula.

2.2.3 Working with the Simple Interest Formula

To get a feel for how simple interest compares with other interest plans, which will be discussed later, we consider a few examples.

Example 2.1 Determine the amount of interest that Maurice gains on a \$5500 deposit at an APR of 7% if left in the account for one year, assuming simple interest. How much will Maurice have in his account after the one-year period?

Solution 2.1 To determine the amount of simple interest, we need the principal, the interest rate, and the time given in years. When we solve, we change the interest rate from percent to a decimal. Hence, in the formula, we use 0.07 instead of 7%. The interest is calculated as follows:

$$\begin{aligned} I &= P \cdot r \cdot t \\ &= 5500(0.07)(1) \\ &= 385 \end{aligned}$$

The accumulated interest in this scenario is \$385 under simple interest.
The total amount Maurice will have in his account after one year is given by:

$$\begin{aligned} A &= P + I \\ &= 5500 + 385 \\ &= 5885 \end{aligned}$$

So the total amount in Maurice's account, or the maturity value, is \$5885 after one year.

Example 2.2 Determine the amount Daphne borrowed if the total interest was \$800 and the APR was 12% over the span of eight months, assuming simple interest.

Solution 2.2 We solve the interest equation for P. However, we recall that in the formula, we must express time in years. So we convert eight months to the equivalence in years:

$$\frac{8 \text{ months}}{1} \times \frac{1 \text{ year}}{12 \text{ months}} = \frac{8}{12} \text{ years} = \frac{2}{3} \text{ years}$$

And we now substitute the appropriate values in the interest equation and solve for the initial amount borrowed, or P.

$$\begin{aligned} I &= P \cdot r \cdot t \\ 800 &= P(0.12)\left(\frac{2}{3}\right) \\ 1200 &= P(0.12) \\ 10{,}000 &= P \end{aligned}$$

The initial amount Daphne borrowed was \$10,000.

We can continue to use the simple interest formula to gain experience in solving for each component. Of particular concern is solving for the interest rate given all other components. We allow you to practice solving for this value in the student exercises at the end of this chapter.

2.3 Compound Interest

Simple interest is the most basic and easiest savings strategy for which to calculate formula values. The interest strategy for savings that resembles more of a real-life situation is that involving **compound interest**.

2.3.1 The Compound Interest Formula

With **compound interest**, the interest is added into the account such that, over the course of compounding, the interest rate acts on new mini-principals within the compounding time frame. What makes compounding interest so unique is the fact that interest accrues to the account at several points within a specified time period. We again assume with compound interest that there has been a one-time deposit, and interest is acting on this one-time deposit, as opposed to having recurring deposits in an account. We address the effect on interest on recurring deposits in Asset 3.

Definition

In **compound interest,** *interest accrues on the principal and also on any interest that has been earned on the principal; interest accrues at a frequency that must be specified (e.g., quarterly, monthly). The compound interest formula is given by:*

$$A = P\left(1+\frac{r}{c}\right)^{ct}, \qquad \textbf{Equation 2.5}$$

where A is the amount accumulated (also referred to as the future value) after t years. P is the original principal, and r is the APR. In the equation, c is the compounding period (or how many times the interest rate is compounded within one year).

2.3.2 Working with the Compound Interest Formula

Essentially, money under the influence of compound interest has more of an opportunity to grow. For example, in compounding interest, if we have an APR of 7% compounded monthly, we apply equal amounts of the 7% rate per month for 12 months, as opposed to applying the entire 7% at the end of the 12 months. We take a look at an example using compound interest and make several observations after applying the formula. For teaching purposes, we use the same values as we do in Example 2.1.

Example 2.3 Determine how much Maurice has in his account after one year if he makes a $5500 deposit, which is subject to an APR of 7%, compounded monthly.

Solution 2.3 In this instance, we are solving for A. The initial deposit or P is $5500. Our interest rate, r, is 7% (or 0.07 in decimal form). Our time, t, is 1 ($t = 1$). Since we are compounding monthly, our value for c is 12 because there are 12 months in a year (or this is how many times our 7% interest rate is compounded in one year). Using the compound interest formula, we have the following:

$$\begin{aligned} A &= 5500\left(1+\frac{.07}{12}\right)^{12(1)} \\ &= 5500\left(1+\frac{.07}{12}\right)^{12} \\ &= 5897.60 \end{aligned}$$

In this scenario, Maurice will have \$5897.60 in his account after one year.

When solving with the compound formula, it is important not to round off values until the very end, if possible. Truncating decimals before the end can alter the final answer significantly. Any good scientific, nongraphing calculator (like the TI-83 or HP 10s) should allow you to solve these equations without rounding until the end. Several online scientific calculators are accessible to use as well. Any simple Google search will locate them.

Conceptually, one may wonder what is the difference in applying the entire 7% interest at the end of the 12 months versus applying $\frac{1}{12}$ of the 7% at the end of each month for 12 months. In other words, why did we not get the same answer for Example 2.3 as we did for Example 2.1? Or why is it that Maurice will have \$5885 under simple interest but will have \$5897.60 under interest compounded monthly? He has the same amount of money; the interest rate is the same, and so is the investment period. We take a look at Table 2.2 to try to clarify the distinction between interest strategies, illustrated by cumulative money amounts per month. In both cases, we assume a one-time initial deposit or principal of \$5500.

TABLE 2.2 Maurice's Money: Simple Interest vs. Compounding Monthly (End-of-Month Totals)

Month	Simple Interest	Compounding Monthly
January	\$5500	\$5532.08
February	\$5500	\$5564.35
March	\$5500	\$5596.81
April	\$5500	\$5629.46
May	\$5500	\$5662.30
June	\$5500	\$5695.33
July	\$5500	\$5728.55
August	\$5500	\$5761.97
September	\$5500	\$5795.58
October	\$5500	\$5829.39
November	\$5500	\$5863.39
December	\$5885	\$5897.60

As Table 2.2 illustrates, in the case of simple interest, the interest rate is not applied until the end of the year (in December). When compounded monthly, a portion of the interest rate takes effect at the end of each month. In January, for example, $\frac{1}{12}$ of the interest rate takes effect on \$5500, yielding \$5532.08 at the end of that month. This value becomes the "new" principal at the start of February. Now, another $\frac{1}{12}$ of the interest rate takes effect on this "new" value, yielding a value of \$5564.35 at the end of February. Continuing in this fashion, Maurice's money grows to \$5897.60 by the end of the year. This is the advantage of compounding: the effect of interest is evident at each compounding period, not just the end of the specified time period.

We keep in mind the different values for c for various compounding periods. Table 2.3 highlights these values for c in the compounding formula for different periods.

TABLE 2.3 Some Compounding Period Values

Compounding Period	Value of c
Semiannually	2
Triennially	3
Quarterly	4
Monthly	12
Weekly	52
Daily	365

We consider two more types of examples for problems involving compound interest. In one, our goal is to calculate the time (t); the other focuses on our finding the interest rate.

Example 2.4 Ravi made an initial deposit of \$8925. If the APR was 6.2%, how long did it take for the deposit to grow to \$13,400, assuming quarterly compounding?

Solution 2.4 We place each value appropriately into the compound interest formula. We solve for t.

$$13,400 = 8925\left(1 + \frac{.062}{4}\right)^{4t}$$
$$\Rightarrow \frac{13,400}{8925} = (1.0155)^{4t}$$

From this point, we must apply one of the key rules concerning logarithms, which is directly related to information concerning exponential functions in the opening chapter. We use the following property to help us solve for t:

$$\begin{aligned} a &= b^x \\ \Rightarrow \log a &= \log b^x \\ \Rightarrow \log a &= x \log b \end{aligned}$$

Property 2.1

Property 2.1 suggests that we can take the *logarithm* (denoted as *log*) of both sides without changing the equation's truth value. If there is an exponent, we are able to bring it in front of the *log* operation and proceed with solving.

We apply Property 2.1 in the solution:

$$\Rightarrow \quad \frac{13{,}400}{8925} = (1.0155)^{4t}$$

$$\Rightarrow \quad \log\left(\frac{13{,}400}{8925}\right) = \log(1.0155)^{4t}$$

$$\Rightarrow \quad \log\left(\frac{13{,}400}{8925}\right) = 4t\log(1.0155)$$

$$\Rightarrow \quad \frac{\log\left(\frac{13{,}400}{8925}\right)}{4\log(1.0155)} = t$$

$$\Rightarrow \quad 6.6 = t$$

So it takes 6.6 years or 6 years, seven months for Ravi's deposit to grow to \$13,400. (We convert the 0.6 years to months by using the following:)

$$\frac{0.6\,\text{years}}{1} \times \frac{12\,\text{months}}{1\,\text{year}} = 7.2\,\text{months} \approx 7\,\text{months}$$

Example 2.5 Jose's money grew from \$3455 to \$5210 in three years. What was the APR if compounding on the account was monthly?

Solution 2.5 Inserting the appropriate values into the compound interest formula, we have:

$$5210 = 3455\left(1 + \frac{r}{12}\right)^{12(3)}$$

$$\Rightarrow \frac{5210}{3455} = \left(1 + \frac{r}{12}\right)^{36}$$

In order to continue, we make use of another algebraic property that is beneficial in our quest to solve for the interest rate.

$$a = b^x$$

$$\Rightarrow (a)^{\frac{1}{x}} = \left(b^x\right)^{\frac{1}{x}}$$

$$\Rightarrow (a)^{\frac{1}{x}} = b$$

Property 2.2

Property 2.2 expresses that when we raise a power to a power, we multiply the exponents together. Of course, when we raise one side of the equation to a power, we raise the other side to the same power. We notice that in Property 2.2, the exponents on the right side of the equation "disappear." Upon a closer look, when we multiply x by $1/x$ the result is 1. So after multiplying both exponent values, we end with b^1, which is the same as b.

We use this information to continue solving:

$$\begin{aligned}
\frac{5210}{3455} &= \left(1+\frac{r}{12}\right)^{36} \\
\Rightarrow \left(\frac{5210}{3455}\right)^{\frac{1}{36}} &= \left(\left(1+\frac{r}{12}\right)^{36}\right)^{\frac{1}{36}} \\
\Rightarrow \left(\frac{5210}{3455}\right)^{\frac{1}{36}} &= 1+\frac{r}{12} \\
\Rightarrow \left(\frac{5210}{3455}\right)^{\frac{1}{36}} - 1 &= \frac{r}{12} \\
\Rightarrow 12\left[\left(\frac{5210}{3455}\right)^{\frac{1}{36}} - 1\right] &= r \\
\Rightarrow 0.1377 &= r
\end{aligned}$$

So we have that $r = 0.1377$. This means that Jose's APR was 13.77% (move decimal twice to the right).

2.4 Continuous Compound Interest

If we take a look at the compound interest formula and begin increasing the frequency with which compounding occurs, something interesting transpires. In mathematics, especially calculus, increasing the frequency is interpreted as "taking a limit." We explore this notion in the following section.

2.4.1 The Continuous Compound Interest Formula

In this case, to increase the frequency of compounding means that the time, t, gets larger and larger or approaches infinity. For example, if t goes from four to eight, it means compounding goes from four times to eight times that year. Mathematically, we see what happens when t gets even larger:

$$A = \lim_{t\to\infty} P\left(1+\frac{r}{c}\right)^{ct}$$

By introducing a new variable, $k = \frac{c}{r}$ (or $c = kr$), we can substitute into and simplify the right side of the equation to get:

$$\begin{aligned}
A &= \lim_{k\to\infty} P\left(1+\frac{r}{kr}\right)^{krt} \\
&= \lim_{k\to\infty} P\left(1+\frac{1}{k}\right)^{krt} \\
&= P\left[\lim_{k\to\infty}\left(1+\frac{1}{k}\right)^{k}\right]^{rt}
\end{aligned}$$

In the brackets, we notice that this limit value gets closer and closer to the value in algebra referred to as e, which is an irrational number (like π). In mathematics, the value of e has a rough value of 2.718 (as π has a rough value of 3.14). Replacing this value in the bracket with the equivalent value of e provides us with the formula for **continuous compounding**.

Definition

In **continuous compounding,** *interest accrues on the principal and also on any interest that has been earned on the principal; in theory, interest accrues every instant or on a constant, perpetual basis. The formula for continuous compounding is given by:*

$$A = Pe^{rt}, \qquad \textbf{Equation 2.6}$$

where A is the future value; P is the original principal; r is the APR; and, t is time given in years. We recall that e is an irrational number and not a variable.

2.4.2 Working with the Continuous Compound Interest Formula

We see that in continuous compounding, interest does not wait to be compounded at the end of a given month, or week, or day, or even second. As the name implies, in continuous compounding, interest is added in an ongoing, continuous fashion throughout the given time period. This would suggest that at the end of the time period, we would expect more money to be in the account when compared to compounded monthly, quarterly, and the like. Again, we assume a one-time deposit in the scenario of continuous compounding. We take a look at an example similar to the one we examined in Examples 2.1 and 2.3.

Example 2.6 How much will Maurice have in his account after one year if he makes a \$5500 deposit, which is subject to an APR of 7%, compounded continuously?

Solution 2.6 Of course, we substitute the appropriate values into the continuous compounding formula, solving for A. We have:

$$\begin{aligned} A &= 5500e^{.07(1)} \\ &= 5898.79 \end{aligned}$$

After one year, Maurice will have \$5898.79 in his account with continuous compounding.

When entering values in the calculator, we should use the e^x key, which may or may not require use of the second-function key. Most calculators allow you to place the entire string of values of the equation in at once.

When we take a collective glance at Maurice's account in each of the three scenarios, we are able to compare the three interest strategies and how they match up. Summary values come from solutions to Exercises 2.1, 2.3, and 2.6. Table 2.4 highlights this comparison. As we might guess, the amount in Maurice's account under continuous compounding is greater than the other two amounts. As discussed, this is because interest accrues at a more frequent rate here than in the other two. Even though we start with the same deposited investment amount at the same interest rate, this simple example shows how some accounts can outperform others, depending on how the notion of interest is applied.

TABLE 2.4 Maurice's Account ($5500 Initial Investment; 7% Annual Interest Rate)

Interest Strategy	Account After One Year
Simple interest	$5885.00
Compounded monthly	$5897.60
Continuous compounding	$5898.79

We consider a different type of example that we often encounter when working with the continuous compound interest formula. As in the case with compounding interest, we need to be able to solve for values found in the exponent position.

Example 2.7 Sue makes an initial deposit of $1120. Given continuous compounding, how long would she have to leave the money in the account before it doubles, if the APR is 7.13%?

Solution 2.7 Using the continuous compound interest formula, we substitute appropriately. Doubling the initial investment means we end up with $2240 in the account:

$$\begin{aligned} 2240 &= 1120e^{0.0713t} \\ \Rightarrow \quad \frac{2240}{1120} &= e^{0.0713t} \\ \Rightarrow \quad 2 &= e^{0.0713t} \end{aligned}$$

To continue, we use another property tied to exponential functions, especially those involving the irrational number, e. We state here:

$$\begin{aligned} a &= e^x \\ \Rightarrow \quad \ln a &= \ln e^x \\ \Rightarrow \quad \ln a &= x \ln e \\ \Rightarrow \quad \ln a &= x \end{aligned}$$

Property 2.3

Property 2.3 states that, when we have e raised to a power, we can solve for the power by taking the *natural logarithm* (denoted as *ln*) of both sides. In Step 3, we use our knowledge of algebra to bring the entire exponent in front of the *ln* expression. We also recognize that Step 4 exploits the fact that $\ln e = 1$, simply leaving x on the right side.

We finish solving the problem to find t.

$$\begin{aligned} 2 &= e^{0.0713t} \\ \Rightarrow \quad \ln 2 &= \ln e^{0.0713t} \\ \Rightarrow \quad \ln 2 &= (0.0713t) \ln e \\ \Rightarrow \quad \ln 2 &= 0.0713t \\ \Rightarrow \quad \frac{\ln 2}{0.0713} &= t \\ \Rightarrow \quad 9.72 &= t \end{aligned}$$

Expressing our answer in terms of years and months, we discover that Sue should keep her deposit in this account for approximately nine years, nine months if she wants to see her initial investment doubled.

2.4.3 The Exponential Function Revisited

When we consider the compound interest formula and the continuous compound interest formula, we notice their striking similarity to the exponential function introduced in Section 1.2.2. We recall the generic exponential function (Equation 1.2), given by:

$$y = c \times a^x,$$

as stated earlier. When we compare both compound formulas to this exponential function, we clearly note that each component mirrors a similar component in the above equation. Table 2.5 illustrates this comparison:

TABLE 2.5 Components of Exponential Function vs. Compound Interest vs. Continuous Compound Interest

Exponential Function	Compound Interest Formula	Continuous Compound Interest Formula
y	A	A
c	P	P
a	$(1+r/c)$	e
x	ct	rt

The graph showing how much is in Maurice's account month by month with continuous compounding resembles Figure 1.2, another exponential function. We recall that at the end of 12 months, his account has grown to $5898.79. Figure 2.1 shows the growth pattern leading up to this amount. For compounding monthly, the graph for Maurice's account would also display a similar exponential curve but would not grow as quickly when compared to continuous compounding.

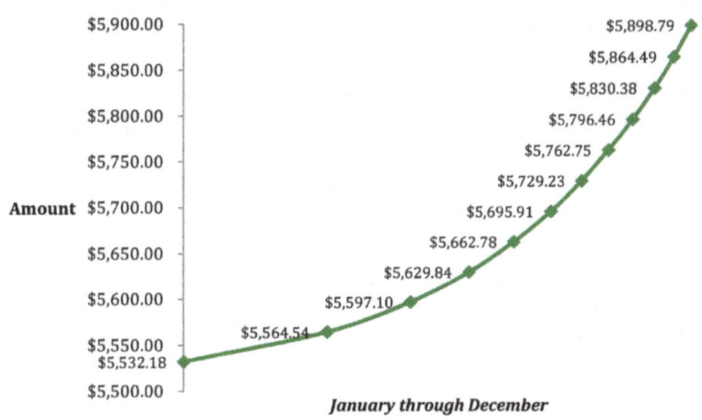

FIGURE 2.1 Maurice's Account with Continuous Compounding (Monthly Growth, Logarithmic Scale)

Money Talk

Savings 101

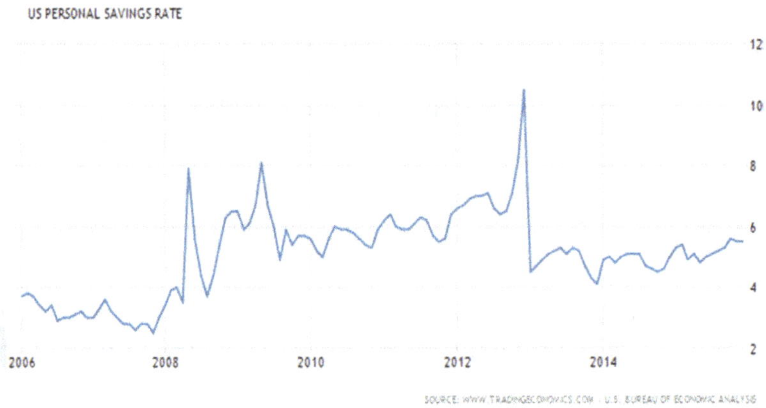

FIGURE 2.2 **Savings in US Households: The Trend, The Reality**

Source: **http://goo.gl/DcqEzZ**
(Line Graph – 10Y)

Saving money can always pose a challenge. Even for adults, putting money aside is easier said than done. According to the Bureau of Economic Analysis, the rate at which US households are saving money has declined overall but recently has been making a slow but steady comeback, as illustrated in Figure 2.2:

According to the Bureau, the savings rate for US households hovered around 5.48% in 2016. Interpreted, this means that for every $100 earned in US households, $94.52 is spent while about $5.48 is saved. Although this rate has improved from a downward trend over recent years, it is far from what these households need to maintain a sense of security and financial independence.

With tuition costs continuing to rise, students can still arm themselves with the knowledge of various low-risk savings plans that will help their money grow once they graduate and secure a job. Low-risk savings instruments are merely those financial programs that carry relatively low interest rates and guarantee an increase in the originally invested principal. We discuss four of the most popular low-risk savings programs:

- A *basic savings account* is an account in which customers make a deposit or series of deposits and receive interest payments at the end of each month. Customers may be required to maintain a certain balance to avoid monthly maintenance fees. More than six withdrawals per month are prohibited; otherwise, banks may close the account and refund any balance to customer.
- A *certificate of deposit account* (or *CD*) is an account in which customers make a one-time deposit and receive interest reward only after a specified, fixed time period. CD investments may range from as little as three months to as much as five years. If money is withdrawn before maturity, substantial penalties are incurred. Generally, you cannot add money to an existing CD account.
- A *money market (deposit) account* (*MMA* or *MMDA*) is an interest-bearing savings account that requires a higher minimum monthly balance than regular savings accounts. Banks impose fees or close accounts if this balance is not maintained. Interest rates often mirror those in the money markets. Often, customers can write checks against this type of account but can exceed no more than six per month. Since a higher minimum is required, a higher interest rate is often used to reward investors.
- *Savings bonds* (or *zero-coupon bonds*) are savings instruments issued by the federal government and are sold for a discount off of the face value. At a fixed interest rate, the investor is able to redeem them after the set period of time (as many as 10 or 15 years). Despite how the economy fairs, these bonds guarantee a prescribed amount to be received on a specified date.

With respect to interest benefits of the four savings plans discussed, MMAs tend to offer higher interest rates than the other three plans on average, given similar amounts deposited and over similar investment times. Special programs, however, offer higher interest rates for regular savings plans, especially for those under the age of 18 years. Each person should consider his/her own financial situation to determine which savings plan is best for him/her. Out of the four, bonds would generally produce higher yields since they are invested at a longer time and for a guaranteed amount.

Whichever low-risk savings plan you choose, you should always make sure that the institution in which you place your money is what is referred to as *FDIC-insured*. This term stands for "Federal Deposit Insurance Corporation" and guarantees that up to $250,000 per depositor per bank is safe or retrievable in the event that some financial catastrophe happens. Like car insurance, this is savings insurance. Although savings bonds are not FDIC-insured, they are strictly backed by the government and will always yield agreed-upon value if held until maturity.

More and more individuals are turning to online institutions for their savings plan versus banking with brick-and-mortar banks. Since this is the case, it is becoming easier for imposters to pose as banks and put themselves in positions to steal from unsuspecting victims. It becomes even more imperative that customers assure that banks—online or not—display the FDIC logo to lessen the chances for fraud and theft and to assure you that your savings are safe and in good hands.

Student Exercises: Interest and Savings

2.1 **a.** Under simple interest, determine the amount of interest Jill earns in her account if she deposits \$2230 at a 2.45% annual interest rate, which matures after three years.
b. What is the maturity value of Jill's account after this three-year period?

2.2 Determine the annual interest rate applied to Samone's savings account if her initial deposit of \$5600 grew to \$6412 after two years, six months, assuming simple interest.

2.3 Assuming simple interest, determine Alvin's initial deposit if his account grew to \$7700 in four years at an annual interest rate of 3.54%.

2.4 An investment group of 15 college students at Duke University decided to contribute \$255 each into a regular savings account. Determine how much would be in the account after four years at a 1.23% annual rate of interest, assuming monthly compounding.

2.5 **(Excel)** Assuming weekly compounding, how long (in years and months) does it take for \$1784 to grow to \$2290 with an annual interest rate of 6.11%?

a. Find without using Excel **b.** Find using Excel

2.6 Joshua deposited \$3238 into a savings account. After six years, it grew to \$5119. What annual interest rate was in effect on his account, assuming daily compounding?

2.7 Assuming continuous compounding, how much would Roberto have to deposit into his account if it grew to \$3109 over four years, three months with an annual interest rate of 2.99%?

2.8 How long (in years and months) would it take Carmen's account to triple, assuming an annual interest rate of 4.2% with continuous compounding with quarterly compounding?

2.9 **a.** If Derek deposited \$2900, how much would he have in his account after seven years at an annual interest rate of 4.01%, assuming continuous compounding?
b. How much would he have to deposit for his account to reach this new amount found in **a.**, given the same time frame but at an annual interest rate of 6%, assuming continuous compounding?

2.10 If Beth invested \$20,000 at 6% interest, how much more time would it take for her account to grow to \$30,000 with semiannual compounding than it would under the same conditions with continuous compounding?

2.11 **(Excel)** Compare the growth of a \$1000 investment at different interest rates *with simple interest.*

a. Make a chart showing the future value after 15 and 30 years at interest rates of 2%, 3%, 4%, 5%, 6%, 7%, and 8% (*Hint: Use some form of the \$ sign*).
b. Determine how much you would have to invest at 2% to obtain the same future value as \$1000 invested at 8% (for t = 30 years).
Amount needed to be invested is ____________________.

2.12 (Excel) Compare the growth of a $1000 investment at different interest rates *compounded monthly*.

a. Make a chart showing the future value after 15 and 30 years at interest rates of 2%, 3%, 4%, 5%, 6%, 7%, and 8% (*Hint: Use some form of the $ sign*).

b. Determine how much you would have to invest at 2% to obtain the same future value as $1000 invested at 8% (for t = 30 years).
Amount needed to be invested is ________________________.

2.13 (Excel) Compare the growth of a $1000 investment at different interest rates *compounded continuously*.

a. Make a chart showing the future value after 15 and 30 years at interest rates of 2%, 3%, 4%, 5%, 6%, 7%, and 8% (*Hint: Use some form of the $ sign*).

b. Determine how much you would have to invest at 2% to obtain the same future value as $1000 invested at 8% (for t = 30 years).
Amount needed to be invested is ________________________.

2.14 In problems 2.11–2.13, discuss any two (2) realities you observe when taking a look at all of the results.

Asset Three

Present Value of an Annuity

Chapter Outline

'Tis against some men's principle to pay interest, and seems against others' interest to pay the principal.

Benjamin Franklin

3.1 College Students and Credit Scores

When applying to enter college, you were required to submit several pieces of information concerning your performance in high school. Maybe you had to write an essay, get teacher recommendations, and take the Scholastic Aptitude Test (SAT). In addition, you were required to make known your grade point average (GPA) from the high school that you attended. This GPA, ranging normally from 0.0 to 4.0 provided a quick numerical summary of how successful and diligent you were during these years. What makes the GPA so useful to colleges is the fact that the number represents how you performed in the *past* and would probably be a good indicator as to how you would perform in college in the *future*. When college officials have to determine which students receive entry into the college or which students receive scholarships, the GPA stands as one of the crucial criteria for doing such.

In the world of personal finance, one single number helps creditors and banks determine how well you have handled matters in the past concerning your financial matters. This number is your **Fair Isaac Corporation (FICO) score**.

Definition

The **Fair Isaac Corporation (FICO) score** *is a three-digit number, which is used to assess overall how well individuals have handled their finances in the past. It helps lenders determine how much of a credit risk people may be.*

The FICO score is to personal finance what the GPA is to college admissions. The FICO score gives those who will lend money a good sense about how an individual has handled his or her monies in the past. The idea is that if people have handled their finances in a responsible manner in the past, they will more than likely continue to handle their finances responsibly in the future. A person who has a relatively high score has paid all previous loans back to the lender or has consistently paid on the loan each month. A person who has a relatively low score has been very slack on the repayment of bills and loans in the past as noted by late payments or no payments on the loan at all. It is widely known that major banks use your social security number to check your credit when applying for a car or a home. What may not be as widely known is that businesses may check your credit for your application for an apartment or something even as small as a cell phone. Potential employers will check your credit, especially if you are applying for a job that requires accounting and budgeting. They believe that you cannot handle their finances if you cannot handle your own. It seems as if possible lenders are placing more and more emphasis on your ability to manage the things that transpire in your financial world.

3.1.1 FICO Score Subranges

A FICO score may range from 300 to 850. In general, the higher the score, the more you can borrow and the less you will have to pay to borrow the money. Much like the high school GPA, information related to the FICO score is best interpreted by looking at the meanings of the subranges of the overall range. Two tables follow, which provide a general understanding of these subranges. Table 3.1 shows the subranges of the score and how creditors tend to "grade" those who fall into said subranges.

TABLE 3.1 The FICO Score as a "Grade"

FICO Score	Grade
720–850	Excellent
700–719	Very Good
675–699	Good
620–674	Fair
560–619	Bad
500–619	Very Bad
Under 500	Horrific!

This table reveals, for example, that someone who has a FICO credit score of 717 has done a very good job in the past of paying bills and handling personal financial matters. This score only reflects personal financial information that was submitted to one of the three credit reporting agencies. We say a word about these agencies in Section 3.1.2.

Table 3.2 takes a closer look at FICO score subranges in light of a few interesting statistics as of 2012.

TABLE 3.2 The FICO Score Personified

FICO Score	Population Percentage	Delinquency Rate
800–850	13%	1%
749–799	27%	2%
700–749	18%	5%
650–699	15%	15%
600–649	12%	31%
550–599	8%	51%
500–549	5%	71%
300–499	2%	87%

Source: **http://goo.gl/dO3dTa**

The table reveals, for example, that 18% of the population has FICO scores between 700 and 749; and only 5% of those in this category are delinquent on accounts. So, out of a population of 100,000, we would expect 18,000 (18% of 100,000) of them to have a FICO score between 700 and 749, and we would expect 900 of the 18,000 (5% of 18,000) to make late payments on accounts. The key trend revealed in the data is that the higher the credit score, the less likely that people will make late repayments on their credit accounts.

3.1.2 The Anatomy of a FICO Score

Each month, creditors update credit report agencies concerning your repayments. If you are late paying a credit card, this information is submitted to three agencies, which keep record of your overall repayment history. These three agencies are:

1. Experian (www.experian.com)
2. TransUnion (www.transunion.com)
3. Equifax (www.equifax.com)

Everyone is entitled to a free credit report per year at http://goo.gl/WDDER1. Many have even managed to get more than one free from this site per year since it is an automated site. Regarding the credit score, it is a little more difficult to get the credit score itself without paying; however, some sites like http://goo.gl/Ngg8jc provide credit scores free for those who register at their site. One should not pay any money to register, but you will have to enter your social security number and answer a few questions before being authenticated. Some credit card companies offer to provide credit scores for free if you use their credit card services. It is vital that everyone request to see credit reports from all three agencies to see the story behind the credit score. If any errors exist, you should immediately contact each agency and start the process to challenge any errors that appear.

Regarding the FICO score, it is crucial to be aware of the factors that make the credit score what it is. Knowing the anatomy of this important score helps you to stay diligent concerning financial matters and to guard against situations that may hurt the score. Figure 3.1 helps us visualize the five categories that are instrumental in shaping the credit score:

History of Payments

This category accounts for 35% of the credit score and is the most important factor in determining the credit score. In a nutshell, the bulk of your score is based on how responsible you are in repaying your bills. In this category, your score is influenced by whether you pay credit card bills on time or not (or pay them at all). If overdue or nonpaid bill balances are sent to collection agencies, your score takes a hit in this category.

Debt Capacity or Debt Utilization

At 30%, this percentage of your credit score exploits how much debt you have compared to the limit you have on your credit cards. If you have a credit limit of $2000 on a credit card, for example, and your balance on the card is $1900, your debt utilization is high. This would tend to be viewed as a disadvantage because you are using most of your debt capacity. If your balance in the same scenario is $200, your debt utilization is low, which would be viewed positively and would generally raise your credit score. This category, essentially, gauges your ability to manage having access to credit without abusing it.

Length of Credit History

This piece of the credit score puzzle takes into account how long you have maintained good credit with certain accounts. Typically, the longer you have kept current on credit card payments, the higher the credit score. The credit score generally decreases once accounts that have been opened the longest are closed. This component contributes to 15% of the credit score.

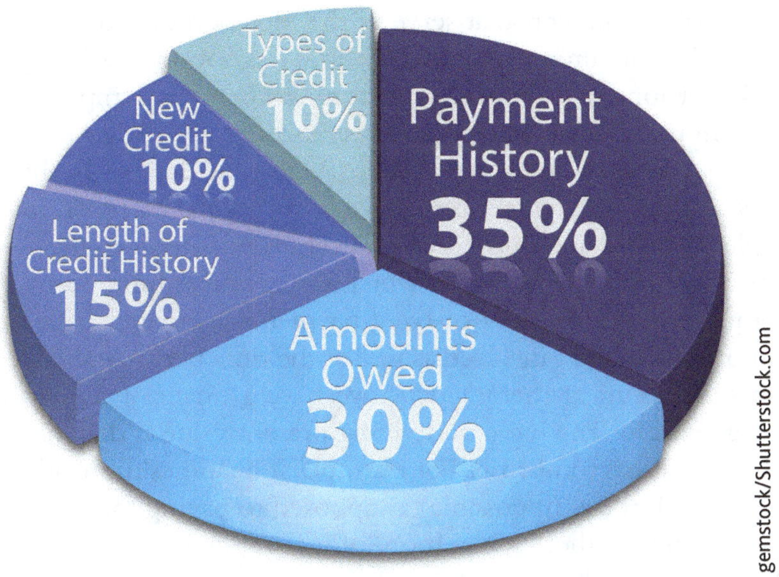

FIGURE 3.1 The Breakdown of a FICO Score

New Credit

When you become eligible for credit, you have to be aware of and guard against the temptation to apply for every credit card that strikes your fancy. Ten percent of your score is directly related to how frequently you apply for new credit cards. These new requests for credit are referred to as inquiries. In general, a constant stream of inquiries for new credit would tend to lower your score because it shows the potential for a new capacity for debt and possible abuse of it.

Types of Credit

Over time, you will not just demonstrate your creditworthiness through use of credit cards. You may have to take loans on cars, homes, and other items. This mix of different types of credit helps to determine 10% of your credit score. It is not advisable to deliberately set out to be sure you have a good mix of credit to raise your score. Becoming an adult and taking on adult financial responsibilities would generally ensure that this mix occurs naturally over the course of time.

These five pieces of the credit puzzle are key to understand what the credit score is, what factors contribute to it, and how it can remain in stellar shape.

3.2 Annuities Defined

Perhaps the most important decision you will make during and after your college years will center around your understanding of an **annuity**. Although the term itself may be a bit foreign to most, its impact is more significant than many realize.

Definition

At its core, an ***annuity*** *is a flow of fixed payments over a determined period of time. An annuity is drafted such that this flow of payments terminates after the time period expires.*

Annuities are financial instruments that serve as the lifeblood of today's economy and drives most financial decisions. Annuities are unique in that they have the notion of a "lump sum" attached to them. What categorizes different annuities, at their base nature, is where this lump sum appears or occurs. What differentiates annuities from the financial strategies we encountered earlier is that in asset two, payments made were made only *once*, and interest accrued to that one-time deposit. In this asset, a flow or series of payments are made; *more than one* payment is made at fairly regular intervals. Interest, then, is applied to this notion of multiple payments and thus becomes a significant factor in this type of financial scenario.

The first instances we observe are those in which the annuity's lump sum appears at the beginning of the determined time period. The flow of fixed payments associated with this financial situation is influenced by the amount of interest involved as well as the time period itself. We investigate this further.

When the lump sum occurs at the *beginning*, we have a financial situation that is categorized as the present value of an annuity. The logic underlying present value is that a certain amount of money today has more value than it has tomorrow. For example, it becomes more advantageous to pay for the total amount of a car in cash today (if possible) as opposed to paying for it over time through multiple payments. Your money "goes further" when more of it is applied toward the total cost today.

Mathematically, we use a well-known formula to assist us in calculating certain values associated with the present value of an annuity.

Definition

Mathematically, the present value of an annuity is represented as follows:

$$PVA = \frac{PMT\left[1 - \left(\frac{r}{c} + 1\right)^{-ct}\right]}{\frac{r}{c}}, \qquad \textbf{Equation 3.1}$$

where PVA is the present value of the annuity, PMT is the regular payment made, r is the APR, c is the compounding period per year, and t is the total time of repayment in years.

Again, we use this formula when the lump sum of the annuity occurs at the beginning of the financial scenario. Such instances that fall into this category are those primarily dealing with loans (car payments, credit cards, and mortgages) and even lottery payouts. We take a look at most of these instances in the next few sections.

3.3 Repaying Your Student Loans

If you are like most college students, you have had to use the help of student loans at some point in your college career. In addition to grants, scholarships, and work–study opportunities, loans are critical components of your financial aid package as you travel on the road to securing your degree. As helpful as student loans are in assisting you to accomplish your academic dreams, you should be well advised that it is important to realize that after graduating, you will be required to pay the loan back to the federal government. The type of student loan you receive—**subsidized** or **unsubsidized**—will determine how much you will have to repay after walking across the stage on graduation day and celebrating such a spectacular feat.

Definition

A **subsidized loan** *is one in which the federal government pays interest for the loan from the initial loan date through six months after the student's graduation date. An* **unsubsidized loan** *is one in which the student pays interest for the loan from the initial loan date.*

Subsidized loans are earmarked for financially needful undergraduate students who are embarking upon completing their educational degrees for the first time. Unsubsidized loans are for those who are continuing their education beyond their undergraduate careers. Undergraduate students who are not in financial need (according to financial aid application results) may also qualify for unsubsidized loans. Whether paying their interest back sooner or later, students should always be aware of the interest rate associated with their school loan, as it influences how much will be paid back during the repayment period. According to Federal Student Aid, an office of the US Department of Education, the interest rate for subsidized loans issued after July 1, 2016 and before July 1, 2017 was 3.76%, a decrease from the 4.29% rate the year before (Lobosco 2016).

Six months after graduation for the undergraduate experience, students pay back funds that were already distributed. So this is an instance where the lump sum of the annuity occurs at the *beginning* of the loan period, thus falling in the category of the present value of an annuity. We consider an example that involves repaying a loan over a specific period of time at a certain interest rate.

Example 3.1 Carly was set to begin repayment of her student loan from her studies at North Carolina Central University. Over the course of her college undergraduate career, her total in loans grew to $26,600. Assuming the interest rate is 3.76% for the entire loan amount, determine how much she will pay per month if she desires to pay off the loan in 15 years.

Solution 3.1 We use Equation 3.1 and solve for *PMT*:

$$26{,}600 = \frac{PMT\left[1-\left(\dfrac{0.0376}{12}+1\right)^{-12(15)}\right]}{\dfrac{0.0376}{12}}$$

$$\Rightarrow \quad 26{,}600 = \frac{PMT\left[1-(1.003133333)^{-180}\right]}{0.003133333}$$

$$\Rightarrow 83.3466578 = PMT[1-0.569430704]$$

$$\Rightarrow 83.3466578 = 0.430569296\ PMT$$

$$\Rightarrow \quad 193.573 = PMT$$

To pay back the loan in 15 years, Carly's monthly payment will be $193.57.

Even though interest rates have declined over the past few years, much debate has continued to ensue about lowering them even further. Students and politicians alike have weighed in on the issue in hopes of lightening the financial burden of the average college student in America. The issue of lowering interest rates tied to student loans has become such a vital concern in America that the 2016 US presidential candidates included some aspect of student loans and their affordability in their campaigns.

Evan El-Amin/Shutterstock.com

Barack Obama and Hillary Clinton

Joseph Sohm/Shutterstock.com

Donald Trump

Until interest rates for student loans significantly decrease, financial advisors have encouraged many college students, after their graduation, to reduce how much they pay back overall by using the technique of **loan consolidation**. Doing so promises to save students considerably on the amount of interest that students pay back. Often, an **origination fee** is employed when loans are consolidated into one.

Definition

Loan consolidation *is the process whereby which separate loans are combined into another loan, so as to ease the burden of paying separate monthly payments at a lower interest rate. It is essentially refinancing your loan. An* **origination fee** *is the initial charge one pays to consolidate separate loans in another one. The fee is often folded into the overall amount that is consolidated or refinanced.*

Consolidating loans and paying one easy monthly payment have proven to be a great financial alternative than paying multiple monthly payments for different loans. In general, more money is saved in the long run, and variable interest rates become fixed (if any of the private loans have variable interest rates). However, consolidating loans are frowned upon if you have to pay an exorbitant origination fee or if you are already close to paying off the different loans being considered for consolidation. One should also note that in order to get a very low interest rate with the consolidation loan, one's credit score comes into play, whereas it does not with student loans.

Example 3.2 Carly was set to begin repayment of her student loan from her studies at North Carolina Central University. Over the course of her college undergraduate career, her total in loans grew to \$26,600. She also had private loans totaling \$6500. Assuming the interest rate is 3.76% for her student loans and 4.9% for her private loans, determine how much she saves in interest if she consolidates both loans into one. Assume she would have paid the two separate loans off in 15 years, and assume she will pay the consolidated loan off also in 15 years. Since she has a decent credit score, the bank offers her an interest rate of 2.14%. Last, assume the consolidation loan has an origination fee of \$450.

Solution 3.2 (i) For the two separate loans, we see how much she would have to pay back per month; we use Equation 3.1 and solve for PMT in both scenarios. We already found that she would pay back $193.57 per month for her student loans. For her private loans, we have:

$$6500 = \frac{PMT\left[1 - \left(\frac{0.049}{12} + 1\right)^{-12(15)}\right]}{\frac{0.049}{12}}$$

$$\Rightarrow 51.06 = PMT$$

For the private loan, Carly's monthly payment will be $51.06.
We now find how much in interest she pays on both loans separately if they are not consolidated:

a. Interest paid back on student loans: (193.57)(180) – 26,600 = 8242.60
b. Interest paid back on private loans: (51.06)(180)–6500 = 2690.80

Hence, the total interest paid back for both loans separately is **$10,933.40**.

(ii) When both loans are consolidated, the total amount of the loan to be financed (including the origination fee) is $33,550.00 (26,600+6500+450). Equation 3.1 reveals the monthly payment:

$$33{,}550 = \frac{PMT\left[1 - \left(\frac{0.0214}{12} + 1\right)^{-12(15)}\right]}{\frac{0.0214}{12}}$$

$$\Rightarrow 218.0668 = PMT$$

After consolidating, Carly's monthly payment would be $218.07.
We now find how much in interest she pays on the consolidated loan. We find it by solving the following: (218.07)(180)–33,550 = 5702.60. Hence, the total interest paid back for the consolidated loan is **$5702.60**.
Finally, the total amount Carly saves in interest by consolidating into one loan is the difference between how much interest is saved in both scenarios (i) and (ii), which is $5230.80 ($10,933.40 – $5702.60).

For consolidating two loans into one, Carly saves **$5230.80** overall in interest.

You should remember that whether you decide to consolidate loans or keep them as separate loans, they should be paid back on time each month until paid off. You do not want to get in a place where you are skipping payments, making payments late, or ignoring payments altogether. Continually being delinquent on student loans will result in **loan default**, which can cripple your financial health.

In addition to damaging your credit score, a status of being in default on your student loan is never forgiven until the actual loan is paid off. This means that your credit score will never recuperate from this type of default until you take responsibility and resume payments until the balance is paid back.

Definition

Student loan default *is the situation in which students fail to repay their student loans according to the rule of the contract (promissory note). This default status is reached after approximately nine months of delinquent (late or ignored) payments.*

It also means that your delinquency will be reported to collection agencies, and they may pursue avenues of getting their money back (e.g., account seizures).

3.4 Your First Car

Acquiring your first car will be one of the most important purchases made during your adult years. There are many different financial routes you could follow to get the car from the lot to your residence. Whether you decide to lease a car and return it to the dealership once the lease term has expired, or to buy a preowned vehicle, or to purchase a brand new one with no miles, or to buy Uncle Randy's old-school Mustang, you will have to give some thought into how you will pay for it. You will have to decide if the lease-and-return option, the lease-to-own option, the preowned-purchase option, or the brand-new-purchase option is best for you based on your transportation goals. However, we explore in this section a few payment option scenarios given different financial realities.

As we mentioned earlier in this asset, one's credit score contributes greatly to the annual interest rate that banks will require you to pay. Your credit score is crucial as you negotiate the best interest rate for the life of the car loan. Several car commercials have even advertised a 0% APR for a certain portion of the payback period of the loan. You would have to take a look at the guidelines for such financing and be sure to read the fine print in the contract or on the bottom of the TV screen to see what stipulations need to be met to guarantee what is advertised. For example, it may be that your credit score has to be over 700 and that it is required that you put a certain amount of money down to ease the bank's mind about what you are willing to invest at the moment. Either way, it becomes important to take a look at how a great credit score can translate into money saved over the term of the car loan.

Unless you were born with a silver spoon in your mouth or if you have not saved enough money on your own, you will probably have to finance all or part of the amount of the car you are purchasing. In an ideal world, you receive the car as a gift or can simply pay cash for it and do not have to worry about paying for it over time. Until then, you will have to work the best financial scenario that fits within your budget and requires you to pay the least amount of interest of the life of the car loan. From test-driving the car to finally signing on the dotted line, this represents a major purchase and should be handled with care.

After reviewing financial details and signing for the car, a bank essentially fronts the bill and expects you to pay back all monies with interest. So, this is an instance where the lump sum of the annuity occurs at the *beginning* of the loan period, thus falling in the category of problems to be solved with formula for the present value of an annuity. We consider a few examples to illustrate the use of the present value formula. The examples below assume no money was used toward the down payment.

Example 3.3 Determine Tom's monthly payment on a \$19,500 Nissan Sentra, which has been financed at an interest rate of 4.2% over a four-year period.

Solution 3.3 We again use Equation 3.1 to solve for *PMT*. We note that the amount financed, \$19,500, is *PVA*. Our interest rate is 4.2% or 0.042 (use the decimal form in equation), time *t* is 4, and interest is compounded monthly so *c* is 12:

$$19{,}500 = \frac{PMT\left[1-\left(\frac{0.042}{12}+1\right)^{-12(4)}\right]}{\frac{0.042}{12}}$$

$$\Rightarrow 26{,}600 = \frac{PMT\left[1-(1.0035)^{-48}\right]}{0.0035}$$

$$\Rightarrow \quad 68.25 = PMT[1-0.845601827]$$

$$\Rightarrow \quad 68.25 = 0.154398173\ PMT$$

$$\Rightarrow \quad 442.04 = PMT$$

Tom's monthly payment will be \$442.04.

Example 3.4 If Tom's credit score increases by 50 points, the bank has agreed to decrease the APR to 2.6%. What would Tom's new monthly payment be?

Solution 3.4 We use Equation 3.1 and solve for PMT:

$$19{,}500 = \frac{PMT\left[1-\left(\frac{0.026}{12}+1\right)^{-12(4)}\right]}{\frac{0.026}{12}}$$

$$\Rightarrow \quad 42.25 = PMT[1-0.901326695]$$

$$\Rightarrow \quad 42.25 = 0.098673305\ PMT$$

$$\Rightarrow 428.18 = PMT$$

Tom's new monthly payment would be \$428.18.

Upon first glance, the savings in Example 3.4 do not seem considerable when we just consider savings for one month. However, upon a second look, what Tom saves over the four-year period is a testament to the benefits of having a better credit score. We leave it as one of the student exercises to figure out two ways to calculate how much Tom saves over the life of the car loan, given his new credit score.

3.5 Crunching the Credit Card Numbers

In 2009, President Obama signed the Credit Card Accountability, Responsibility, and Disclosure (CARD) Act. The Act, among other advantages, restricts credit card companies from imposing unfair rate hikes and forces the companies to talk about contract terms in noncryptic, plain language (Office of the Press Secretary 2009). In addition, the Act is responsible for protecting college students and young adults. Companies that issue credit cards and universities alike are now required to reveal contract agreements concerning marketing or distribution of credit cards to students. Long overdue, this government legislation makes it impossible to dupe students into signing up for credit cards without proper agreement disclosure. Before, credit card companies used to swarm in on unsuspecting college students at campuses nationwide and allowed students to sign up for credit cards on a whim with the elusive promise of financial freedom and a corny T-shirt, key chain, or water bottle.

The mentioned legislation now protects college students and at least helps them have full knowledge of the financial situation upon which they are about to embark. Though parents are ideally responsible for schooling their children regarding financial matters, it often resorts to the "blind leading the blind" since parents themselves are steeped in debt and can offer no real guidance in that respect. In order to make for a more informed society regarding credit card advantages and disadvantages, we have to work toward increasing the financial knowledge base of college students, which comprise a huge segment of the population at large. The message is clear and basic: it is hard to get ahead in your savings if all of your money is going to fatten the pockets of your credit card companies through interest payments (Mack 2010).

Such an undertaking would take more time than is realistically possible in one textbook. However, we illustrate a few examples, which may shed light on the overall picture of credit card usage and ramifications tied to it.

3.5.1 Making the Minimum Monthly Payment

You will find that swiping the credit card at Macy's or using it online to purchase that must-have airline ticket is the easy part attached to using someone else's money. You will soon discover, however, that the looming death trap associated with using credit cards unwisely is the interest repayment of the debt from what was so easily charged. We consider a simple but realistic example of making a charge and paying the minimum monthly payment that the bank requires for the purchase:

Example 3.5 Najid completed his Introduction to Robotics final exam and decided to reward himself with a flat screen TV, valued at $538.48, including taxes. Since he recently received a Visa card that guaranteed a certain amount of airline miles per purchase, he charged the entire amount of the TV. Determine how long it will take him to pay the debt in total if his card has an APR of 16.89% and he makes only the minimum monthly $15 payment. We assume no extra daily percentage fees for balances that carry over into the next pay period, which may not be the case in real life.

Solution 3.5 When Najid chose to pay for the purchase via his credit card, his situation became one that fit in the category of the present value of annuity. Essentially, the bank that awarded him the credit card fronted the $538.48, so the lump sum appears at the beginning. We should use Equation 3.1 and solve for t, the time (in years) that the debt is repaid. Since Najid is paying the bill monthly, the compounding period is 12; the PVA is $538.48. PMT is $15 and r is 0.1689. The equation reveals the following value for t:

$$
\begin{aligned}
538.48 &= \frac{15\left[1-\left(\dfrac{0.1689}{12}+1\right)^{-12t}\right]}{\dfrac{0.1689}{12}} \\
538.48 &= \frac{15\left[1-(1.014075)^{-12t}\right]}{0.014075} \\
\Rightarrow 0.5053 &= 1-(1.014075)^{-12t} \\
\Rightarrow -0.4947 &= -(1.014075)^{-12t} \\
\Rightarrow 0.4947 &= 1.014075^{-12t} \\
\Rightarrow \log(0.4947) &= -12t\log(1.014075) \\
\Rightarrow t &= \frac{\log(0.4947)}{-12\log(1.014075)} \\
\Rightarrow t &= 4.2
\end{aligned}
$$

Based on the minimum monthly payment, it will take Najid 4.2 years to pay back the debt for the TV. We convert the decimal part of the answer to months based on the following:

$$\frac{0.2 \text{ years}}{1} \times \frac{12 \text{ months}}{1 \text{ year}} = 2.4 \text{ months}$$

Hence, it will take Najid four years and approximately three months to pay off the credit card balance from his TV purchase if he makes the minimum payment of \$15 per month.

Note that Solution 3.5 makes use of several algebraic properties introduced in asset one, the algebra review section. We have to use basic properties of isolating the unknown variable as well as those involving logarithms. A look at the introductory chapter may prove useful if you are still somewhat confused with the calculation of t.

Example 3.6 Determine how much Najid paid in interest after he paid the balance off, according to the minimum-payment repayment plan. We assume no extra daily percentage fees for balances that carry over into the next pay period, which may not be the case in real life.

Solution 3.6 Najid paid \$15 per month for four years and three months, which equals approximately 51 months. We see then that:

$$\frac{\$15}{\text{month}} \times \frac{51 \text{ months}}{1} = \$765$$

We quickly notice that Najid's initial purchase of \$538.48 has risen to \$765, yielding total interest payments of \$765 – \$538.48, or \$226.52. Najid has paid not only for the flat-screen TV that he wanted but also close to half the value of another TV altogether in interest. What a way to celebrate the completion of a final exam!

"The next few days are critical. We're going to slowly introduce her to cash."

3.5.2 Credit Card Perks

Credit card companies have wised up in their efforts to attract more and more customers. Banks have become more aware that customers are realizing their own spending power and the credit outlets where they choose to wield it. Consequently, some banks now offer certain perks to make associations with them appear more worthwhile.

Definition

A **credit card perk** *is an incentive that credit card companies use to encourage consumer use of credit. Perks are often in the form of a monetary reward or in some other intangible form having its own sense of value or worth.*

These perks may take on several forms and can entice the most straightlaced of buyers to participate in the use of credit. Several of these perks follow (Fitzpatrick 2011):

1. Free airline miles or flight vouchers
2. Cash back
3. Tickets for theme parks
4. Gift cards
5. Access to airport lounges
6. Phone discounts
7. Free ID fraud protection

These represent only a few perks that accompany varying credit cards. And let's shoot straight. These companies are not just offering benefits or perks because they love you so much. Their goal is to seduce and encourage more and more charging with the hopes that you will carry a balance over to the next month, so they can impose interest and earn money off of purchases. What's more, as discussed earlier, your credit score possibly decreases every time you apply for a credit card, so do your research and decide which card has the right fit for you.

There are as many different possible perks or rewards as there are credit card companies. You will just have to investigate on your own and ask the right questions to see which perk program is right for you. For example, you would have to understand the guidelines that come with airline miles accumulated through usage of the card. Often, customers realize too late that there are certain blackout dates for travel for certain rewards programs, which could defeat the purpose of accumulating miles altogether. In addition, credit cards with great perks often have high interest rates; so beware! Cash back rewards seem the most beneficial, as money itself can contribute to the financial goals one may have, irrespective of what they are.

It is important to realize that we steer clear of strictly equating the notion of a credit card with debt. Used wisely and with discipline, you can get "free" rewards from credit companies. If you are disciplined and pay the total due each month, the rewards can add quickly, and you can beat the credit card agencies at their own game. You can make money off of them as opposed to their making money off of you. For example, some Visa cards give 1% cash back for every purchase. Since grocery purchases are unavoidable, for example, you can make these purchases on the card regularly and pay the balance in full each month. After a certain amount of purchases, the cash back reward amount will have grown to a point where you will be able to redeem them. A request is then generally made online to redeem rewards, and the reward is applied directly as a credit to the account or is mailed as a paper check. And the cycle continues. If you were slack concerning paying the balance off each month, accumulated rewards would be offset by any interest that may have accrued over the repayment window. So you just have to use much discipline and a little common sense to make sure you are *really* receiving the perks that the card promises.

3.5.3 Transferring Balances and Teaser Rates

During the summer of 2011, the author found himself between a rock and a hard place. He had been preparing and saving for over a year to make a major purchase, totaling around $7000. Funds were secure in an online savings account, so he would not have access to them any earlier than two business days' notice, which was the time it generally took to move funds to his checking account. He knew that he had to make this purchase during the short time he had flown home to North Carolina. The date for the plane ticket back to New York was set, and he had two days left to make the transaction happen. His credit score was very high, so financing would be no problem—so he thought.

He had not realized that the time it takes to process financing for the major purchase could not be done in a day or two. It would take at least four days, which he did not have, unless he paid extra monies for a plane ticket alteration.

He made a drastic decision within the circumstances and time period that he faced. Since he knew he had access to the monies in a savings and that he had a very high credit limit, he did the unthinkable by charging the entire purchase to his credit card. This was a decision he made only because he knew he would be responsible for the repayment of *all* of the debt.

The problem that existed was that subconsciously, he still could not stomach such a huge balance as a result of a gigantic purchase, which was now subject to a 19% interest rate. Although he planned on paying the balance off immediately, he still wanted to shield himself in the event that another emergency arose, and he needed some of the funds on reserve. The worst-case scenario for him was that he would take no more than two months to pay the balance off, which would mean there would be some portion of the balance carried into another month. Essentially, he searched for the best situation in which he would be able to conduct a **balance transfer**.

Definition

A **balance transfer** *is a transaction in which all or a portion of the balance on one or more credit cards is transferred to another one.*

Although this financial situation is not ideal, it has its place in helping to deal with possible emergencies, especially if you know the emergency will be short-lived. You will have to do some serious research when finding the right card to transfer your balance to because, often, there is an automatic transfer fee that can be as high as 3% of the balance outright, regardless of what the interest rate is on the new credit card. But after considering the transfer fee, you should indeed be aware of the interest rate attached to the card. Interest rates associated with credit cards in this situation of transferring balances could have a seductive 1.9% interest rate, which is virtually unheard of. Often, however, this interest rate is a **teaser (or introductory) rate**.

Definition

A **teaser (or introductory) rate** *is a reduced interest rate that is bestowed to a customer during the early stage of a loan. It is not permanent and will increase to a "normal" rate after a specified time period.*

Teaser rates do just that: entice and taunt. If we are not careful and responsible, they become like worms on the end of fishing poles, luring the big-mouthed, unsuspecting catfish to take a bite. Once caught, prey can easily get snagged and pulled out of any sense of stability, leaving them like fish out of water, gasping and clinging to dear financial life. We explore an example:

Example 3.7 Paula vowed to straighten out her financial life and pay off her credit card debt. Over time, she amassed a debt totaling \$657.23 on her Master Card, \$786.20 on her American Express, and \$248.21 on her Visa. She decided that she would transfer all balances to a separate credit card after receiving two balance transfer offers, outlined as follows:

> Offer One: This credit card imposes a 3% one-time balance transfer fee per balance transferred or \$10 per balance transferred, whichever is higher. Once transferred, the balance is subject to a 1.9% teaser APR for the first six months and increases to a standard interest rate afterward.
>
> Offer Two: This credit card has no balance transfer fee. Once transferred, the balance is subject to a 5.9% APR for the first six months and then increases to a standard interest rate afterward.

Determine which credit card offer saves Paula the most money if her goal is to transfer all existing balances to one card and to pay off the consolidated balance in *six months* (assume no other charges are made to the new card and equal payments each month).

Solution 3.7 Offer One

Each balance is subject to a 3% one-time transfer fee:

$$\$657.23 \times 3\% = \$19.72$$
$$\$786.20 \times 3\% = \$23.59$$
$$\$248.21 \times 3\% = \$7.44$$

So after initial transfers, the total balance subject to the APR is: \$657.23 + \$19.72 + \$786.20 + \$23.59 + \$248.21 + \$10 = \$1744.95 In the third balance transfer, we use \$10 instead of \$7.44 since guidelines require us to use the higher value between the 3% fee and \$10. We are reminded that this \$1744.95 is a lump sum that occurs in the beginning of the loan phase, so we use Equation 3.1 to help us solve. We determine the amount we need to pay each month in order to pay the transferred balance in six months, using the balance, teaser rate, compounding period, and time:

$$1744.95 = \frac{PMT\left[1-\left(\frac{0.019}{12}+1\right)^{-12(0.5)}\right]}{\frac{0.019}{12}}$$
$$\Rightarrow 292.44 = PMT$$

Remember that compounding is monthly, so $c = 12$. And we wish to pay off the balance in six months, which equates to ½ of a year; so our time is 0.5, or $t = 0.5$. Our calculations reveal that we should pay \$292.44 per month to pay off the balance.

Finally, we determine the total amount Paula pays in fees and interest by subtracting her total debt before transferring from how much she paid during the six-month payment window (including transfer fees). Her total debt before transferring is \$1691.64, which is the total amount owed on all cards before transferring. After transferring, she makes six payments of \$292.44, totaling \$1754.64. The total amount in fees and interest she pays in order to transfer under Offer One is \$63:

$$(292.44)(6) - 1691.64 = 63.00$$

Offer Two

There is no transfer fee, so we simply start applying interest to the total amount transferred, which is \$1691.64. For the first six months our APR is 5.9%, and our time should again reflect paying this rate for six months, expressed in years. So t again is 0.5. Our equation then yields:

$$1691.64 = \frac{PMT\left[1-\left(\frac{0.059}{12}+1\right)^{-12(0.5)}\right]}{\frac{0.059}{12}}$$
$$\Rightarrow \$286.81 = PMT$$

In this case, the total amount Paula pays in fees and interest under Offer Two is \$29.22:

$$(286.81)(6) - 1691.64 = 29.22$$

Paula would save more money (about $34) by transferring her debt to the card under Offer Two.

Example 3.7 is a real-world situation that many face daily as they juggle the realities of their expenses. Companies issuing credit have stepped up their game to chorale as many customers as possible. In this example, it is very tempting for Paula to choose Offer One since the teaser is much less than in Offer Two. However, the impact of the balance transfer fees weighs more than most people realize and can significantly influence the overall bottom line. It behooves each of us to pay close attention to guidelines concerning teaser rates and perform relevant calculations before making a decision that can impact us for months, even years.

3.5.4 Deferred Interest

Often, certain companies (like furniture companies) offer heavy discounts during key holidays. Customers are targeted during these times since they are feeling generous and in the purchasing mood. Among its strategies to lure these customers is the opportunity for them to pay for purchases in a "convenient" manner, one that challenges customers' sense of discipline and focus. This method of repayment is referred to as **deferred interest**.

Definition

Payment plans that offer to delay (or defer) payment of interest during a specified period of time are **deferred interest** *plans. In the retail sector, these are often advertised as charging "no interest until" a certain date. After that date, however, interest that has been accruing since the purchase date is charged to the account and is applied to the original amount of the purchase.*

Used wisely, this repayment strategy can make the purchase of major items more possible, especially if one does not have the entire lump sum readily handy. Ignored, however, deferred interest can be a slow-moving train, which can eventually pick up steam and speed. Often referred to as a hidden time bomb, this payment method can wreak havoc on even the most thrifty and most frugal person. Since the specified time of repayment can be so long (often spreading over years), creditors bank on buyers' forgetfulness or lack of discipline in the repayment of the debt. Although you may start paying back well, your focus for the remaining time period may be full of challenges: other financial matters, emergencies that may have arisen, or changes in family or work situations.

Three key elements are generally at work in deferred-interest ads to lure the customer in to visit the store, thus increasing the likelihood of a purchase.

The Element of Urgency

Ads promoting deferred interest generally are extended for a limited time only. They often use jargon that states something to the effect of, "Hurry! Sale Ends Saturday!" or "One Day Sale." This is meant to force buyers to feel a sense of unnecessary anxiety. These ads urge customers to make a decision *now* and think about the consequences later.

The Element of the Fine Print

Somewhere on the ad, in very small print, are stipulations about the purchase that may not have been obvious upon first glance. Often, a minimum purchase amount is required in order for one to make good on the deferred-interest offer. This fine print is very inconspicuous or appears not at all on the ad itself. When customers arrive at the store and only want to purchase a $500 loveseat using deferred interest, for example, they may discover that they must purchase at least $2500 worth of furniture in order to qualify for the delayed-interest repayment deal. It becomes crucial to investigate the fine print to get a complete picture of what the company requires with respect to the advertised financing opportunity.

The Element of Delayed Financial Responsibility

In generally, customers who use the deferred-interest program are not "responsible" for paying any interest for a certain time, say 48 months. Customers will only be required to make minimum monthly payments, which will not necessarily be the total financed amount divided by 48. Some banks have begun implementing plans where customers make equal payments per month or the total financed amount divided by 48 in this case. However, this is relatively a new phenomenon. Banks generally charge monthly amounts so that the total financed amount is not paid by the end of the promotional period. But the bank does this for a reason. It has something up its financial "sleeve" when doing this. Although the luxury of paying using deferred interest can work to customers' advantage, it can come back to haunt them later if they do not exercise strict, financial discipline. We discuss the possible backlash that often comes along with paying with this method in the following example concerning the purchase of a laptop.

We offer as a general rule a way of attacking such a repayment plan so that you always come out on top:

1. Divide the total financed amount by the number of months in the deferred-interest promotional time window;
2. Be consistent with paying this monthly amount so that the final payment is processed right before the "no interest until" date approaches.

Here is a real-life example, illustrating this technique based on another purchase the author made. In January of 2011, the author decided to purchase a laptop. The store's offer was one in which the laptop charges could be paid back within one year. The benefit was that monies could be left in a savings account without having to shell out the total cost of the laptop up front. As long as discipline was exercised, the author would not have to sacrifice earning interest on his own money each month while paying off the laptop in equal payments. The opportunity had come to finance the purchase for "free."

The total laptop amount was $1472.19. As per the stated strategy, the total was divided by 12, which made monthly payments around $122.68. Even if the author did not pay this amount each month, the bank would still require a minimum monthly payment, say $25. If this minimum payment went unpaid each month, there would be a penalty of paying upwards of 30% in interest, and the opportunity to continue paying interest on a deferred timeline would be revoked. Hence, deferred interest does not mean that you make *no payments* over the time period. It just meant that as long as the minimum payments are made each month, a deferred repayment timetable would still be in effect. Table 3.3 outlines the author's actual payments for each month, other charges made during the 12-month interval, cumulative deferred interest charges, and the running balance remaining on the account after each payment.

Note in the months of August and September, respectively, the credit card was used to make $66.11 and $49.76 in additional charges. Remember that although the laptop was financed over 12 months, it was still a credit line that could be used to make everyday purchases via the credit card attached to the account. One has to guard against the temptation to start using this credit card

TABLE 3.3 Monthly Payments Toward Laptop Purchase (Jan 2011–Jan 2012)

Month	Cumulative Deferred Interest Charges if Remaining Balance Not Paid by Feb. 7, 2012	Monthly Payment Rendered	Other Charges	Remaining Balance
Jan. 2011	$0	$0	$0	$1472.19
Feb. 2011	$17.53	$122.68	$0	$1349.51
Mar. 2011	$41.93	$122.70	$0	$1226.81
Apr. 2011	$65.22	$122.70	$0	$1104.11
May 2011	$86.59	$122.70	$0	$981.41
June 2011	$106.19	$122.70	$0	$858.71
July 2011	$122.96	$122.70	$0	$736.01
Aug. 2011	$137.79	$122.70	$66.11	$679.42
Sept. 2011	$150.43	$188.81	$49.76	$540.37
Oct. 2011	$160.42	$172.46	$0	$367.91
Nov. 2011	$168.15	$122.70	$0	$245.21
Dec. 2011	$173.38	$122.60	$0	$122.61
Jan. 2012	$176.19	$122.61	$0	$0 (yay!)

irresponsibly because interest on new purchases can get confusing with interest in the deferred case. As Table 3.3 shows, the payment for September took into account the normal payment of $122.70 plus the total amount charged in August ($66.11) for a payment of $188.81. Likewise, the payment for October reflected the normal payment of $122.70 plus the total amount charged in September ($49.76) for a payment of $172.46. Since no more charges were made on that card after September, monthly payments went back to the normal $122.70. In January of 2012, the final payment of $122.61 was made, which brought the balance on the financed laptop purchase to zero. The account was finally paid off! Thankfully, none of the charges in the deferred-interest column of Table 3.3 mattered since all of the initial balance was paid in full by February 7, 2012. We say a word, however, about what would have happened in the event that any portion of the balance was carried past the promotional cutoff date.

Figure 3.2 is a portion of the author's January 2012 statement. From Table 3.3, the remaining promotional balance in the amount of $122.61 was due by the deferred financing expiration date, which was February 7, 2012. If this total amount was not paid by this date, then the total interest that had been accumulating over the promotional period ($176.19) would have to be repaid.

Instead of paying $122.61 as the last payment before February 7, let's suppose a payment was made in the amount of $122.60 with no other payment until after the deferred financial expiration date. The last two rows of our table would look as follows, illustrated in Table 3.4:

Deferred Financing Promotion Summary/Deferred Interest Charge Calculation

Thank you for taking advantage of the Deferred Financing promotional offer. Your Deferred Financing promotion began on the date of the applicable transaction. **You must pay your Deferred Financing promotional balance in full by the Expiration Date shown below to avoid paying the accrued interest charges.** To keep your account in good standing you must also pay the Minimum Payment Due each month by the Payment Due Date. The Deferred Financing Expiration Date and the due date of your Minimum Payment Due are different. If the due date of your Minimum Payment is before your Deferred Financing Expiration Date please make sure you make at least the Minimum Payment Due by its Payment Due Date to avoid a late charge.

Deferred Financing Transaction Date & Original Amount	Remaining Promotional Balance	Balance Subject to Deferred Interest	Deferred Interest Charge for this Billing Cycle	Total Deferred Interest Charge*	Deferred Financing Expiration Date
01/21/2011 $1,308.93	$122.61	$143.90	$2.81	$176.19	**02/07/2012**

*Deferred interest charges have not been included in your account balance. Deferred interest charges will post to your account if you do not pay your Deferred Financing promotional balance in full before the Expiration Date and/or you make a late payment.

FIGURE 3.2 Deferred Financing Promotion Summary for Final Month

TABLE 3.4 Making a Payment of $122.60 as Opposed to $122.61

Month	Cumulative Deferred Interest Charges if Remaining Balance Not Paid by Feb. 7, 2012	Monthly Payment Rendered	Other Charges	Remaining Balance
Dec. 2011	$173.38	$122.60	$0	$122.61
Jan. 2012	$176.19	$122.60	$0	$0.01

Note that the remaining balance would only be a penny. We assume no other payments were made until the next statement, which would be after the February 7 promotional cutoff date. One would think that the only interest that accrued to the account would be the interest on the remaining balance or on one cent. However, according to the rules and guidelines of deferred interest for the card, if there is a remaining balance from the initial purchase after the promotional cutoff date, *even if that balance is only a penny*, the amount to be repaid is the total amount of interest shown for January 2012, which represents all interest applied to the original purchase amount. A balance of one cent would force repayment of *all* of the interest that had accrued on the initial $1472.19.

We see now that deferred interest can be a beneficial asset if we stay on top of payments and keep abreast of the promotional expiration date. Otherwise, such a repayment plan can explode and do more harm than good, defeating the purpose of saving on paying interest altogether.

3.6 Financing a Home: The American Dream ... Or Is It?

The largest investment you may make after graduating from college will be that of your very own home. Dubbed the American dream, a home represents a sense of comfort and stability. It can be one of the greatest joys one experiences and provides satisfaction for those who work tirelessly day after day to make their money mean something. Before deciding on buying a home, however, you should be sure that it is a purchase that you are mentally and financially ready to make. During the Great Recession of 2008, upwards of seven million Americans lost their homes (Sullivan 2015). The reality is that purchasing a home is a major undertaking and should be done after much thought and preparation. Until then, it may be advisable to consider the benefits and luxuries of renting. Section 3.6.1 discusses benefits of renting and how one prepares for the process of home ownership. Section 3.6.2 delves into some of the basic mathematics behind financing a home, giving special attention to amortization schedules.

3.6.1 Playing House

Arguably, one of the best ways to prepare for home ownership is to go through the process of renting your own apartment. There was a time when renting was frowned upon by those who believed strongly in the notion of home ownership. People who rented were seen as lazy and as ones who were not serious about their financial future. The proverbial refrain concerning renters was that they were content with essentially flushing their money down the toilet by aiding property owners in their quest to become rich. With the downturn of the American economy, however, more and more individuals have used the vehicle of renting to position themselves for home ownership and to stabilize their financial condition amid the economy's recovery from the 2008 recession hit. In essence, renting allows you to "play house" and discover if you have the discipline, endurance, and financial wherewithal to maintain your own living quarters without the heavy commitment attached to a mortgage.

As with any major decision, it is advantageous to consider both pros and cons as they relate to renting and whether it is a right move for you. Think of possible benefits and disadvantages of renting and jot them down in the space given. See if any of your responses match any of the ones that follow in Table 3.5:

Example 3.8 List three pros and three cons associated with renting as opposed to purchasing a home, condo, loft, or townhome.

Solution 3.8

Pros of Renting	Cons of Renting
1.________	1.________
2.________	2.________
3.________	3.________

How did your answers match up with ours? There are quite a few pros and cons associated with renting. Hopefully, you thought of some that were not listed in Table 3.5. The more benefits and disadvantages you can think of, the better off you will be when the time comes to start the renting process.

"Playing house" involves testing your ability to pay bills on time and live independently in other financial respects. It is advisable to set aside an extra amount of money each month (say $150) to see if you are still able to live comfortably without needing it. With the purchase of a home, you will be responsible for your own repairs and replacements. This $150 represents the money each month you earmark for these imaginary repairs. If you can still live comfortably each month while renting without

TABLE 3.5 Pros and Cons of Renting

Pros of Renting	Cons of Renting
1. Tenant generally not financially responsible for major repairs (i.e., structural damage, leaks, etc.)	1. No tax write-off benefits
2. Allows one to live in a certain area for a short period in order to test if (s)he wants to establish permanent residency in the same vicinity or move	2. Monthly rent payments not applied to tenant's ownership of the property
3. Can save money for down payment of home purchase	3. May have to deal with noisy neighbors and/or their pets
4. No headaches or worries associated with selling the property when the need arrives to move	4. Charged for making major changes to apartment (painting walls, installing ceiling fans, etc.)
5. Not financially responsible for paying property taxes on homes or association fees for condos, lofts, or townhomes	5. May have to move more frequently to different apartments due to rent increases (to keep monthly rent payments relatively the same)

needing this $150, you are well on your way to readying yourself for home ownership. Other expenses you will need to consider for home ownership are property taxes, private mortgage insurance (which you will have to get if you do not put much money down), and/or association fees. If you are not able to set aside and not touch money while renting (in addition to your regular rent payment and utilities), you should consider again whether you are ready to move to the step of home ownership. The upside to this idea of "playing house" is that you are doing it in the safe confines of a situation where you are renting in contrast to one where you are locked into the financial responsibility of paying for a mortgage.

3.6.2 Some Basic Mortgage Calculations

Karl: "So, what's the verdict?"

Loan Officer: "Well, Mr. Dixon, looks like with your income, you can afford a 1.5 million dollar house."

Karl: "Really? That's fantastic. Looks like my years of working are finally paying off. I can finally get my dream home. One … point … five. I can't wait to start. Let's go take a look at some of these million dollar dream homes."

The previous short conversation could possibly reveal much about Karl Dixon, an overjoyed soon-to-be home-buyer. The loan officer has just informed him that the amount of house he can afford to buy is upwards of $1.5 million. What Mr. Dixon may not realize is that just because you qualify for a $1.5 million house does not mean that you have to buy one that costs that amount. Karl can be just as content with purchasing a $500,000 house and still have some financial breathing room to enjoy life. Many, like Karl perhaps, operate under the assumption that the more money is made, the more money should be spent. In his *Rich Dad, Poor Dad*, Kiyosaki mentions that this "process of increased spending throws families into greater debt and into more financial uncertainty, even though they may be advancing in their jobs and receiving pay raises on a regular basis" (2000).

So let's help out Mr. Dixon figure out a more comfortable loan ceiling amount for his mortgage based on how much he can pay per month, so that he can still have some financial flexibility with paying other bills, eating out, and saving for vacation. We'll address most of these ideas in Asset Five, where we discuss budgeting. In the meantime, let's say that Karl has determined that he is comfortable with paying $1300 per month in rent and decides that he will finance the house for 30 years, which is not uncommon. Although there are different interest options available to him, he decides to go with the **fixed APR** offered of 3.0% since his credit score is 710. We determine how much loan he qualifies for based on Equation 3.1, our present value of annuity formula. Again, we use this formula because the bank will eventually front the money as a loan, and equal payments will be used to repay the debt.

Definition

A **fixed APR** *is an interest rate that does not fluctuate over the time period in which the loan is to be repaid. A* **variable APR** *is an interest rate that fluctuates over the time period in which the loan is to be repaid.*

Example 3.9 Determine how much loan Karl needs if he can afford $1300 per month at a fixed APR of 3.0% for a 30-year repayment term. Assume he puts no money down.

Solution 3.9 Since the loan (lump sum) will be provided by the bank up front, we use Equation 3.1:

$$
\begin{aligned}
PVA &= \frac{1300\left[1-\left(\frac{0.03}{12}+1\right)^{-12(30)}\right]}{\frac{0.03}{12}} \\
&= 308,346.20
\end{aligned}
$$

Karl would need a loan of $308,346.20 from the bank.

It may be that Karl feels comfortable enough in his ability to take the loan officer's advice and purchase a home valued at $1.5 million dollars. Let's take a look at the increase in Karl's monthly payment if the conditions of the loan are similar as in Example 3.9:

Example 3.10 How much more will Karl's monthly payment be if he finances a $1.5 million home at a fixed 3.0% APR for 30 years (with no down payment)?

Solution 3.10 We use the present value of an annuity formula and solve for *PMT*:

$$
\begin{aligned}
1{,}500{,}000 &= \frac{PMT\left[1-\left(\frac{0.03}{12}+1\right)^{-12(30)}\right]}{\frac{0.03}{12}} \\
6324.06 &= PMT
\end{aligned}
$$

In this example, Karl's monthly payment would be \$6324.06. This means that he would pay \$5024.06 more each month (\$6324.06 – \$1300 = \$5024.06).

In both of these scenarios with Karl, we assumed that there was no down payment on his home purchase. This assumption is not particularly valid as a general rule in the home-buying process in real life. If there is no down payment made, lenders often force customers to pay something called **private mortgage insurance** (**PMI**).

Definition

Private mortgage insurance (PMI), *paid by the borrower, is lender protection against default on a mortgage loan. It is often put in place when borrowers put down less than 20% on the purchase of a home.*

This insurance is often added monthly as a part of the mortgage payment. After approximately two years, you can request that PMI be discontinued since the bank sees you are making good on your payments. Lenders nowadays, however, strongly favor applicants who can put at least 20% down on the home purchase. This gives those awarding the loan some assurance that you are absorbing some of the financial risk of the purchase and are making an undeniable investment in the overall mortgage experience. Hence, PMI becomes unnecessary in that case. Let's see how the down payment factors into Karl's initial situation, in which he chooses to pay 8% down.

Example 3.11 Determine Karl's monthly payment if he is awarded a 30-year, \$308,346.20 home loan at a fixed 3.0% APR, assuming that he will put 8% down toward the purchase.

Solution 3.11 Since Karl is putting down 8%, we subtract the equivalence of that from the total loan before financing:

$$308{,}346.20 \times 8\% = 24{,}667.70$$

So, we have \$308,346.20 – \$24,667.70 = \$283,678.50. In our formula, we now determine the monthly payment using this new value as our present value of the annuity, as opposed to the original amount:

$$283{,}678.50 = \frac{PMT\left[1 - \left(\frac{0.03}{12} + 1\right)^{-12(30)}\right]}{\frac{0.03}{12}}$$

$$1196.00 = PMT$$

When Karl puts 8% down, his monthly payment decreases to \$1196.00 (in comparison to \$1300 he pays in Example 3.9).

3.6.3 Amortization Schedules

Once approved for a mortgage, we begin making payments back to the bank. In addition to the interest that we pay, which is determined by the fixed or variable APR, our payments of course are applied to the principal. Over time, we are excited to see the amount of the principal and interest vanish and to finally lay hold of a property that we can call ours. What we may not realize as we are repaying the mortgage debt is that the amount of the monthly payment that goes toward the principal and interest is not of the same ratio. When we take a glance at the **amortization schedule** for the mortgage repayment, we may be shocked to see monthly how much of our payments are applied to the interest and to the principal.

Definition

An **amortization schedule** *is a detailed table showing how much of each monthly mortgage payment is applied to the interest and principal. It typically also shows the payment number, the payment itself, and the amount remaining on the loan.*

Amortization schedules provide a visual overview and summary of mortgage debt repayment. Several online amortization calculators exist. One of them is available at http://goo.gl/yiaIhJ. It provides the calculated monthly payment, gives detailed monthly repayment information, and even tells how much in interest is paid each year. Although such calculators are very useful, it is still necessary for us to grapple with the mathematics behind the calculations, so we can arrive at such answers ourselves. We take a look at an example.

Example 3.12 Megan was approved for a $259,490 loan for a mortgage to be paid off in 15 years at a fixed APR of 4.2%. We assume she put 20% down. Show the amortization table for her first two monthly payments on the loan.

Solution 3.12 We must complete Megan's entries of the amortization schedule for the first two payments. The schedule appears in Table 3.6 and is partially completed:

TABLE 3.6 Megan's Amortization Schedule Showing PMT and Starting Balance

Period	Monthly Payment	Amount Paid Toward Interest	Amount Paid Toward Principal	Remaining Balance
0				$207,592.00
1	$1556.42			
2	$1556.42			

We determine the beginning balance to be financed, based on how much she is putting down on the approved loan amount. Since she is putting down 20%, her starting balance is $207,592, as indicated in the table above (20% of $259,490 is $51,898; this amount subtracted from $259,490 is $207,592). This amount of $207,592 is the only value appearing in the row for *Period 0* because no payments will be made until *Period 1*, which represents the first month's payment.

The table also shows a monthly payment of $1556.42 that Megan pays for *Periods 1* and *2* (or months one and two). We calculate this by solving for *PMT* using the present value of annuity formula to which we are accustomed. We observe three facts when solving for this value:

1. For *PVA*, we use the value of $207,592, the amount determined after applying the down payment.
2. We substitute the value of 15 for *t* since she is paying off the loan in 15 years.
3. Since payments are monthly, our value for *c* is 12.

$$207{,}592 = \frac{PMT\left[1 - \left(\frac{0.042}{12} + 1\right)^{-12(15)}\right]}{\frac{0.042}{12}}$$

$$1556.42 = PMT$$

Amount Paid Toward Interest

For *Period 1*, we compute how much of Megan's payment for that month is paid toward interest. We calculate this by simply applying the loan's APR for that month to the remaining balance from the month before. In this case, the APR for the year is 4.2% (or 0.042); however, the APR for that month is given by $\frac{4.2\%}{12}\left(or\ \frac{0.042}{12}\right)$. The amount paid toward interest, then, would be the APR for that month applied toward $207,592, or $726.57.

$$207{,}592 \times \frac{0.042}{12} = 726.57$$

Amount Paid toward Principal

For *Period 1*, we compute how much of Megan's payment for that month is paid toward the principal or remaining balance. To find this, we simply subtract the amount Megan paid in interest for that month from her actual payment. In this case, the amount paid toward the principal is $829.85, the calculation of which is shown below:

$$1556.42 - 726.57 = 829.85$$

Remaining Balance

For *Period 1*, we compute Megan's remaining balance as of that month. We arrive at this value by subtracting the amount actually paid toward principal for that month from the remaining balance from the previous month. In Megan's case, her remaining balance after making her first payment is $206,762.15, the computation of which appears below:

$$207{,}592 - 829.85 = 206{,}762.15$$

The updated amortization schedule, which now includes *Period 1* calculations, is given in Table 3.7:

TABLE 3.7 Megan's Amortization Schedule Almost Filled

Period	Monthly Payment	Amount Paid Toward Interest	Amount Paid Toward Principal	Remaining Balance
0				$207,592.00
1	$1556.42	$726.57	$829.85	$206,762.15
2	$1556.42			

Note two observations:

1. The total amount paid toward interest plus the amount paid toward principal will always equal the monthly payment for that month.
2. Not all of what is paid for the monthly payment goes directly toward paying the principal off each month. In some cases, depending on how long the loan is financed, the amount paid toward interest for a given month can exceed the amount paid toward the principal.

We provide more details on the amortization schedule for Megan, which includes information for *Period 2*. Remember that, when calculating the interest for *Period 2*, we have to consider the interest rate for that particular month. And when computing the amount paid toward the principal, we use a value from the month prior. We show the completed schedule in Table 3.8:

TABLE 3.8 Megan's Amortization Schedule Completely Filled

Period	Monthly Payment	Amount Paid Toward Interest	Amount Paid Toward Principal	Remaining Balance
0				$207,592.00
1	$1556.42	$726.57	$829.85	$206,762.15
2	$1556.42	$723.67	$832.75	$205,929.40

For the two periods in Example 3.12, what do we observe concerning the trend for the amount paid toward interest and the amount paid toward principal? See if you can figure out the total amount in interest that Megan pays over the life of the loan. You should be able to determine this mathematically without seeing all of the entries of the amortization schedule. Think algebraically, given the information that is provided in the example.

Whether you are calculating values of the amortization schedule by hand, by online calculator, or by software, this financial tool becomes key in helping borrowers keep close tabs on the eradication of their mortgage debt and get one step closer to financial freedom!

3.7 Equity in the Home-Ownership Equation

As mentioned, home ownership is not for the faint of heart. There are many financial hoops through which you have to jump even before moving into the home. Once you move in, you have then become responsible for any maintenance involved—tasks as small as cutting the grass to as large as replacing the roof. One of the main reasons buyers put up with the challenges of owning property is the added *possible* benefit of gaining equity in the home.

Definition

The **equity** *in a home or property refers to the current value of a home minus any lingering debt or amount owed on the same home or property.*

Building equity in a home can be one of the sharpest weapons in the arsenal of a person who wants to invest her money to make money. Gone are the days when homeowners bought a home with the intention of living in the same home for 30 years, the general life span of a mortgage. Generally, people moved in homes to start and raise families, having no desires to leave the city or state. Stability was the goal, and very little would stand in the family's way to seize the stability desired. Homes were just the investment people made that symbolized anchoring, stability, and family.

Today, many buyers (especially recent college graduates) have no immediate desire to "settle down" and "play house." Many feel as though they are upwardly mobile and do not need, in their mind, a house to weigh them down. Job prospects could flood in at any moment. If you were purchasing a home, these opportunities could limit what you may perceive to be the best break of a lifetime. As a consequence, buyers purchase homes, knowing that in about five years or so, they will sell it (they hope) and be rewarded financially.

3.7.1 The Upswing

Suppose, for example, you go to the bank to close the deal on your home purchase. Let's say the home you are purchasing is for $500,000 over the course of 30 years. You complete the paperwork and begin making payments each month, as agreed to by the loan contract. After four years, let's say you have paid your mortgage loan down to $476,000. Most of the payments have gone toward paying mortgage interest. You apply for a job in another state and get it. Now, you have to move. You wish to see how much your property is worth now because you need an idea of what to sell it for. Wait! Why are you concerned about how much it is worth? It *should* be worth $476,000 or the amount owed at this point, right?

Wrong! It is possible that the value of the home could now be worth $520,000, which is more than it was worth when you bought it. This means that the home that sat in one place and did not move has somehow managed to become worth more now than it used to be. The home's equity or value of the home has increased. How can this be? One way is less scientific and more subjective.

You should try to gauge the area you are moving to before signing off on any home loan agreement. You would hope that the area shows signs of growth and development. Are there other homes being built in the neighboring area? Is there a lot of trees and underdeveloped land around where you are moving? Are there retail business chains (especially Starbucks!) nearby or being built? Answering "yes" to these questions could very well lead to an increase in equity of your own perspective home over time because it suggests that the surrounding community is on the upswing. This makes the area more attractive in general and inflates the value of all properties attached to it. This component to building equity in your home is somewhat out of your hands. You cannot predict what builders will erect in your area, but being observant and keen concerning the area surrounding where you want to purchase your home will serve you well.

Other suggestions that can increase the probability that your home will increase in equity are discussed as follows (Baron 2015). We address only a few:

1. **Create Some Space**
   Getting rid of the kitchen island or knocking out a wall can open up the home area tremendously without too much of an out-of-pocket investment. It can pay dividends when trying to sell the home.
2. **Make Regular Maintenance Pay Off**
   Address the basics. Make sure plumbing is adequate and the attic is insulated. Repair leaky windows, and inspect the furnace and septic systems. Performing regular maintenance guards against having to make huge repairs/replacements in the future, thus keeping the value of your property high.
3. **Adopt a Green Mentality**
   More and more people are becoming green-conscious. Consider upgrading heating and air conditioning systems to more green-efficient ones. Consider a solar-powered water heater. Going green can tack on huge amounts of utility savings, making your home a more desirable catch than nongreen ones when the time comes to sell.
4. **Do Easy Bathroom Upgrades**
   We're not talking about a complete bathroom overhaul. Minor changes like applying fresh caulk, replacing faucets, and installing a low-flush toilet can tune up a bathroom and make it look as good as new.
5. **Remember Landscaping**
   Tangled and neglected landscaping does not do well to attract buyers. As most judge a book by its cover, buyers judge your property by surrounding foliage. Plant a tree or two when you first move in, and let time add value to your property as the trees grow. But it is important to manage all greenery and make sure it does not block key views of the home.

3.7.2 The Downtick

On the flip side, it is also possible for your home to acquire negative equity. There is nothing definite that says that your home will always appreciate in value. If you neglect it and are not careful, your home's value will depreciate. In the example from the previous section, let's say that you had purchased the home for $500,000 and made the same payments over four years, leaving you with a mortgage remaining at $476,000 as before. You get the same job opportunity in another state. Once you research and find out the value of your home, you discover that your home is only worth $450,000. Somehow, the value of your property has decreased by $50,000. If you sell it (assuming you receive your asking price of $450,000), you will still owe the remaining $26,000 of the mortgage loan ($476,000 – $450,000). This is a condition known as being "under water." Owning a home has become one of your worst nightmares!

Factors contributing to the depreciation of your home value are various. Many of them are outside of your control and depend on variables driven by the economy (e.g., high foreclosure rate in nearby area, rising unemployment). It is important to note that there are certain factors that contribute to a situation in which the value of your home plummets over time.

1. **Property Neglect**
   Although any home will be subject to basic wear and tear, it is your responsibility to upkeep the home as best as possible. Making necessary repairs and replacements in a timely manner keeps your property appealing and its value up. Also, if homes in the surrounding area have been neglected, your property value will suffer, even if you keep your property maintained.
2. **Neighbors From Hell and/or Crime**
   It is true that you cannot control anybody's behavior but your own. But this does not mean that you should not be proactive. Drive through the neighborhood where you are thinking of buying the home; be sure to drive around during the late evening hours, especially during the summer months. The heat outside does not cause nefarious behavior; but it sure does provide an opportunity for it to rear its ugly head. The National Sex Offender Registry online is a solid and proven way you can also vet your neighbors before making a final decision to purchase the home that you want.
3. **Substandard Schools**
   This is of particular interest to you if you have children. The quality of the schools in the neighborhood is an important contributor to your property value. Schools that are closed down, boarded up, or ranked low tend to tear away at property values of the homes around them. Do your research and investigate the quality of schools surrounding where you live. It may be one of the deciding factors that determine whether you move into the home you are considering or not.

Much of whether your home experiences positive or negative equity change is up to you. Let the variables outside of your control mind themselves. But you have a responsibility to stay vigilant and make the best decision with the best information available so that you can turn a profit on one of the best investments that exists in America today: your home.

Money Talk

College Students and Credit Cards: Friends or Foes?

Through the years, banks have aggressively sought out college students to obtain and use credit cards. In all honesty, credit cards themselves are not to be shamed or despised. Responsible college students can use the four years in college to establish and strengthen their credit score, placing them in prime position to purchase a home or car in the future. Without guidance and wisdom, however, college years can turn into stressful ones that can cast a shadow on students' financial well-being and health. Often, where students fall on this financial continuum depends a great deal on students' knowledge and application of what they know as it relates to credit cards.

According to a study, college students maintained an average credit card balance of $499 in 2013, with freshmen ($611) and seniors ($610) contributing the highest amounts toward that total (Sallie Mae 2013). Since most college students do not have credit histories, banks characterize them as being risky but still pursue them since the volume of college students is huge. All banks tend to see concerning countless college students are dollar signs galore; as a result, they stick them with interest rates that push toward some of the highest rates in the country. In a way, it is unfair that banks know that few college students have no credit history because they are young but "penalize" them anyway by attaching rates as high as 22% to their cards. Students must do their research, then, when it comes to choosing which credit cards would better suit them.

Smart college students will research different credit cards online that cater to goals and perks that pertain to them as students. They will gird themselves with as much information as possible so that they can take advantage of the credit card companies as the companies take advantage of consumers. Students should seek out perks from credit cards such as:

1. First and foremost, locate a credit card that has no fee. Sometimes, you can find great perks from a credit card that waives the fee for the first year and restores it after the year span. If you are disciplined and will remember when the year expires as it relates to the fee, you can enjoy the benefits that come along with the card and cancel it right before the fee hits.
2. Find a card that has cash back rewards or travel rewards. This is fairly simple. These programs reward you a certain percentage of your purchases and allow you to redeem either as cash or toward airline miles for a future trip. Be careful, however, because these programs can force you to try to overspend to reach the reward benchmark. So you could do yourself a disservice by spending $2500 just to get a $25 credit or check in the mail.

Further, students must deliberately commit to paying off balances at the end of each month to avoid effects of exorbitant interest rates and to keep them out of a financially depressing vortex. Banks hope that students will pay only the minimum amount due at the end of the billing cycle so that they pay interest fees. For example, if a student makes a $1000 purchase using a credit card that has a 21.4% interest rate and pays only the minimum payment each month, it will take over seven years to pay back, and the total amount repaid will be $1941 (Lowry 2014). Ridiculous!

In a nutshell, credit cards are neither friend nor foe. How you as a college student decide to use them will determine their effect on your life. They are simply unbiased tools that can help steer your credit score in a financial direction that can immensely benefit you; or they can help drive your score in a direction that will lead you into a reality of anxiety, pain, and regret. Ultimately, the choice is yours.

How will you choose to use your credit card freedom?

Student Exercises: Present Value of an Annuity

3.1 In Table 3.2, assume that we have a population of 250,000.

a. About how many people would we expect to have a FICO score that is between 650 and 699?
b. For those who have a FICO score between 500 and 549, about how many people would we expect to make late payments or go delinquent on credit account?

3.2 Wayd currently has $37,001 in student loans he has to repay at an interest rate of 3.76%. He also has private loans totaling $4588 at an interest rate of 4.9%. He would like to pay both off in 20 years. A bank representative offered him an opportunity to consolidate both loans into one at an interest rate of 4.01% with an origination fee of $785. If the consolidated loan would be paid back over the same 20 years, would it be a good financial decision to merge both loans into one? Show mathematically why it would or would not in terms of the total interest he would repay in both scenarios.

3.3 In Example 3.4, Tom saved on his monthly car payment since his credit score was 50 points higher than in Example 3.3. Show two different methods of calculating Tom's total savings over the four-year period. (Hint: In one case, consider how much he saves each month and make calculations based on that. In the second case, think about the total amount Tom pays in interest in Example 3.3 only and then how much he pays in interest in Example 3.4 only. Now, make calculations based on these values.)

3.4 Determine how much Natalie would be required to pay monthly to afford a $23,555 car loan at 5.09% over five years, assuming monthly payments. Assume she puts no money down.

3.5 Jared's Mastercard balance is $2198.26. How much would he have to pay back each month in order to pay the balance off in a year and a half, assuming an APR of 19.77%? We assume no extra daily percentage fees for balances that carry over into the next pay period, which may not be the case in a real life.

3.6 Sheremy planned on paying off her car loan of $24,981 with monthly payments of $699.14. At an APR of 5.2%, how long will it take her to pay the loan back?

3.7 How much does Manuél pay in interest overall on a $329,800 house if he makes monthly payments at an interest rate of 4.1%? How much would he save in interest overall if the APR was 3.66% instead? Assume in both cases that he pays off the mortgage in 30 years.

3.8 Jessica was granted a home loan in the amount of $429,050 to be paid back in 30 years. Assume she put down $30,100 for a down payment. For an APR of 3.13%, complete the following amortization schedule for the first three payments:

Period	Monthly Payment	Amount Paid Toward Interest	Amount Paid Toward Principal	Remaining Balance
0	—	—	—	
1				
2				
3				

3.9 TY&G Bank approved Charlie for a home loan in the amount of $841,000. He was curious to find out how much his monthly payments for the loan would differ if he paid the loan off in 30 years as opposed to 20. He also wanted to know how much interest he'd pay overall for both repayment periods. Assume the APR in both scenarios is 3.94%. Complete the chart below regarding Charlie's monthly payments and interest.

Charlie's Home Loan	Monthly Payment	Total Interest Paid
20 years		
30 years		

3.10 (Excel) Portia has an unpaid credit card debt of $461. The interest rate she carries is 17.55%. Make a table showing her payment number, monthly payment, interest, and remaining balance. We assume no extra daily percentage fees for balances that carry over into the next pay period, which may not be the case in a real life.

a. (Scenario 1) Assuming no extra purchases, how long will it take to pay off the loan if you make the minimum payment of $19 per month?

b. (Scenario 2) Would it take exactly half the time to pay off the credit card debt if Portia doubled up on payments each month? If not, how much sooner does she pay the debt off in this case when compared to Scenario 1?

c. Determine how much she saves in interest when doubling up on the payments (comparing the two Scenarios).

d. In Scenario 1, assume she makes seven minimum payments and then decide to transfer the balance to another card. There is a one-time transfer fee of 1% of the current balance. She resumes minimum monthly payments for eight months, during which she enjoys a 2.35% interest rate. After these eight months, she continues making minimum payments at an 18.4% interest rate until the balance is finally paid off. Was it worth it for her to switch cards (when compared to a Scenario 1 payoff strategy)? Why or why not?

3.11 (Excel) Use Excel to complete the following:

a. Make a table that shows *monthly payments* of a $100,000 loan as the interest rate varies from 3% to 10% at 1% increments as the term of the loan varies from 10 years to 30 years at five-year increments (*Hint: Use some form of the $ sign*).

b. Make a table similar to the one described above that shows the *total interest paid* during the life of the loan (*Hint: Use some form of the $ sign*).

3.12 (Excel) Create an amortization schedule for a 20-year, $200,000 loan at 7.5% interest with monthly payments.

a. During which payment number does the amount applied to the principal exceed the amount paid to the interest?

b. *True or False?* After half of the time has passed in making payments, we also note that exactly half of the overall balance has been paid off. Explain.

c. After completing the schedule, show two different ways for finding the total amount of interest paid over the 20 years.

References

Baron, Jeanne. 2015. "Brokers Tell All: 10 Ways to Boost House Value." *This Old House Online*. Accessed July 28, 2015. http://goo.gl/VYjfWr.

Fitzpatrick, Alana. 2011. "Credit Card Perks: Warranties, Protection, Freebies …" *Moneysavingexpert.com*. Accessed January 3, 2012. http://goo.gl/yrSqif.

Federal Trade Commission (FTC). 2015. "Identity Theft Tops FTC's Consumer Complaint Categories Again in 2014." *Federal Trade Commission: Protecting America's Consumers*. Accessed February 20, 2016. https://goo.gl/nXZWQ3.

Kiyosaki, Robert T. 2000. *Rich Dad, Poor Dad*. New York: Warner Books, Inc.

Lobosco, Katie. 2016. "Student Loan Interest Rates Are Going Down." *CNN Money*. Accessed August 13, 2016. http://goo.gl/Nzxqvd.

Mack, Ryan C. 2010. *Living in the Village*. New York: St. Martin's Press.

Office of the Press Secretary. 2009. "Fact Sheet: Reforms to Protect American Credit Card Holders." *The White House*. Accessed May 12, 2017. https://goo.gl/s6mMvl.

Pascual, Al, Kyle Marchini, and Sarah Miller. 2016. "2016 Identity Fraud: Fraud Hits an Inflection Point." *Javelin Strategy and Research*. Accessed April 1, 2016. https://goo.gl/Ef6uvU.

Sullivan, Bob. 2015. "Boomerang Buyers: Is There Homeownership After Foreclosure?" *Credit.com*. Accessed April 1, 2016. http://goo.gl/ItRFLw.

Asset Four

Future Value of an Annuity

Chapter Outline

The question isn't at what age I want to retire,
it's at what income.

George Foreman

4.1 Annuities Revisited

Previously, we addressed annuities in their relation to the repayment of debt through the use of credit cards, car loans, and the like. When we revisit the definition, however, we see that an **annuity** is not a financial instrument solely used for debt repayment. We restate the definition below.

Definition

At its core, an **annuity** *is a flow of fixed payments over a determined period of time. An annuity is drafted such that the said flow of payments terminates after the time period expires.*

An annuity, then, is not limited to fixed payments set for the eradication of debt. Over a certain time period, annuities may also be instruments used to secure one's financial future. Savings plans and different types of retirement vehicles serve as annuities whereby time assists in the growth of money to the investor's favor.

We recall that the notion of a "lump sum" is attached to all annuities. We remember that *more than one* payment is still made at fairly regular intervals, and interest is still applied to this notion of multiple payments. In this case, however, we explore instances in which this lump sum occurs at the *end*, leading us to financial situations categorized as the future value of an annuity.

Mathematically, we use a well-known formula to assist us in calculating certain values associated with the **future value of an annuity**.

Definition

The **future value of an annuity** *is represented mathematically as follows:*

$$FVA = \frac{PMT\left[\left(\frac{r}{c}+1\right)^{ct}-1\right]}{\frac{r}{c}}, \qquad \textbf{Equation 4.1}$$

where FVA is the future value of the annuity; PMT is the regular payment made; r is the APR; c is the compounding period or frequency of payments per year; and t is the total time (in years) of repayment.

Again, we use this formula when the lump sum of the annuity occurs at the end of the financial scenario. Such instances that fall into this category are those involving some savings plans and most retirement accounts. Ahead, we take a look at a few of these instances.

4.2 Never Too Young to Think About Retirement

According to *Public Agenda*, a publication whose mission is to assist average citizens understand policy issues, most college students became dropouts not because they were lazy or could not make the grade. On the contrary, many of them are rather industrious. The stress of balancing work and school, however, took its toll, as many of them had become their own breadwinners (Johnson and Rochkind 2008). Quite naturally, very few college students have the luxury of storing up money for the sake of retiring since they are trying to eke out an existence day to day during their college years. It may be somewhat inspirational, though, to explore a few scenarios in which college students are able to start earmarking funds in their early twenties in smaller amounts. In the following sections, we discuss the role and effect of time on retirement investment strategies. Through basic examples, we attempt to analyze how one's retirement savings are affected by whether accounts are, in fact, interest-bearing and are influenced by when said retirement accounts commence.

4.2.1 Planning Today for Tomorrow

We consider a simple example in which Joey, a 20-year-old college junior, decides to set aside \$100 per month in a retirement account, say a Roth Individual Retirement Account (IRA), which retains a fixed APR of 1.4%, compounded monthly, over the life of the investment. Assuming that he continues to contribute to this account each month until the age of 65 without making any withdrawals, it becomes interesting to see how much is available to him at the end of this time period. Assuming regulatory rules of a typical Roth IRA, Joey does not have to worry with paying taxes on what is available to him since money that funds Roth IRAs typically comes from after-tax dollars. The goal of this example is simply to observe how much Joey's account has accumulated over time because of interest when compared to his stashing away the same amount in a shoebox or safe.

Example 4.1 Determine how much money Joey has in his account at the end of his contributions.

Solution 4.1 Here, we see this is a situation in which the lump sum occurs at the end of the contribution period. Since this is true, we use the future value of an annuity formula (Equation 4.1). In the equation, *PMT* would be the \$100 monthly contribution, the r value would be 0.014 (for the 1.4% interest rate); since we are compounding monthly, c is 12. Our t is 45 or the time in years for the total investment time (65–20 = 45). So we seek the value of *FVA* in:

$$FVA = \frac{100\left[\left(\frac{.014}{12}+1\right)^{12(45)}-1\right]}{\frac{.014}{12}}$$

$$= \frac{100[(1.001167)^{540}-1]}{1.001167}$$

$$= 75{,}164.68$$

Once Joey turns 65, given all previous assumptions, he will have at his disposable a whopping \$75,164.68 to spend as he wishes during his retirement years.

Example 4.2 How much would Joey have accumulated if he would have placed the same amount in a shoebox or safe for the same amount of time (with no interest acting on money)?

Solution 4.2 At \$100 per month over 45 years, Joey's account would have grown to the following:

$$\text{Joey's Account} = \frac{\$100}{\text{month}} \times \frac{12 \text{ months}}{\text{year}} \times 45 \text{ years}$$
$$= \$54{,}000$$

In truth, \$54,000 is not a shabby chunk of change, especially considering that it came about through meager monthly \$100 deposits. However, when compared to Example 4.1, where Joey has access to \$75,164.68, we all begin to take note of the power of interest and the effect on the growth of money. That's a difference slightly over \$21,000, all attributable to Joey's consistency in depositing funds and his decision to place his money in an account that was interest-bearing. And thankfully, since his money is in a Roth IRA, he does not have to pay money to the government on the interest that has accumulated, another striking difference between not placing money in a regular savings account. We speak more about taxation, however, in Asset Five.

4.2.2 Visualizing Prosperity

It becomes increasingly interesting to take a moment to visualize Joey's account over the span of 45 years and witness the exponential growth that is evident in his financial world. When compared to the scenario of his shoebox savings strategy, we see how important such a small interest rate has on his account overall. Figure 4.1 shows Joey's account growth with and without the effect of interest acting on his account over time. The chart shows a running total of Joey's account in both instances, culminating with the total amount accessible at the end of the investment period.

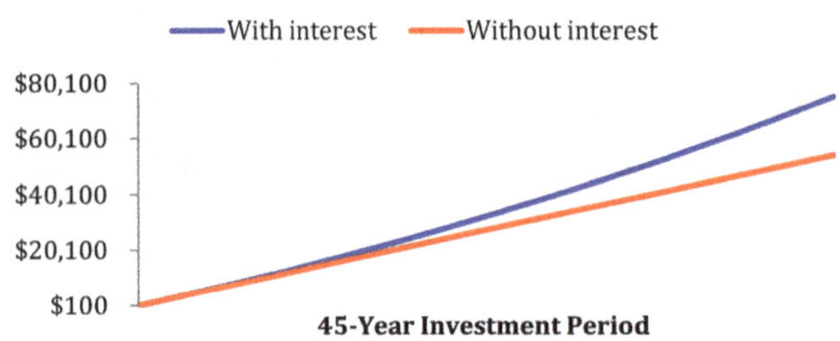

FIGURE 4.1 Joey's Account With and Without Interest Applied

What Figure 4.1 reveals is the power of interest in action. The bottom line in the diagram shows a constant and steady increase in Joey's account. Only what Joey has placed in the account is present. The overall effect of his decision in this situation shows a linear trend, where growth happens but is constant. The top line, however, eventually shows more aggressive growth or exponential growth, where growth occurs slowly but eventually becomes more pronounced over time. In fact, after the first month, Joey's balance is the same with or without interest applied ($100 in each). By the end the 45-year period, as noted, Joey has amassed $54,000 without interest but over $75,000 with it. Oh, that we each learn to visualize and leverage the benefits of interest to our own financial lives!

4.2.3 Time is on Your Side (If You Act Now)

Geary notes that "unfortunately, many of today's workers pass on the opportunity to save for retirement early, when the beauty of compounding interest can work its magic and maximize savings. Hewett Associates discovered that only [thirty-one] percent of ... those in their 20s, who are eligible to place money into retirement savings plan to do so" (2007). Of a truth, this 31% has discovered the true secret behind growth of retirement funds: starting time. We observe two examples, which illustrate this seemingly insignificant variable of starting a retirement plan relatively early.

Example 4.3 Although Alonzo was struggling with working and being a student at Carnegie Mellon, he still managed to open a Roth IRA and make monthly deposits of $285 at a fixed APR of 3.92%. If he is currently 22 years old, how much would be in his IRA when he turns 65, assuming the annual percentage rate (APR) remains the same?

Solution 4.3 Since this is another case in which the lump sum occurs at the end of the payments, we are in the future value scenario. In reality, most IRA investments are subject to variable APRs, which change based on investors' risk tolerance. For the sake of simple comparison, we input values appropriately in Equation 4.1 (Note that $t = 43$, which is the difference in Alonzo's age from the beginning to the end of his deposits):

$$FVA = \frac{285\left[\left(\frac{0.0392}{12}+1\right)^{12(43)}-1\right]}{\frac{0.0392}{12}}$$
$$= \$382,209.85$$

Over this 43-year period, Alonzo has amassed close to $400,000 in retirement savings. And since these funds are in a Roth IRA, Alonzo does not have to pay any of this to Uncle Sam!

Example 4.4 Suppose Tyla decided to wait to start contributing to her retirement until after graduating from Spelman College and landing a job. Suppose she had quite a bit of student loans to pay back and decided to open the Roth at age 45, after having been on the job for a while. Assuming an $855 monthly contribution and an APR and stopping age that are the same as Alonzo's, how much will be in Tyla's retirement account?

"I always hoped retirement would look like this."

Cartoonresource/Shutterstock.com

Solution 4.4 We use Equation 4.1 to determine how much would be in this account (note here that $t = 20$):

$$FVA = \frac{855\left[\left(\frac{0.0392}{12} + 1\right)^{12(20)} - 1\right]}{\frac{0.0392}{12}}$$
$$= \$310{,}788.71$$

We see then that in order for Tyla to have a decent-sized retirement account, she is forced to pay more per month. Since she is only saving for twenty years, she must sacrifice more of her month-to-month earnings in order to make up for a late start. Note that she is contributing three times as much as Alonzo; however, the fact that Alonzo started contributing early (in his twenties) allows him the benefit of contributing less and having more monthly financial flexibility since a smaller portion of his earnings are earmarked for retirement. In fact, we observe that Tyla has $71,421.14 less funds than Alonzo by the time she reaches 65, although she is contributing considerably more per month. Figure 4.2 illustrates Alonzo's and Tyla's money growth over time; Alonzo's slow-and-steady growth outperforms Tyla's portfolio because he decides to make a move and start contributing much earlier than Tyla does.

In essence, the notion of time becomes an invaluable factor that one can leverage to make the retirement account grow aggressively. Making contributions early on can offset the limitation of not having enormous amounts of money to set aside for a comfortable retirement season.

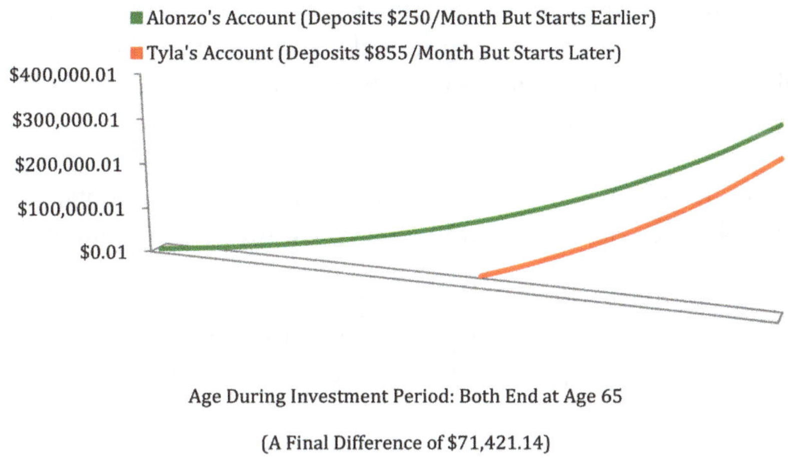

FIGURE 4.2 **Alonzo's and Tyla's Roth IRA Contributions: Slow and Steady Wins the Race!**

4.3 Finding Time

As one might guess, we can also use the future value of an annuity formula in our quest to find the value of time, t. We recall that in order to find time, we must exploit our knowledge of algebra. We tackle a few examples to remind us of the algebraic manipulations we must undergo.

Example 4.5 Ranjeet wanted to put away $650 quarterly in an effort to save $210,550 in his retirement account. If he saved at a fixed APR of 2.99%, how long would it take him to reach his goal?

Solution 4.5 We use the future value of an annuity formula and substitute the appropriate values therein. Note that $c = 4$ since the compounding period or frequency of payments is four times per year. We solve the following:

$$210550 = \frac{650\left[\left(\frac{0.0299}{4}+1\right)^{4t}-1\right]}{\frac{0.0299}{4}}$$

$$2.42133 = \left(\frac{0.0299}{4}+1\right)^{4t}-1$$

$$\log(3.42133) = 4t\log(1.007475)$$

$$\frac{\log(3.42133)}{4\log(1.007475)} = 41.29$$

It will take Ranjeet approximately 41 years and 4 months for his account to reach $210,550.

Example 4.6 As part of her assignment for her finance class, Marisa had to determine at what age she would have to start investing in order to guarantee \$500,000 in retirement funds. She planned on contributing \$550 per month, given a fixed APR of 4.44%. Assume she wants to retire at age 60.

Solution 4.6 Since the lump sum would occur at the end of the payments, we would have to use Equation 4.1. So Marisa would need to solve for t in the following:

$$500{,}000 = \frac{550\left[\left(\frac{0.0444}{12} + 1\right)^{12t} - 1\right]}{\frac{0.0444}{12}}$$

Based on the equation above, we determine that it will take Marisa approximately 33 years and 3 months to guarantee \$500,000 in her IRA. This means she will have to start her contributions around age 27. We leave details of this solution as part of the student exercises.

Money Talk

Roth vs. Traditional: The Right IRA for You

Given today's economy, it becomes increasingly difficult for individuals and families to contribute regularly to retirement accounts. The uptick is that Americans are living longer; according to the National Center for Health Statistics, the average life expectancy rose from 78.6 in 2009 to 78.8 (2016). The downside, however, is that they are saving less, thus outliving what retirement they have accumulated. According to the National Institute on Retirement Security, "Americans between the ages of 40 and 55 have retirement savings of $14,500" (Ghilarducci and James 2016). This low savings amount equates to pennies with respect to how much is really needed to sustain a life during retirement years. It becomes advantageous, then, to consider two primary types of retirement accounts and discuss their intricacies.

Many experts agree that the Roth IRA is geared more toward young adults who are in the beginning stages of saving for retirement. The account is funded with after-tax dollars, which means that Uncle Sam has already taken his cut before money enters the account. This means that you will not be taxed on what you contribute (i.e., contributions) if you need to withdraw it. It is recommended that these contributions be left alone so that they may grow and reap the benefit of interest; however, there is no further tax to pay on these contributions if they need to be used. The interest that accumulates (i.e., earnings) from the Roth is tax-free only if you wait to withdraw it at age 59½ or older and if the money has been in the account for at least five years. Otherwise, you will have to pay a 10% penalty and pay taxes on these earnings. As of 2017, the most one can contribute to a Roth is $5,500 per year, given that the income does not exceed $132,000 for single people. This makes it, according to some, the best retirement savings route for the college student or those who recently graduated from college.

Another big advantage of the Roth is that, as long as the money has remained in the account for at least five years, you can withdraw up to $10,000 to use toward the purchase of a home penalty and tax-free, thanks to the 1997 Taxpayer Relief Act. This is a once-in-a-lifetime courtesy extended to assist those in their quest to capture the American dream. After this provision has been used once, it may never be used again; however, it is an alternative way of saving for a home if the regular savings account is not available. And since interest rates overall in Roth IRAs tend to outdo those in regular savings accounts (depending on risk tolerance), money would tend to reach the $10,000 max quicker in the Roth account.

Unlike the Roth, the traditional IRA is funded with pre-tax dollars. This means that the money that funds this account is removed from the paycheck before taxes are removed. Unlike the 401(k), the employer does not match your contribution to the traditional IRA. But like the 401(k), your salary for the year reflects your gross income minus what you contributed to the IRA. The benefit of this funding strategy is that it lowers your tax bracket for the current year, thus decreasing what you owe Uncle Sam. Referred to often as a "salary reduction plan," this account, like the 401(k), has the effect legally of making your salary seem less than what it was, permitting you to pay taxes from a lower income class (Sasanow 1996). Granted, you will have to pay federal taxes on what you withdraw (contributions and earnings) from this account during retirement, but many experts believe this retirement tax bracket will be less than what one would face otherwise. If funds are withdrawn before retirement age, a 10% penalty in enforced, along with your having to pay federal income taxes on said funds.

Like the Roth, the traditional IRA carries with it the same flexibility of allowing first-time homebuyers to withdraw up to $10,000 toward the purchase without penalty, generally speaking. However, the government restricts your borrowing against this traditional account. This traditional IRA is good for those who may lack the discipline of not touching monies saved for retirement and who need an extra "incentive" (i.e., the immediate penalty incurred) to stay financially focused. Though the Roth is more flexible and less restrictive, it arguably lacks the "mean face" to keep your hands out the retirement cookie jar. The traditional IRA stands stern and strict and dares you to touch it. Its no-nonsense setup stands as a drill sergeant, whipping you into financial shape with a promise of fiscal fitness in your years to come.

Maximum contributions in traditional IRAs may not exceed $5,500 per year as in that of Roth IRAs. In fact, if you have both types of retirement accounts, the total for both together may not exceed this $5,500 limit as of 2017. As long as you are not covered by another plan at work, there is no income limit that controls how much you can contribute if you are single. Finally, monies in a traditional IRA will face another penalty if the funds have not started being withdrawn by age 70½. A minimum amount is required to be taken or else the feds keep half of this mandatory withdrawal amount (strange, I know!).

At any rate, we only address a small portion of what makes Roth and traditional IRAs tick. You will have to do your own research and consider your own financial situation before deciding which is best for you. There are more types of retirement plans in existence (e.g., the SEP IRA, the 401(k), the 403(b), and the Roth 401(k)). We only address the basic two to give the student a general idea as to how these types of financial instruments work. Regarding the Roth IRA and the traditional IRA, the following link is recommended to distinguish both at a glance: http://goo.gl/yzdR6G.

Student Exercises: Future Value of an Annuity

4.1 Patrick put $411 per month in an IRA at an APR of 1.14% for 25 years. How much will he have in his retirement account at the end of the investment period?

4.2 Gloria attempted to figure out how much money she would lose if she decided to save her money for retirement in a non-interest-bearing checking account as opposed to investing in an IRA. She wanted to save for 20 years. The IRA would be compounded monthly at an APR at 2.66%. Determine how much money she would lose if she went the route of saving money in the checking account instead of the IRA. Assume $310 monthly contributions. Assume that both accounts are untouched over the life of the investment and are subject to no fees to have the account open.

4.3 Maury's retirement portfolio accumulated to $189,440. If he had been saving for 17 years at an APR of 2.19%, what were his monthly contributions into his account?

4.4 A certain IRA was funded with $800 in semiannual contributions. If it grew for 33 years and 8 months, how much would be present in the account, assuming an APR of 1.98%?

4.5 Denise wanted to amass $400,000 in her retirement account, having an APR of 3.52%. She wished to save over a period of 35 years.

a. How much would she need to contribute if she made monthly contributions?
b. How much would she need to contribute if she made quarterly contributions?

4.6 In Example 4.5, how much time would Ranjeet save in reaching his goal if he contributed monthly instead of quarterly (assume the same investment conditions outside of contribution frequency)?

4.7 In the solution for Example 4.6, we determined that Marisa would have to start saving around age 27. Show mathematically how we arrived at this solution.

4.8 In Examples 4.3 and 4.4, we discussed Alonzo's and Tyla's IRAs based on different starting times.

a. Determine how much money Alonzo's account earned in interest over his investment period.
b. Determine how much money Tyla's account earned in interest over her investment period.

4.9 Zak's retirement goal was $315,000, which he wanted to reach in 40 years of monthly investing at an APR of 3.2%. He determined how much he would have to pay monthly to reach this goal but later decided to increase his retirement goal to $415,000. How much more would he have to contribute per month to his account to reach his new goal as compared to his old one? (*Hint: Compare one monthly payment to another.*)

4.10 (Excel) Use Excel to simulate your retirement account as you fund it over the course of your life. This is a Roth IRA (assumes after-tax dollars).

You should research at least three institutions online (e.g., T. Rowe Price or Vanguard) in order to secure the best interest rate offering. Make sure that all are FDIC-insured. Decide which of the three you will do business with, and discuss what factors influenced your choice.

Begin funding your account. You should assume that growth of your funds follow a strategy that is compounded monthly.* You also cannot exceed $5,500 in contributions any given year (based on 2017 contribution limits). You may establish any dollar amount as the retirement goal you would like to achieve by the time you retire. You may choose the age at which you would like to start contributing and also the age you would like to retire.

Make sure you make the initial deposit required by the bank that you choose and continue making contributions as you see fit. Make any changes that you deem necessary in order to reach the financial goal that you set (i.e., alter the number of years you work, change the amount of contributions).

Discuss

1. What dollar amount is the goal you have set for yourself?
2. What interest rate did you find?
3. At what age did you start contributing? At what age did you set for yourself to retire?
4. How much do you have to contribute each month?
5. How much have you accumulated in the account by retirement?
6. Show a graph that illustrates the total amount of money you have in your account each year from start to finish (*FVA* values).

* Note: This is not really a real-life financial setup. In real life, if you are a big risk-taker, you can invest at a variable interest rate that is more aggressive than a static APR. You can invest in something called a money market, in which you can gain a lot of money quicker than with compounding monthly, but the risk is that it becomes possible to lose a portion or all of the money you have invested. Most people who are young invest aggressively. As they age and reach retirement age, they can switch to a more conservative (less risky) portfolio. We discuss this more in Asset Seven.

References

Geary, Leslie H. "Retirement Planning for 20-somethings." *Bankrate.com*, April 23, 2007. Accessed March 5, 2016. http://goo.gl/YCRii7.

Ghilarducci, Teresa, and Hamilton E. James. "A Smarter Plan to Make Retirement Savings Last." *New York Times*, January 1, 2016. Accessed March 5, 2016. http://goo.gl/v0sMHF.

Johnson, Jean, and Jon Rochkind (with Ott, Amber and DuPont, Samantha). 2009. *With Their Whole Lives Ahead of Them: Myths and Realities About Why So Many Students Fail to Finish College.* New York: Public Agenda.

National Center for Health Statistics. Centers for Disease Control and Prevention. February 25, 2016. Accessed March 5, 2016. http://goo.gl/sO8uOJ.

Sasanow, Richard. 1996. *The 401(k) Book.* New York: Henry Holt and Company, Inc.

Asset Five

Budgeting and Taxation

Chapter Outline

My mom has always been my champion. She said, "Save your money. Pay your taxes. Don't put everything in one basket," but she let me explore and be creative.

Queen Latifah

5.1 Needs vs. Wants

Are you addicted to your cell phone? A study by researchers at Baylor University found that female college students spend ten hours on their cell phone, on average, in comparison to the eight hours that their male counterparts spend (Roberts, Yaya, and Manolis 2014). Part of the study suggested that increased use of cell phones (e-mailing, accessing the web, checking social-media sites, etc.) showed a linkage to lower grades. Further still, an overdependence on cell phones with young adults and college students may indicate that use of cell phones may be becoming an addiction, a step up from being a habit. Arguably, this shift of importance as it relates to cell phones in the lives of college students complicates matters when it comes to whether students see cell phones as **needs** or **wants**.

Definition

A **need** *is something that you must have in order to survive. The absence of it would result in a serious dysfunction or death. A* **want** *is something that is considered a luxury and does not have any bearing on one's survival. The absence of it would not result in serious dysfunction or death.*

Hence, according to the respective definitions, one would more than likely place cell phones in the category of "need," although college students may very well feel as though they are severely dysfunctional without it. The point here is not to argue about the category to which cell phones belong. The goal is to have you understand the notion of needs versus wants and answer questions truthfully as they relate to which direction your money goes. In other words, once you yourself develop a firm grasp of the definitions of "need" and "want," you will be in a great position to prioritize financial matters in your life and make your money flow in the direction that is most important.

ALMAGAMI/Shutterstock.com

Example 5.1 Determine whether each of the following is a need or want.

iPhone 6	________	Water	________
Shelter	________	Cable	________
Vitamins/Minerals	________	Clothing	________
Concert Tickets	________	WiFi	________

Solution 5.1 These solutions for some of these may be arguable.

iPhone 6	Want	Water	Need
Shelter	Need	Cable	Want
Vitamins/Minerals	Need	Clothing	Need
Concert Tickets	Want	WiFi	Arguable*

*The Ruiz (2015) article in the References section provides interesting arguments on both sides as it relates to whether having WiFi is a need versus a want, especially in impoverished communities, where access to Internet can mean the difference between getting and not getting a job.

Once you establish the lists of needs and wants, you are able to use wisdom as it relates to channeling the flow of your money in your life. How your money flows to varying destinations in your life is key to becoming financially free and independent. When we say "flow," we are not just speaking about the way in which money comes to us via our jobs, careers, or inheritances. This is but one aspect of money flow in our lives. In another sense, it has to do with how money drifts away, leaving us to take care of the financial responsibilities that we have day to day.

In fact, there are a number of terms that we can substitute for the word "money." For example, money is referred to as cash, legal tender, banknotes, coins, loot, or dough. One very interesting term that often gets overlooked as it relates to money is the term *currency*. When we look deeper at that term, we see at its root the term "current." In nature, a current simply refers to a flow of water impacted by gravity as it goes in a downward fashion. A current is always moving and never stops. It symbolizes mobility and constant movement.

Galyna Andrushko/Shutterstock.com

In the context of money, your money should flow into your world with no stoppage. Although we do not focus so much in this textbook on money flow and your career, we suffice it here to encourage you to pursue work in which you are not dependent on a paycheck each pay period to make ends meet. The goal is to have the type of work situation in which you are the owner or where you have several sources of income that constantly flow into your financial life. Although you may have to start with a basic job where you get paid a certain amount of money per hour, you want to position yourself eventually into a situation where you are not paid by the hour but rather paid by your ideas. This often translates into more money overall because now you are an entrepreneur as opposed to one who simply clocks in and out of a nine-to-five job or even one who is salaried.

In addition, once you secure a steady current of funds, you have to know how to make money flow away from you as you pay your bills each month. The goal is to have the right percentage of your money flowing to the appropriate destinations. Having a lot of money coming in to your possession is probably an important goal, but it is just as important to make sure that the money current that is flowing away from you does so in a wise manner so as to keep you in the best financial shape possible.

5.2 Obtaining Freedom Through Budgeting

It is well known that many celebrities were unable to maintain the lifestyles they had at one time because of the lack of financial planning and unwise use of their money. Certain stars like 50 Cent, Abby Lee Miller, and Larry King reportedly had more money than they ever could have imagined but made not-so-wise decisions concerning their money and wound up in precarious financial situations. Most found themselves in positions where they had bought huge homes and other assets that they may not have needed. Perhaps they did not take into account that their money flow would not always be as strong when they reached certain stages in their life. Hence, they were not able to support the lifestyle they had known so well and decided to declare bankruptcy.

Everett Collection/Shutterstock.com

50 Cent

Kathy Hutchins/Shutterstock.com

Abby Lee Miller

s_bukley/Shutterstock.com

Larry King

Managing and monitoring your money inflow and outgo are crucial to being financially successful. Whether you are a celebrity or just a "regular" individual, your forward movement financially must be based on level-headed thinking and sound financial monitoring of your day-to-day life. One key way to manage the inflow and outgo of your money is through the financial strategy of budgeting.

5.2.1 Budgeting Defined

We begin by taking a close look at what a **budget** is and how it is designed to help us in our financial endeavors.

> **Definition**
>
> *A **budget** is a financial plan of action that accounts for how money flows into and out of your life. It is an action plan that spans a specific time and for a specific goal or purpose.*

When we think of budgeting, most of us cringe because we think of being restricted and bound. We want to be free and spend as we please without anything holding us back. However, the idea behind budgeting is that we put financial limits on ourselves temporarily so that we can eventually achieve a larger financial goal. One key notion to remember is this: budgeting should always be goal-driven. Is your goal to save money? pay off credit cards? travel? It is a good idea to always have a goal in mind when doing a budget so that you have motivation to stay focused while the budget is in motion.

The preeminent word in budget is "budge." To budge means to make room or to make or cause the slightest movement. When you are swamped with debt and bills, it becomes important to do what is needed to make room in your financial life for more success. So as opposed to viewing budgeting as a negative concept, see it as doing what you need to do to cause financial movement in the right direction, to exercise self-control when it comes to your spending.

5.2.2 Budgeting Guidelines for the Young

Now, before we look at a sample budget form, let's consider what researchers say concerning how your income should flow away from you, generally speaking. Of course, every budget is different based on the goal of that particular budget. However, it may be a good idea to have some sense of a starting place. Although you still may be struggling to find a job after graduation, you will have to think about how you will survive in light of having to live life as well as needing to pay back student loans if you have them. Figure 5.1 shows suggested percentages for the money flow in a typical budget for a recent college graduate.

What? Only 5% for clothes? Most of you probably stopped looking at the guidelines once you saw that. But there are more important things to focus on once you start living on your own. When you are fresh out of college, you probably will not have a home, but you will probably share an apartment with someone while you are trying to get on your own financial feet and establish your independence. You'll also need some sense of transportation to get back and forth to your job. Taking public transportation may be a good idea because it frees up your funds and allows you to direct your money to other areas that may need it more since you are a fresh college graduate.

At any rate, take a moment to look over the recommended percentages. Are there any percentages that seem shocking to you? Where do you think you may have the most problems sticking to the percentage recommended? Why?

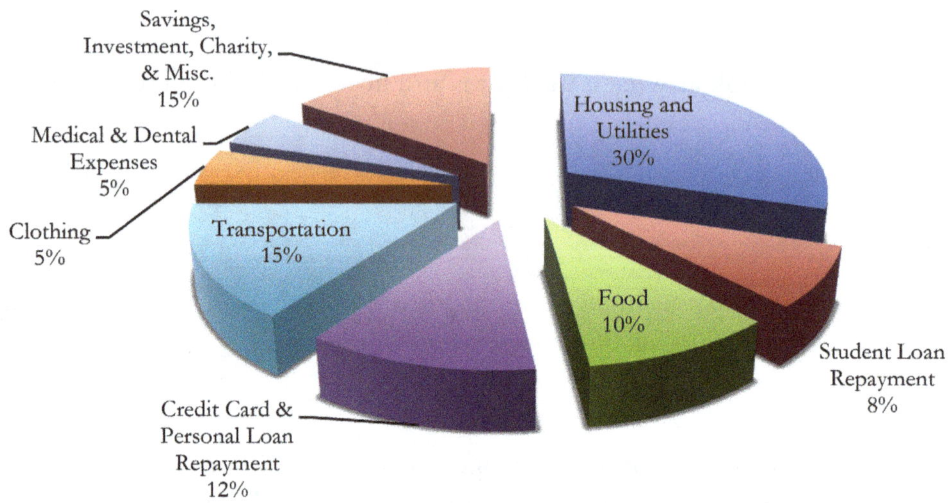

FIGURE 5.1 General Budget Guidelines for the Recent College Graduate

Source: Adapted from College Board Budget Worksheet at http://goo.gl/dB9BsS.

Example 5.2 Suppose you land your first job out of college as an entry-level team associate at Citigroup. As a salaried employee, you get paid twice per month. After taxes are taken out, each paycheck is \$1267. For the month, determine how much of your check in dollars equates to each category in the suggested budget in Figure 5.1 based on the percentages provided. Round to the nearest cent, and make sure totals add up to overall income amount.

Solution 5.2 If we consider the budget for the month, we determine your income for the month. Since you get paid twice per month, your pay would be $\$1,267(2) = \$2,534$. From this amount, we figure out how much should be allocated for each category, based on percentages in Figure 5.1.

Housing and utilities	30% of \$2534	=	\$760.20
Savings, investments, charity, and misc.	15% of \$2534	=	\$380.10
Medical and dental	5% of \$2534	=	\$126.70
Clothing	5% of \$2534	=	\$126.70
Transportation	15% of \$2534	=	\$380.10
Credit card and personal loan repayment	12% of \$2534	=	\$304.08
Food	10% of \$2534	=	\$253.40
Student loan repayment	8% of \$2534	=	\$202.72
		TOTAL	**\$2534**

In the situation presented in Solution 5.2, we do not know in which city you are living. Depending on where you live, housing expenses of $760.20 will not go far, especially in a thriving city like New York. However, the cost of living is not as steep in less populated cities. Also, it may be that you have no student loans to repay or any credit card debt. In these cases, you can transfer the money in those categories into housing, or savings, or any others you deem important. This is why eradicating debt is highly important. It allows you more flexibility when it comes to how much of an apartment you can rent or home you can live in. If all you can give to housing is the $760.20, you can get creative and live with a roommate or settle for a smaller apartment. There are many ways to make your budget work. You just have to get and stay creative!

5.2.3 Getting Your Budgeting Feet Wet

Now, when it comes to budgeting, we have to be clear about one thing. It needs to be something you can see. Your budget is not some abstract idea in your head. It has to be something written down, typed out, or visible from a computer or app. If you are completing a budget in any of these instances, you should be flexible when constructing it and allow for changes. So you should fill out paper budgets in pencil. No one system is any better than another. You have to find the right one that is for *you*. Besides, you are the one who will be using it. There are tons of budgets you can use online. Either you can complete them online and print them out, or you can strictly complete and make changes online. Several budgeting sites exist, which we soon address.

Whatever strategy you use, it is imperative that you commit yourself to monitoring what you actually spend so that you can make appropriate changes the next month when you complete a new budget. The most important aspect of budgeting is monitoring. Honestly, the only real monitoring you will have to do will be for items in the budget where you are spending on a daily basis (food, clothing, gas, etc.). You only pay some items in the budget once during that cycle, so there is nothing really to monitor there. However, keeping tabs on eating out and other purchases can give you a sense of where your daily funds are going. Depending on which budget system you use, you can monitor online and enter values as you spend. You can also use credit cards, which detail purchases. You can then later look through statements and determine how much you are spending on each category.

Casper1774 Studio/Shutterstock.com

You will have to decide whether you are one who does better doing budgets online or if you do better with physically writing things down. The author uses a very simple, old-fashioned strategy when doing budgets. He literally takes a sheet of paper and writes down each category each month, starting with a beginning income and subtracting expenses that apply for that month. Any overages are immediately placed into savings. He strives to ensure that the balance in his checking account at the end of each month has only $1.00 in it, enough to keep the account open. In his situation, it is important to have every penny in a situation that is earning him interest, which is not in his checking account.

Note

If your checking account is noninterest-bearing, shift extra funds to an interest-bearing savings account at the end of the budget cycle to maximize earning potential.

Moneymatics: Where Money and Mathematics Meet

(based on Figure 5.1; may not be used for profit, only educational use)

$ Monthly Budget Worksheet $

Month and Year ____________________

INCOME

Employment ____________________ (after taxes/deductions)
Gifts ____________________
Reimbursements ____________________
Other ____________________
TOTAL INCOME ____________________

EXPENSES

1. **Housing and utilities**
   Rent/mortgage ________
   Insurance ________
   Electricity ________
   Gas ________
   Water ________
   Cable ________
   Maintenance/repairs ________
   Total ________

2. **Transportation**
   Car payment ________
   Insurance ________
   Gas ________
   Maintenance/repairs ________
   Total ________

3. **Food**
   Eating in ________
   Eating out ________
   Total ________

4. **Credit card and personal loan repayment**
   Card one ________
   Card two ________
   Other ________
   Total ________

5. **Student loan repayment**
   Total ________

6. **Savings, investments, church, etc.**
   Savings ________
   Investments ________
   Church ________
   Other ________
   Total ________

7. **Clothing**
   Total ________

8. **Medical and dental expenses**
   Medical ________
   Dental ________
   Total ________

9. **Miscellaneous**
   Misc 1 ________
   Misc 2 ________
   Total ________

TOTAL INCOME ________

minus

TOTAL EXPENSES ________

equals

*BALANCE** ________

*If final balance amount is **positive**, consider putting this amount in the savings category (#6) or in paying off debt (#4 or #5). If final balance amount is **negative**, you will have to reduce spending in some of the budget categories (like cable, eating out, etc.) until this balance becomes zero.

Once you determine whether you are more of a person to do budgets by hand the old-fashioned way or in a more automated fashion online, you are on your way. There are a host of free budget sites to assist you in structuring and monitoring your budget. A Google search will provide a myriad of options. A few of those sites are listed below for your perusal:

1. **Buxfer (www.buxfer.com)**
   This service has been touted as the best for college students and twentysomethings who want to start out right and keep their finances under control. You can set short- and long-term goals and manage group expenses. You can split up different bills, figure out who owes what, and make payments online.
2. **Budget Worksheets (www.budgetworksheets.org)**
   Here, you can find a simple, printable budgeting worksheet that allows space for setting up categories and actual spending amounts. There is no online linking to financial accounts.
3. **Budget Tracker (www.budgettracker.com)**
   You do not need to link to financial accounts using this budget sheet either. Use this site to keep track of where your money is going using your computer, mobile phone, or iPad.
4. **Mint (www.mint.com)**
   Use this resource to link to your financial accounts. Here, you can manage your money, pay your bills, and even track your credit score. Some people have reservations using this service because of the need to enter credit card information, though a free service. Credit card info is needed only if you do not want to link a bank account for paying bills using Mint services.
5. **SavvyMoney (www.savvymoney.com)**
   This site specializes in helping you with a proactive approach to reducing your debt and to quicken your savings. It helps you understand your current situation and create a debt-repayment plan based around what works best for you.

Again, these are only five of countless online aids to assist you in organizing your financial life through planning and monitoring. Do your own personal search and experiment with different sites so that you can customize the experience to fit best with your financial situation.

Example 5.3 Suppose your monthly income is \$3455 after taxes. You locate a gorgeous apartment that you would like to rent. The monthly rent is \$1236.50. Consider the following questions:

1. What percentage of your monthly income is the rent for this apartment?
2. Is this more or less than the recommended percentage amount for housing, as outlined in Figure 5.1?
3. If the percentage is more than that suggested in Figure 5.1, what way could you still justify moving forward with renting the apartment?

Solution 5.3

1. To find the monthly rent percentage, we find the following and then convert to a percent: $1236.50 / 3455.00 = 0.358 \times 100 = 35.8\%$. The total percentage in rent is 35.8%.
2. Figure 5.1 suggests that no more than 30% be allotted for housing expenses, so the percentage allotted for rent is more than what is recommended.

3. Although we have not taken into account living expenses (e.g., electricity, gas, water, cable, etc.), we could still justify renting the apartment as long as we have no credit card debt or car payments. This would mean that we could transfer those unused percentages to the housing category, thus increasing how much rent we could afford.

5.3 Where Did My Dough Go?!

Ji Eun had recently secured her first salaried job after college and was ecstatic to get her paycheck. She was hired by Jackson Energy Supply, Inc. in Jackson, Mississippi and was finally able to succeed without the help of her parents. She negotiated with the company an annual salary of $49,837.00. After she did the math, she could hardly stop grinning because she knew her check would be approximately $4153.08 per month. Her mind was spinning as she thought of all the wonderful things she would be able to buy. After her first month on the job, she anticipated seeing the results of her hard work for the month. As she had signed up for direct deposit, she checked her e-mail to view her paystub. When she did, she felt sick to her stomach because Figure 5.2 reveals what she saw.

COMPANY NAME			EARNINGS STATEMENT		
Jackson Energy Supply, Inc., 111 Lombard Drive					
EMPLOYEE NAME	SOCIAL SEC. ID	EMPLOYEE ID	CHECK NO.	PAY PERIOD	PAY DATE
Ji Eun Chang	XXX-XX-9653	1383	66792	12/30/14-01/30/15	02/02/15

INCOME	RATE	HOURS	CURRENT TOTAL	DEDUCTIONS	CURRENT TOTAL	YEAR-TO-DATE
GROSS WAGES			4,153.08	FICA MED TAX	60.22	60.22
				FICA SS TAX	257.49	257.49
				FED TAX	639.83	639.83
				MS ST TAX	185.99	185.99

YTD GROSS	YTD DEDUCTIONS	YTD NET PAY	CURRENT TOTAL	CURRENT DEDUCTIONS	NET PAY
4,153.08	1,143.53	3,009.55	4,153.08	1,143.53	3,009.55

FIGURE 5.2 Ji Eun's Paystub for Her First Month on the Job

She was under the impression that each month she would be taking home her annual salary promised divided by 12. Nobody told her that the painful truth, as she soon realized, is that the amount she would be taking home would be about $1000 less than what she had originally thought. Poor Ji Eun! She quickly learned the terms associated with how much she thought she would be paid and how much she actually got paid. We discuss her **gross pay** and **net pay**.

Definition

The **gross pay** *is the estimated pay that one receives before any taxes or deductions are subtracted. It includes any salary, overtime, bonuses, and commissions. The* **net pay** *is the gross pay minus all taxes, deductions, and fees.*

One of the harshest realities that college students like Ji Eun realize as they graduate from college and enter the world of work is that they will have to pay their fair share of **taxes**. Unfortunately, paying taxes to the Internal Revenue Service (IRS) is not an option. Benjamin Franklin perhaps said it best when he said that the only things certain in life were death and taxes. Now, we need to distinguish between the taxes you pay when you buy a particular item in a store (like a dress) or when you purchase a delectable meal at a restaurant. Taxes in those situations are unavoidable and carry little to no weight as they relate to your financial responsibilities to the government. You also have an obligation to be accountable for the amount of money you make personally and must pay your fair share of local and federal taxes to assist the government in its efforts to financially run the affairs of the country.

Definition

Taxes *are mandatory, government-imposed monetary fees or charges that are used to help finance government services and activities.*

If you are not responsible and fail to file your federal and state taxes each year, you will suffer a number of consequences. You will incur a late fee for each month your tax return is late (after the normal annual April deadline). In addition, the IRS can freeze your account (make it impossible for you to deposit or withdraw funds), garnish all of your wages, and put what is called a lien against your home. This prohibits you from being able to sell or refinance your property. Finally, if you continue to avoid filing taxes or fail to pay them, you will possibly face jail time (as in the cases of Lauryn Hill and Martha Stewart).

JStone/Shutterstock.com

Lauryn Hill

Everett Collection/Shutterstock.com

Martha Stewart

Ji Eun's paycheck in Figure 5.2 also shows two other deductions: FICA Med Tax ($60.22) and FICA SS Tax ($257.49). FICA stands for Federal Insurance Contributions Act. The two taxes that make up the Act ensure that the older generation of America is taken care of. In a nutshell, these taxes were taken out of Ji Eun's paycheck to pay older people in America social security retirement funds and Medicare benefits (for health insurance). It also helps to pay for those who are disabled and for children whose parents are deceased. Yes, part of Ji Eun's check is put into a federal pot to take care of others and make sure they are okay financially. There is great debate going on currently concerning whether social security and Medicare will be around for young people like Ji Eun once they become retirees. We explore this issue further in the *MoneyTalk* discussion at the end of this asset.

"That $20 deduction is for new benefits – like the $10 raise you just got."

Example 5.4 Suppose your annual salary is $34,378.00. Assume that you get paid once per month. On your paycheck stub, you notice that the amount withheld for FICA Med Tax is $41.54, and the amount withheld for FICA SS Tax is $177.62.

a. Determine your monthly gross salary.
b. Determine the percentage of this monthly gross salary that is taken out for the FICA Med Tax and also for the FICA SS Tax.

Solution 5.4 a. Since you get paid each month, you divide your annual salary by twelve to get: $\$34,378.00\ /\ 12 = \$2864.83$.
b. The FICA Med Tax is $41.54. To find out what percent this amount is of the $2864.83, we simply solve for x in the following:

$$\frac{\$41.54}{\$2,864.83} = \frac{x}{100}$$

After cross-multiplying and dividing, we get $x = 1.45\%$.
The FICA SS Tax is $177.62. To find out what percent this amount is of the $2864.83, we simply solve for y in the following:

$$\frac{\$177.62}{\$2,864.83} = \frac{y}{100}$$

After cross-multiplying and dividing, we get $y = 6.2\%$.

As it turns out, it is standard in America that 1.45% of every person's paycheck funds the Medicare reserve, while 6.2% of every person's paycheck goes to fund the social security program.

5.4 Understanding Your Tax Bracket: Federal and State Obligations

The American government has been collecting taxes from its citizens for over 150 years. The Revenue Act of 1862, signed by President Abraham Lincoln, was put into law as a strategy to assist the North in its efforts to fund the Civil War (Giroux 2012). Starting as a flat-rate tax for all citizens (where everyone pays the same percent in taxes), this Act eventually gave way to collecting taxes in a way that required people to pay a different percentage in taxes depending on income level. This tiered plan of paying taxes based on income level has a fairly popular name in the world of finance.

Definition

A **progressive tax system** *is one in which the percentage paid in taxes rises as the level of income rises and lowers as the level of income falls.*

Over the years, there has been intense debate concerning the pros and cons of employing a tax system such as the **progressive tax system**. We list a few perspectives from both sides (Mundra 2012).

Pros

1. Individuals who pay more into the federal government help keep the income gap less polarized between the rich and the poor.
2. Morally, it is no more than right that those who can afford to pay more in taxes should do so. This means that people who have more money are able to help out those who have less, leading to a more "happy" society.
3. A progressive tax system is beneficial for the government because the income yield is significantly more than any other form of taxation.

Cons

1. It is fairer to have all citizens pay the same percentage. Making wealthier people pay higher percentages in tax is "penalizing" them for being wealthy. Even if people make more income, paying the same percentage would still translate into more dollars being paid from wealthier people. Hence, there is no need to increase the percentage too. It's a double whammy!
2. There is in inherent double standard. The government makes people pay a higher percentage in taxes if they make more money, but it does not afford them the political influence that is in concert with their financial ability. In other words, the government does not allow the wealthy more than one vote during elections, so why should it require them to pay a higher percentage in taxes?
3. This tax system assumes that money has the same significance and usefulness to all taxpaying individuals within the same income group. Since different taxpayers have different circumstances, levying taxes in this manner becomes problematic.

5.4.1 Paying Federal Taxes

So depending on a specific income range inside which your salary rests, you are required to pay your fair share of taxes. We recall Ji Eun's annual salary of $49,837.00. This amount, which we referred to as her gross salary, is the starting amount that the government uses to determine how much she owes in taxes. According to the progressive tax system, a specific percentage in taxes is applied to salaries falling within a certain salary tier. The tax percentage is applied to a specific range between which the salary amount falls. This salary range that the government applies the tax percentage onto is called the employee's **tax bracket**.

Definition

In a progressive tax system, **tax brackets** *are sets of income ranges that are taxed at a certain percentage rate (according to that range tier).*

We take a look at the schedule of tax brackets for Ji Eun's salary to see how much she owed the federal government in taxes. Before determining such, however, we must address a slight change in the amount that is to be used to calculate how much tax is due. We discuss the most basic scenario in which she pays taxes. This basic scenario is one in which she uses the **standard deduction** and the **personal exemption** for her state.

Definition

The **standard deduction** *is a fixed amount of money that the IRS allows taxpayers to subtract from their income, which reflects how much in deductible expenses were spent the previous tax year. The amount depends on filing status, age, and some health conditions. A* **personal exemption** *is a fixed amount of money that the IRS allows taxpayers to subtract from their income, which ideally helps guard against taxation at an amount needed to survive at a basic level (i.e., food, clothing, shelter).*

The Standard Deduction and Personal Exemption: Gifts from the IRS

These two "gifts" from the federal government help to reduce Ji Eun's taxable salary, thus how federal taxes are due. The federal standard deduction generally changes each year as determined by the IRS. For purposes herein, we use a standard deduction of $6300 and a federal personal exemption of $4050. Once we subtract these amounts from her salary, we now have her **taxable income**, which allows us to finally determine how much is due in federal taxes.

Definition

Taxable income *is typically the gross income minus any deductions and/or exemptions.*

In Ji Eun's case, using only the federal standard deduction and personal exemption, we have:

$49,837 (*gross salary*)
–$6300 (*federal standard deduction*)
–$4050 (*federal personal exemption*)
$39,487 (*federal taxable income*)

This $39,487 is the updated income we use to determine how much tax is due for her.

TABLE 5.1 Sample Tax Brackets and Federal Tax Rates (For Singles)

Taxable Income Between ...	Tax Due Is ...
$0–$9325	10% of taxable income
$9326–$37,950	$932.50 + 15% of amt over $9325
$37,951–$91,900	$5226.25 + 25% of amt over $37,950
$91,901–$191,650	$18,713.75 + 28% of amt over $91,900
$191,651–$416,700	$46,643.75 + 33% of amt over $191,650
$416,701–$418,400	$120,910.25 + 35% of amt over $416,700
$418,401 +	$121,505.25 + 39.6% of amt over $418,400

Table 5.1 takes a look at sample tax brackets and tax rates to be used to assess Ji Eun's situation. (For our purposes here, we assume she is single. Figures and tax rates change for married couples, heads of households, etc.).

Based on that assumption, we see that her taxable income of $39,487 places her in the $37,951-to-$91,900 tax bracket. This means that the tax amount due is $5226.25 plus 25% of the amount of her salary that exceeds $37,950. The exceeding amount is: $39,487 – $37,950 = $1537. And 25% of this amount is: (0.25)(1537) = 384.25. So the amount of federal taxes due for Ji Eun is: $5226.25 + $384.25 = **$5610.50**.

5.4.2 Paying State Taxes

Even though Ji Eun's federal taxes due are $5610.50, this is not her only financial tax responsibility. We also have to determine how much she had to pay in state taxes. Although federal tax guidelines apply to taxpayers regardless of the state in which they reside, state tax guidelines vary per state. Each state has its own set of guidelines for citizens who earn income in that particular state. Specifically, each state has its own amounts for standard deduction, personal exemption, and guidelines to determine how much tax is due. This information may be easily found online for each state.

Just as we took into account the federal standard deduction and personal exemption for Ji Eun, we must take into account the state standard deduction and personal exemption for her with respect to determining her financial obligations at the state level. When we first introduced Ji Eun's situation, we discussed that her job was located in Jackson, Mississippi. We can research online Mississippi's standard deduction for the current year; however, we use sample deductions for purposes here. We assume the standard deduction for the state of Mississippi is $2300 for singles and the personal exemption is $6050. This means her taxable income for Mississippi state taxes is:

$49,837 (*gross salary*)
– $2300 (*Mississippi standard deduction*)
– $6050 (*Mississippi personal exemption*)
$41,487 (*state taxable income*)

So Table 5.2 shows sample state tax guidelines for a single person for the state of Mississippi.

TABLE 5.2 Sample State Income Tax Rates for Mississippi (Singles)

Portion of Taxable Income ...	Tax Due Is ...
The first $5000	3% plus % on next income level
The next $5000	4% plus % on next income level
Above $10,000	5%

The difference here is that each level of the state tax-bracket strategy influences the amount that Ji Eun would pay in state taxes. For example, considering her taxable income of $41,487, we figure out how much in taxes she owes the state of Mississippi when filing her taxes. Using information from Table 5.2, we have the following:

1. 3% of the first $5000: (0.03)(5000) = $150
2. 4% of the next $5000: (0.04)(5000) = $200
3. The amount in excess of $10,000: $41,487 - $10,000 = $31,837

So, 5% of that amount = (0.05)($31,837) = $1591.85

Hence, the total amount Ji Eun owes in state taxes for the state of Mississippi is: $150 + $200 + $1591.85 = **$1941.85**. In sum, when Ji Eun filed her taxes, her taxes due were $5610.50 in federal taxes and $1941.85 in state taxes, totaling $7552.35. Indeed, this was probably not how she anticipated spending a portion of her income.

When we look at Ji Eun's paystub in Figure 5.2, we see that the amount of federal taxes that were taken out for that month was $639.83, and the amount of state taxes was $185.99. For the year, the total amount in federal taxes to be automatically reduced from her paycheck (assuming it is the same amount each month) would be ($639.83)(12) = $7677.96. This means at the end of the year, she overpaid an amount in taxes than she owed the government based on federal tax rates. This means that she will get a refund from the federal government for $2067.46, which reflects the difference in what she already paid and what she owed ($5610.50 – $7677.96 = – $2067.46). The negative suggests a refund is due to her.

For the year, the total amount in state taxes to be automatically reduced from her paycheck (assuming it is the same amount each month) would be ($185.99)(12) = $2231.88. This means at the end of the year, she will receive a refund from the state of Mississippi for $290.03, which reflects the difference in what she already paid and what she owed to the state ($1941.85 – $2231.88 = – $290.03). The negative suggests a refund is due to her.

In the next section, we explore more creative means to further reduce one's taxable income, thus reducing how much tax is due to the government.

5.5 Punching Uncle Sam in the Gut!

Before delving into the details of this section, we pause and offer a strong disclaimer! None of the information presented in this textbook and in this section in particular should be taken as legal tax advice. When it comes to your taxes, you should always consult a certified public accountant (CPA) to assist you in preparing your state and federal tax documents each year. That said, we explore some ways that can ease the financial burden as it relates to how much we pay in taxes. Although there are numerous ways we can do this, we only stick with discussing a few of them.

The overall idea is to *legally* reduce the tax bracket in which the IRS taxes your income. When you reduce your tax bracket, you ultimately reduce the amount of money you owe the government. In the previous section, we saw that Ji Eun's taxable income was taxed to the fullest extent that it could be as a single person using the federal and state standard deduction and personal exemption for herself. The tax bracket in which her income fell determined how much tax was due from her.

We see, however, that Ji Eun could have reduced her taxes due even more by making good on deductions other than standard deductions, which we discuss next.

5.5.1 Softening the Blow with Pre-Tax Deductions

Pre-tax deductions are prearranged deductions that are subtracted from your check each pay period (generally). Often, the total amount for the year is divided by how many pay periods there are in the year and removed from the amount of the check. Other times, a set amount is simply subtracted from the check each pay period without specifying first how much for the year should be subtracted.

> **Definition**
>
> **Pre-tax deductions** *are approved deductions that reduce one's taxable income and, as a result, lower how much one owes in taxes.*

Thus, in addition to viewing your pay stub and noticing reductions for Medicare and social security, you can choose to participate in several of these pre-tax programs (if your job offers them) and reap the wonderful benefits attached to such. We now discuss several of these pre-tax programs.

Retirement Contributions

This is perhaps the most important pre-tax program in which you could ever participate. Some employers match the 401(k) retirement contributions that are directly removed from your paycheck. Your contribution in these cases allows you to save for retirement with funds on a pre-tax basis. You will eventually have to pay taxes on this money when you retire. Hence, this program is called a tax-deferred program. Funds are removed before taxes are taken out of your check. The hope is that the amount you pay in taxes later will be less than the amount you would pay in taxes at the present time when you are paid. Often, this will in fact be the case because most peoples' income is much less during retirement than during working days. Since income will be much less during retirement, then so will the income tax rate that the retirement funds will be subject to. You should keep in mind that there is a limit to this deferral contribution (not counting your employer's part of the contribution). You should contact your employer to find out what this limit is for the current year.

The Health Flex Plan

One pre-tax deduction you can take advantage of is the Flexible Spending Plan (FSA). This is an opportunity that your employer allows for you to pay for certain health care expenses (such as copayments for doctor's offices, prescriptions, eyeglasses/contact lenses, and crowns). You determine for the year how much you would like to contribute and your employer deducts equal amounts from each pay period over the course of that year. Although funds should be used by the end of the year, you can carry over up to $500 to be spent three months into the following year (provided your plan does not already have a stated grace period built in). There are limits to these contributions, as one might expect.

The Dependent Care Flex Plan

Much like the FSA, the Dependent Care Flex Plan (DCAP) allows the employee to work and include the costs to care for tax dependents under the age of 13 or a parent who is elderly. Costs for spouses who are physically or mentally disabled are also allowable if residing with the FSA owner. The same three-month extension applies to DCAPs as in FSAs. Again, contributions from this category may not exceed a certain dollar amount.

Transit

Through an employer benefit program, you can deduct from your paycheck costs to commute, free of tax. As of 2016, you can deduct up to $255 per month for transit passes and $255 per month for qualified parking. Again, your employer must have this program, in which funds come directly out of your paycheck. You may not whimsically pay for such transit and parking services on your own and seek reimbursement or tax benefits later.

These are not the only pre-tax programs that help to lower one's income tax rate. Others include health insurance plans, long-term disability premiums, and qualified union fees. Benefits that come with using pre-tax dollars are undeniable, as they can quickly move you from a higher tax bracket to a lower one. This translates to owing less money to Uncle Sam and enabling you to place more toward saving or taking that much-needed vacation.

Example 5.5 In the previous section, we discovered that Ji Eun owed a total of \$5610.50 in federal taxes. Assuming all things are equal, decide if the amount she owes in federal taxes changes if she participates in the following pre-tax contributions: she signs up for parking at \$200 per month through her employer's transit program; she contributes \$215 per month to her 401(k) plan; she has \$75 taken out each month for copays and dental matters through her employer's FSA plan.

Solution 5.5 We recall that Ji Eun's federal taxable income in the previous section was \$39,487. For the year, we have:

1. Her parking contributions come to: (\$200)(12) = \$2400
2. Her 401(k) plan contributions come to: (\$215)(12) = \$2580
3. Her FSA contributions come to: (\$75)(12) = \$900

Now, her taxable income is: \$39,487 – \$2400 – \$2580 – \$900 = \$33,607. According to Table 5.1, this places her taxable income now in a new tax bracket (\$9326 – \$37,950); so the amount in federal taxes due is determined by the following: \$932.50 + 15% of the amount over \$9325.

Now, the amount over \$9325 is \$24,282 (or \$33,607 – \$9325). And 15% of this amount is (0.15)(\$24,282) = \$3642.30.

So the amount Ji Eun owes in federal taxes using the benefit of her pre-tax contributions is \$932.50 + \$3642.30 = **\$4574.80**. In comparison, this is less than the previous \$5610.50 she owed in federal taxes without the pre-tax contributions.

Sebastian Kaulitzki/Shutterstock.com

5.5.2 Itemized Deductions to the Rescue!

In addition to pre-tax deductions, you can also reduce the amount owed in federal taxes by itemizing your deductions when you complete your tax form. Also dubbed as write-offs, these deductions also help to lower your tax bracket. Although they do not reduce your taxable income on a dollar-for-dollar basis, a certain percentage of each of these deductions reduces how much you pay in federal taxes. Again, we assert that information discussed here is not meant to serve as legal advice. To learn about the full benefit of itemizing deductions, we recommend hiring a CPA. We discuss a few examples of such **itemized deductions** here. It is crucial to keep all paperwork, statements, and receipts when claiming these deductions in case you have to justify to the government that they are legitimate write-offs.

Definition

Itemized deductions *are qualified expenses that taxpayers may use to reduce their taxable income. When filing taxes, either itemized deductions or the standard deduction may be used to determine this taxable income.*

Charitable Donations

Gifts to charity serve several purposes. First, you are able to give to an organization that you feel strongly about helping. Second, your donations to these qualifying charities serve to reduce the bottom line of what you owe in federal tax dollars. Monetary donations to religious groups, veterans' associations, public parks, and nonprofit organizations qualify for tax write-offs in this category. The IRS is very strict when it comes to these deductions, so you *must* keep records of all of these donations in the event you have to prove contributions. The charity should give you an official receipt substantiating your donation, particularly if the contribution exceeds $250.

Student Loan Interest

It may have been the case that you had to pay for most or all of your education through a student loan. Once you graduate, you are able to capitalize from this investment in another way. When you make a loan payment, a certain part of it goes toward paying the interest. This part is what you may write off at the end of the year. Technically, this is not necessarily an itemized deduction, as you may receive this benefit without itemizing. However, we place it here because it is not a pre-tax deduction taken out of your check automatically. At the end of the year, the bank to which you are repaying your loan will send you a form that has the amount in interest that you paid back for the year. This is the amount you report on your taxes as your deduction. If you are single, as long as you make less than $75,000, you are able to make good on this particular deduction. It can reduce up to $2500 from your taxable income.

Mortgage Interest

Once you get your job, you will have to decide if you will rent or buy property. In Asset Three, we talk in-depth about the pros and cons of owning a home. One of the perks is that you are able to deduct interest from your mortgage payments. Similar to the benefits you reap when paying back student loans, you experience awesome benefits through deductions associated with paying back your mortgage. The bank to which you are making mortgage payments will send you a form, which informs you with how much of your loan repayment has been applied to interest. For the first few years (assuming a regular fixed mortgage), most of your payments will go toward interest, as we explained when we discussed amortization schedules. Being able to write this interest off may lower your tax bracket considerably, which, in turn, means that you may owe less in federal taxes. Generally, this deduction maxes out on interest paid on properties whose value does not exceed $1 million.

Previous Year's State Income Tax Paid

When you file your taxes from the previous year, you may have had to pay state taxes. If you did, you will be able to write off the amount that you paid when you file for taxes for the current year. For example, if you paid state taxes for a tax season, you will be able to deduct that amount you paid when you fill out the tax forms that are due in April of the next tax season. Remembering to include this deduction will lower your tax bracket and reduce what you owe the IRS.

Again, this is not an exhaustive list of write-offs. There are many, many deductions you may find useful and advantageous. You may search for an complete list and description of all deduction of items you may be eligible for at http://goo.gl/Yf22.

"Is there any chance that these ancient printers could provide $46,000,000 in depreciation deductions?"

Cartoonresource/Shutterstock.com

5.5.3 Benefiting from Online Tax Calculators

Finally, we revisit Ji Eun's financial situation and see how certain deductions affect the amount she owes in federal taxes. We begin with her gross income again and assume no pre-tax deductions were made. None of the deductions in question come directly from her paycheck. She would have to deduct the following ones on her own. In addition, less and less people do taxes by hand nowadays. They tend to use online tax-preparation aids to enter their financial data, make deductions, and file to the government. Sites such as https://goo.gl/gUf6T and http://goo.gl/hoLhy help to guide you step-by-step through completing your taxes, asking detailed questions at every stage.

As an example, we use a tax calculator to show her income and witness how her bottom line changes concerning how much she owes. We use the tax calculator from the IRS website (http://goo.gl/cfqb2m) to assist us in our efforts. We are reminded that Ji Eun is single and has a gross income of $49,837. When we finish determining how much in itemized deductions we have, we have to decide whether to use the standard deduction or the itemized deductions when deciding on how much taxes are owed (not both!). In general, it is advised to use the higher of the two so that the taxable income becomes lower.

We begin by entering her income and federal income tax withheld from the paystub (Figure 5.2). We assume that the check amount and taxes remain the same each month, so we multiply all values by twelve to arrive at yearly totals. We assume that there is no other source of income. We also enter more financial data as requested.

When itemizing, we start with the gross salary and do not use any standard deduction or personal exemption; the exemption of yourself is already assumed when completing itemized deductions. Ji Eun's gross salary was $49,837. For the year, recall her parking contributions are $2400; her FSA contributions are $900; and her 401(k) contributions are $2580. Figure 5.3 shows this information entered on the calculator.

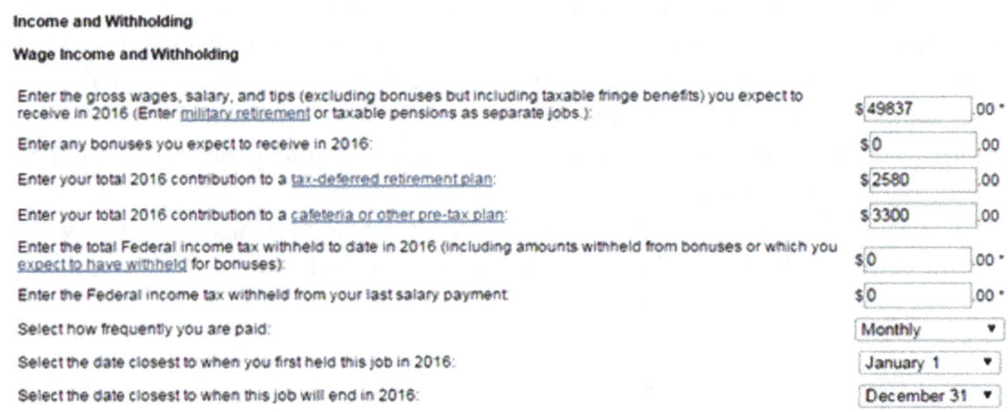
Income and Withholding

Wage Income and Withholding

Enter the gross wages, salary, and tips (excluding bonuses but including taxable fringe benefits) you expect to receive in 2016 (Enter military retirement or taxable pensions as separate jobs.):	$49837 .00 *
Enter any bonuses you expect to receive in 2016:	$0 .00
Enter your total 2016 contribution to a tax-deferred retirement plan:	$2580 .00
Enter your total 2016 contribution to a cafeteria or other pre-tax plan:	$3300 .00
Enter the total Federal income tax withheld to date in 2016 (including amounts withheld from bonuses or which you expect to have withheld for bonuses):	$0 .00 *
Enter the Federal income tax withheld from your last salary payment	$0 .00 *
Select how frequently you are paid:	Monthly
Select the date closest to when you first held this job in 2016:	January 1
Select the date closest to when this job will end in 2016:	December 31

FIGURE 5.3 Ji Eun's Expected Income and Withholdings

For clarity, the $3300 entry for pre-tax contributions represents the total contributions for both relevant costs ($2400 for parking plus $900 for the Flex Plan), while the $2580 entry is for 401(k) contributions. Further, we enter $0 for federal income tax withheld so as not to interfere with how much the calculator decides how much she will owe in taxes. Her paycheck says differently (approximately $640 is taken out each month). Leaving this information blank will not affect how much she owes in federal taxes.

We now take a look at Figure 5.4, which focuses on itemized deductions Ji Eun entered on her tax form. We assume the following situations concerning her are true:

1. She donated a total of $3100 to the church she attends.
2. As a homeowner, she paid a total of $14,755 in interest toward the repayment of her mortgage loan.
3. Each month, she is paying off her student loan. She has paid the debt down almost halfway. The amount she paid on the interest of the student loan was $816.48.
4. The previous year, she paid $2231.88 in state taxes (or $185.99 each month for 12 months)

Deductions

If your standard deduction, $6300, is more than your total itemized deductions, your standard deduction will be used to calculate your withholding. Otherwise, your total itemized deduction amount will be used.

If you want to use your itemized deductions to calculate your withholding, even if they amount to less than your standard deduction, check this box: ☐

Enter an estimate of your 2016 itemized deductions:

Medical and Dental Expenses:	$ 0	.00
Taxes You Paid:	$ 2232	.00
Interest You Paid:	$ 15571	.00
Gifts to Charity:	$ 3100	.00
Casualty and Theft Losses:	$ 0	.00
Job Expenses and Most Other Miscellaneous Deductions:	$ 0	.00
Other Miscellaneous Deductions:	$ 0	.00

FIGURE 5.4 Ji Eun's Itemized Deductions

The amount we enter for interest paid is $15,571.48, which reflects the sum of total loan interest payments she made ($14,755 for the mortgage loan; $816.48 for the student loan). This reflects rounding to the nearest dollar. The worksheet will not let you continue to the next page unless you round in this fashion. Automatically rounded, our entry for state taxes is $2232. When it comes to Ji Eun's deductions, it is important to note that she can use whichever is greater: the total amount of her itemized deductions, $20,903, or the standard deduction plus the personal exemption, which is given in Section 5.4.1 as $10,350 ($6300 + $4050 = $10,350). Of course, in order to receive the maximum benefit of a lower amount due in federal taxes, we would probably use her itemized deductions to determine how much she owes.

Based on the pre-tax deductions and itemized deductions, we observe in Figure 5.5 the total amount now that Ji Eun will owe in federal taxes, as indicated in the first line.

Your Results

Based on the information you previously entered, your anticipated income tax for 2016 is $2,390. You should adjust your withholding on a new Form W-4 as follows:

- For the only job you entered (which has a projected salary of $49,837): 4 allowances.
- Check the "Single" box on your Form W-4

Assuming this recommendation is in effect for the rest of 2016 your expected refund should be about $200. Following this recommendation will ensure that the amount withheld from your wages will cover all of your projected tax liability while minimizing your refund.

Tip Be sure to review your withholding at the beginning of 2017 (or any time there is a change in your tax situation). If you follow the above recommendation and do not check your withholding at the beginning of next year, your withholding for 2017 might be incorrect.

Following is a recap of information entered on the preceding pages on which the above advice is based.
Prepared: March 9, 2016

Filing Status: single	Someone else can claim you as a dependent: no
Number of jobs: 1	Number of dependents: 0
Will you be 65 or older 1/1/2017: no	Are you blind: no
Child & dependent care credit qualifying persons: 0	Child & dependent care credit expenses: $0
Eligible children for child tax credit: 0	Other credits: $0
Total salary: $49,837	Total plans and cafeteria: $5,880
Total tax withheld to date: $0	Total tax withheld from last check: $0
Total earned income other than salary: $0	Nonwage income: $0
Adjustments to income: $0	Total itemized deductions: $20,903
Projected additional withholding if you do nothing: $0	

FIGURE 5.5 Ji Eun's Federal Tax Owed Based on All Deductions

According to the first line of the results in Figure 5.5, we see that she will owe a total of **$2390** in federal taxes, considering her pre-tax deductions and her itemized deductions. One final consideration with regard to itemizing deductions is that it is advisable to keep proof of all itemized deductions. This proof is normally in the form of bank statements, credit card receipts, and other forms of documentation. If the government thinks you are not being truthful about expenses being claimed for itemized deductions, you may become the target of an **audit**.

Definition

An **audit** *is a systemic examination of a person's or a company's financial statement to prove or disprove that all information is accurate.*

If government auditors find that you have not been truthful about information placed on your taxes, you may be fined or, in some cases, may be forced to spend time in jail, depending on what audit results reveal. This is why it is important to keep all documentation to verify information you use when itemizing deductions. In some cases, where audits include justification for job-related expenses, only copies of physical receipts (not credit card statements) are acceptable to support financial claims regarding deductions.

Although this example is somewhat simplified, it loosely proves how beneficial it is to itemize deductions when filing taxes. Again, it is important to seek assistance from an accountant to be sure you are entering the right amounts for the right categories. Mistakes in filing taxes can cost you in financial penalties, which can be very steep. For comparison, we summarize how much Ji Eun will owe the IRS in federal taxes when she (1) uses the standard deduction and personal exemption for herself; (2) uses standard deductions, personal exemption, and pre-tax deductions; and (3) uses pre-tax deductions and itemized deductions. Table 5.3 recaps these bottom-line dollar amounts and presents this information in a clear and concise manner.

TABLE 5.3 Ji Eun's Federal Taxes Owed in Three Separate Instances

Filing Status	Amount Owed in Federal Taxes
Standard deduction and personal exemption	$5610.50
Stand deduction, personal exemption, and pre-tax deductions	$4574.80
Pre-tax deductions and itemized deductions	$2390.00

Hence, we see from this oversimplified example that (all things being equal), Ji Eun owes less money in federal taxes when she incorporates pre-tax deductions and itemized deductions in the filing of her taxes. Hopefully, she and other recent college graduates like her will capitalize on all the benefits that come along with factoring deductions into the overall mix of the tax-filing experience.

Here Today, Maybe Gone Tomorrow: The Plight of Social Security and Medicare

One of the most sensitive discussions in the current world of American finance is whether the benefits of social security and Medicare will still be around for those who reach retirement age. After putting in years and years of service on the job, many cannot fathom that these benefits will possibly no longer be around by the time they reach the end of their work journey.

According to one source, social security benefits are set to expire in 2033 if Congress does not become proactive and introduce measures to extend them (Anderson 2015). According to another source, Medicare benefits will become depleted around 2026; at this time, legislators will have to reduce benefits, raise taxes, or borrow money to continue to provide health services to seniors (Fernholz 2015). If both programs do not expire, experts suggest that programs will only be able to cover a percentage of the benefits that they used to offer in full. In the grand scheme of things and considering how long it often takes for laws to pass on the congressional floor, these dates are closer than one may be willing to admit. We are, hence, staring at a generation that will perhaps not have access to a net of financial security that so many retirees have taken for granted over the years.

Scholars primarily state that two predominant factors contribute to the eminent decimation of both programs: (1) people on average in America are living longer (Barro 2015) and (2) the baby-boomer generation is placing disproportionate stress on the programs because of its huge population (Tankersley 2015). Even though President Reagan signed documents that placed into law the raising of the retirement age to 67 from 65, it did little to offset the strain on the social security pot since average life expectancy rose from 61 to 79 (as of 2015). Moreover, baby boomers, in the next 15 years or so, will contribute heftily to the population of retirees, decreasing the amount of health aid available per retiree. Many have voiced that Congress could have avoided this debacle by being more forward-looking and anticipating that more funding would be needed to take care of America's retirees. It is, however, where the country stands as it relates to these two programs.

In truth, whether social security or Medicare will still be available to retirees in the '20s or '30s is immaterial when it comes to preparation for retirement. In fact, even if both programs were to exist beyond their projected death dates, the financial support they would afford retirees would hardly promise a lifestyle that they may be used to when they worked. Full-fledged benefits of social security and Medicare still leave much to be desired when it comes to meeting basic needs (food, clothing, shelter) and not-so-basic needs (travel, vacation). The overriding lesson is: *Don't depend solely on government support to fund your retirement reality.* When you take proactive steps to contribute to your own 401(k) or 414(h) plan, you are taking deliberate moves to ensure your retirement portfolio is what you want it to be so that you can live how you want when that time comes.

That way, whether social security or Medicare or any other government-sponsored program goes bellied up before you retire will not be a major issue. If the programs still exist when you retire, fine. If they do not, fine. By saving into your own retirement plan (either pre- or post-taxed), you will have taken conscious measures to place your retirement into the person's hands that will be affected by it the most: yours.

Student Exercises: Budgeting and Taxation

5.1 Brad's monthly net income is $3050. According to percentages in Figure 5.1, determine how much he should allot for the following categories:

a. Food
b. Transportation
c. Housing

5.2 Marty makes $1700 a month in net pay. His roommate and he spend $499 each in rent each month. Is the percent Marty pays in rent above or below what is recommended in Figure 5.1?

5.3 Dolly makes $73,729 a year. She gets paid twice per month. Using the percentages at the end of Section 5.3, determine how much is taken out in each paycheck to fund the mandatory Medicare pot (FICA Med Tax) and to fund the mandatory social security program (FICA SS Tax).

5.4 Your net pay for the current month is $3689.42. Using recommended percentages in Figure 5.1, complete the monthly budget worksheet on pages. Assume that you only have $250 in credit card debt and a total of $6500 remaining in student loans. In fact, assume that the overall goal of this month's budget is to pay more toward eliminating this amount in student debt.

Make sure that the total amount of funds in each category is distributed to account for all its subcategories. For example, for Housing and Utilities (30%), be sure that all amounts in that category equal the dollar amount equivalent to 30%, not just the Rent/Mortgage line. You may have to research to see what are the average costs for utilities per month in the area you live.

Be creative! For example, you will determine whether you have a car or catch public transportation. Budget amounts just need to reflect your decision. You will also need to decide what to do with any money that is left over. As a general rule, assume that the goal of this month's budget is to pay down your student loans.

5.5 Gereen's gross salary, at the end of 2016, was $95,820 for her job as an executive at L.L. Bean in Freeport, Maine. How much would she owe:

a. in *federal* taxes, assuming the 2016 federal standard deduction and personal exemption (Hint: Use the link https://goo.gl/1Z2Zg4 to assist in finding the answer)?
b. in *state* taxes, assuming the 2016 state standard deduction and personal exemption (Hint: Use the link http://goo.gl/sSdyvm to assist in finding the answer)?

5.6 Write a half-page discussion on whether you agree or disagree with the progressive tax system in America. State your position and expand on why you feel the way you feel about your position.

5.7 Your annual income in 2016 was $49,355. You made the following pre-tax contributions for the year: $5822 to your 401(k), $1725 to your Health Flex Plan (FSA), and $2400 for preapproved parking. Using Table 5.1, determine how much *more* you would have paid in federal taxes if you did not make those pre-tax contributions (using both the 2016 federal standard deduction and the personal exemption).

5.8 **(challenge)** Loretta's 2016 gross income was $101,263. She made three pre-tax contributions during the year: $7100 into her 401(k), $1060 for preapproved parking contributions, and a certain amount into her Health Flex Plan (FSA). If her taxable income falls between $91,150 and $190,150, use Table 5.1 to determine how much she contributed to her FSA if the amount she paid in federal taxes was $18,752.01. Assume she is single.

5.9 Consider the IRS tax calculator here: http://goo.gl/cfqb2m.

Consider your current financial situation below:

- (i) You are single, and no one else can claim you as a dependent.
- (ii) You have only one job at which you are currently employed, where your annual gross salary is $52,586.39. You are paid twice per month.
- (iii) This year, you expect to contribute $6544 to your 401(k) plan, $2300 to your Health FSA, and $1700 for preapproved parking for your job.
- (iv) You have two children, who are your dependents.
- (v) You are 32 years old and have 20/20 vision.
- (vi) Both of your children are eligible for the Child Tax Credit.
- (vii) So far this year, you have paid $0 in federal income tax withheld to date, and $0 taken out from your last salary payment.
- (viii) You began this job closer to January 1 of the last year, and December 31 is the last day of employment as it relates to financial matters pertaining to this year's taxes.
- (ix) You would always like to use your itemized deductions instead of the standard deduction.
- (x) You paid $1009 in state taxes from last year.
- (xi) As a homeowner, you paid $8271 in mortgage interest and $746 in interest for your student loans.
- (xii) You made a $400 contribution to Community Voice Mail Homelessness.

Determine how much you can anticipate owing in federal taxes at the end of the year. The calculator should show information for the current year you are in.

5.10 Last year, Lamar grossed $190,000 as a stockbroker on Wall Street.

- a. Determine how much he owes in federal taxes when he files on this year. (You should base this on last year's federal tax schedule, which you will need to find online.)
- b. How much would he save in federal taxes if he made the following pre-tax deductions: $1560 for transit passes, $17,800 in retirement contributions to his 401(k), and $2550 into his health FSA.
- c. Determine how much he would save in federal taxes if he made all of the pre-tax contributions in b. and if the following situations hold:
  - (i) He is married filing a joint return and has only one job.
  - (ii) He has four children that he can claim as his dependents. One of the children is adopted.
  - (iii) He and his spouse are both 45 years old and have 20/20 vision.
  - (iv) So far this year, a total of $11,000 has been withheld in federal income tax. A total of $1200 was withheld from his last salary.
  - (v) He is paid every two weeks.
  - (vi) He started his job with Wall Street around February 1, and the closest it will end in the current year is December 31.
  - (vii) He would like to use the higher of his standard deduction or his itemized deduction.
  - (viii) He paid $5788 in state taxes on last year.
  - (ix) He estimates that he will have paid $18,944 in interest from mortgage payments.
  - (x) He estimates that he will have donated $21,000 to his church by the end of the year.

References

Anderson, Tom. "How Social Security Funding Affects Your Retirement." *CBNC: Personal Finance*, March 26, 2015. Accessed July 28, 2015. http://goo.gl/Ni1cwM.

Barro, Josh. "We're Living Longer. That's Great, Except for Social Security." *New York Times*, November 17, 2015. Accessed March 5, 2016. http://goo.gl/g8ed8X.

Fernholz, Tim. "Medicare Is Going to Run Out of Money in About a Decade—But That's What They Always Say." *Quartz*, May 31, 2013. Accessed July 28, 2015. http://goo.gl/u5Hzz.

Giroux, Gary. 2012. "Financing the American Civil War: Developing New Tax Sources." *Accounting History* 17:83–104.

Mundra, Niitesh. "Merits and Demerits of Progressive Tax Income." *Knoji Consumer Knowledge*, February 8, 2012. Accessed March 5, 2016. https://goo.gl/EMwdJX.

Roberts, James A., Luc Honore Petnji Yaya, and Chris Manolis. 2014. "The Invisible Addiction: Cell-Phone Activities and Addiction Among Male and Female College Students." *Journal of Behavioral Addictions* 3(4):254–65.

Ruiz, R. R. "F.C.C. Chief Seeks Broadband Plan to Aid the Poor." *The New York Times*, May 28, 2015, A1.

Tankersley, Jim. "Baby Boomers Are What's Wrong with America's Economy." *The Washington Post*, November 5, 2015. Accessed March 6, 2016. http://goo.gl/5pM4CZ.

Asset Six

Linear Regression

Chapter Outline

Money can't [cause] happiness, but neither can poverty.

Leo Rosten

6.1 Simple Linear Regression

One of the benefits of studying personal finance is the linkage to other crucial areas of mathematics that exist. In particular, finance's relationship with the field of statistics is unique and quite interesting. The fusion between these two fields illustrates just how important one area of study is to the vibrance of another. It becomes key to observe associations and correlations that may exist within one's own financial world. These relationships provide some insight into the scope of influence that some factors tend to have on financial realities. Specifically, the technique of linear regression serves as one of these statistical tools.

6.1.1 The Method Defined

The method of **simple linear regression** dates back as far as the late 1800s and has become increasingly the method of choice for displaying the effectiveness of the relationship between variables (Gibson and Dillard 2016).

Definition

The method of **simple linear regression** *explores and analyzes the relationship of bivariate data in which an explanatory variable is used to predict the response variable.*

The overall mission of this form of regression is to find the least-squares regression line in the form of $\hat{y} = mx + b$*, which illustrates this linkage between the explanatory variable and response variable the best.*

In the simple linear regression equation:

> $\hat{y}$ *is the predicted value given a certain explanatory value* (x);
> m *is the slope of the regression equation;*
> x *is the explanatory value for which we seek a prediction; and*
> b *is the y-intercept of the regression equation.*

Of course, the prefix "bi" means two; thus, bivariate data simply means "having two variables." When we take a closer look at these two variables, we understand clearer their role when it comes to dissecting the method at hand.

The bivariate data we discuss are comprised of explanatory (or independent) variables and response (or dependent) variables. We define both in light of the dataset in Table 6.1, in which we examine two components of the data having to do with one's credit score and the number of credit cards associated with that particular credit score:

TABLE 6.1 Number of Credit Cards Owned and Credit Scores

Credit Card Holder	Number of Credit Cards Owned	Credit Score
Jessica	2	800
Sanjay	6	590
Thomas	4	570
Lisa	0	780
Marge	1	600

According to Table 6.1, it seems as though we have three components of the data. However, the notion of bivariate data suggests that the two aspects of the data we are concerned with are the numeric sets of data on which we can perform mathematical operations. So our interest is drawn to the headings of "Number of Credit Cards Owned" and "Credit Score."

The explanatory variable is that variable which tends to explain results of the other variable. Although we avoid saying that the explanatory variable *causes* results of the other variable, there may be some sense of influential effect onto the other variable. In Table 6.1, our explanatory variable would have to be "Number of Credit Cards Owned" since the number of credit cards that one owns generally tends to explain one's credit score. The response variable of the two, then, must be "Credit Score" since one's credit score somehow generally depends on the number of credit cards one owns.

Example 6.1 In a set of bivariate data, we are given a column of data entitled "Number of Rooms in Home" and another entitled "Initial Mortgage Amount." Which data column represents the response variable? Why?

Solution 6.1 The response variable would be "Initial Mortgage Amount" since data values in this column tend to be influenced by or explained by how many rooms are offered in a home. Generally, the fewer rooms offered in a home, the lower the initial mortgage. The more rooms offered, the more the initial mortgage, generally speaking. Location of home could play a more significant role in a real-life scenario.

The goal of simple linear regression is to find the **least-squares regression line**, which is the line that best summarizes our bivariate data.

Definition

The **least-squares regression line** *is the one and only line that best summarizes the relationship between the two variables in a scenario involving simple linear regression.*

Locating this line involves a number of key steps: constructing the scatterplot, finding the slope and y-intercept, and writing the regression equation in the form of $\hat{y} = mx + b$. We draw the line by using this regression equation.

6.1.2 Constructing the Scatterplot

In simple linear regression, once we identify explanatory and response variables, we show visually the representation of the bivariate data via a **scatterplot**.

> **Definition**
>
> *A* **scatterplot** *shows a visual representation of all bivariate data as a series of (x, y) data points on a Cartesian plane.*

When plotting data on the scatterplot, we place data in the explanatory column on the x-axis, and we place data in the response column on the y-axis. We pair up the appropriate individual values in both columns as separate (x, y) points in order to construct this representation. For example, in Table 6.1, we note that the first credit card holder, Jessica, has a credit score of 800 and owns 2 credit cards. Since the number of credit cards is the explanatory variable and credit score is the response variable, then the point to plot associated with Jessica is (2, 800). We must be careful to place the appropriate point value as the correct value for x and y. Note that it would be incorrect to plot Jessica's point as (800, 2). According to the same table, we would also need to plot the following points: (6, 590), (4, 570), (0, 780), and (1, 600).

In Figure 6.1, we plot these five points to see what the scatterplot looks like concerning our credit card data and label them appropriately.

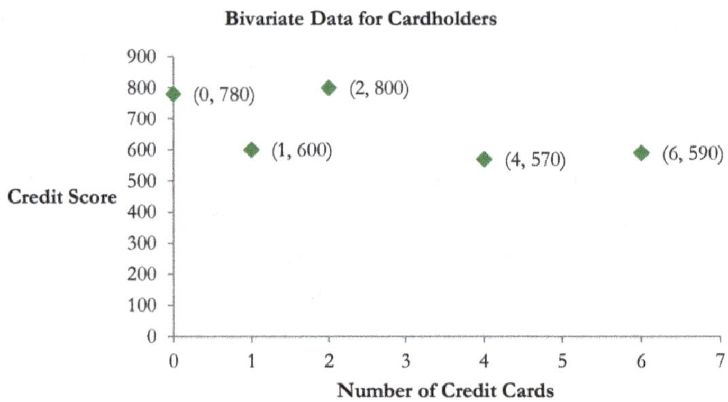

FIGURE 6.1 Scatterplot for Table 6.1

This scatterplot visually represents the bivariate data for all five cardholders. Again, we note that the values for number of credit cards are placed on the x axis, while values for credit scores are placed on the y axis. At the end of Asset Six, we discuss how we use Excel to construct a simple scatterplot.

It further becomes useful to observe several characteristics that can be used to describe the overall trend and features of the scatterplot. In particular, we consider key characteristics of scatterplots with regards to *form*, *direction*, and *strength*.

When we speak of *form*, we consider the question, "Does it resemble some known curve or shape?" For example, we see below that the two scatterplots possess certain well-known forms.

With respect to *direction* for the scatterplot, we ask, "When we scan the data from left to right, does the trend of the points seem to move upward (positive association)? downward (negative association)? without any noticeable direction (neither positive nor negative)?"

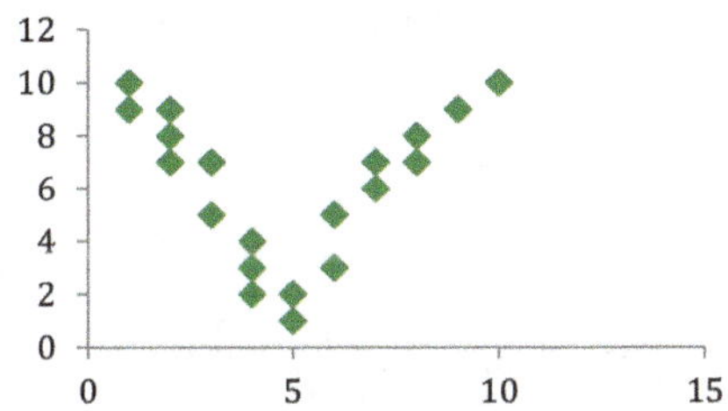

Form of Parabola (Loosely)

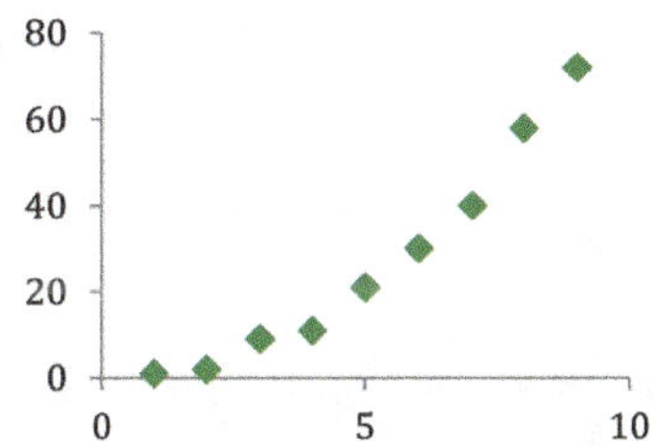

Form of Exponential Function

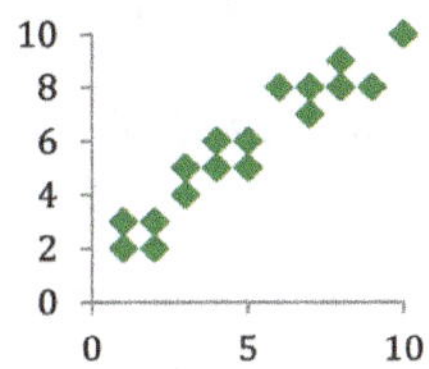

Positive Association

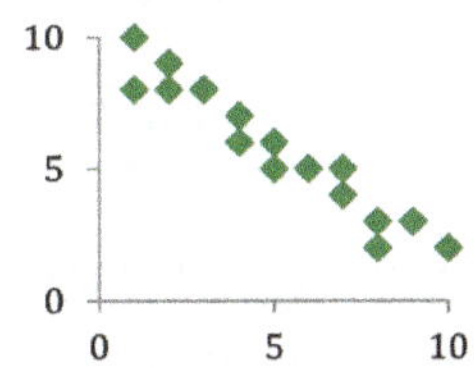

Negative Association

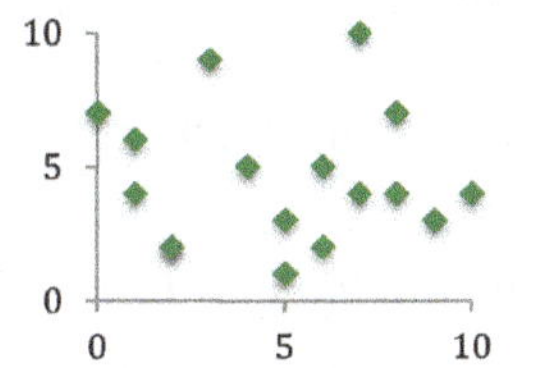

Neither Positive Nor Negative

Concerning *strength*, we observe how well the data seem to be attracted to an imaginary line. To get a sense of the notion of strength, we inquire, "How close do the points in the scatterplot lie to a line that may be drawn through the series of all points?" Section 6.1.5 sheds more light on this idea of strength through discussion of a concept in regression called correlation.

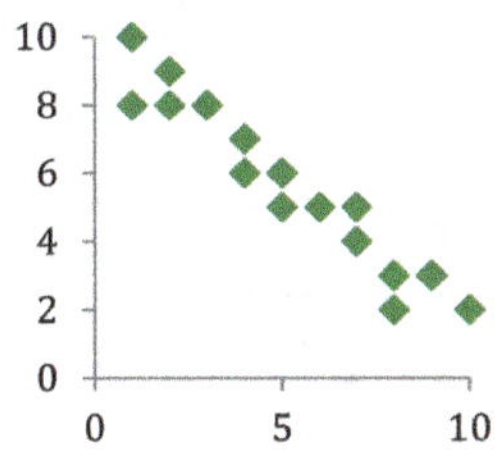

Very Strong

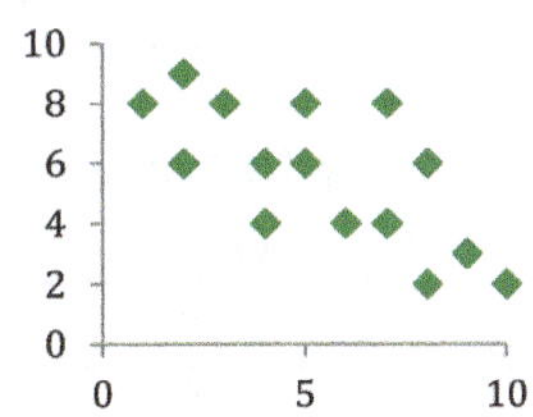

Fairly Strong

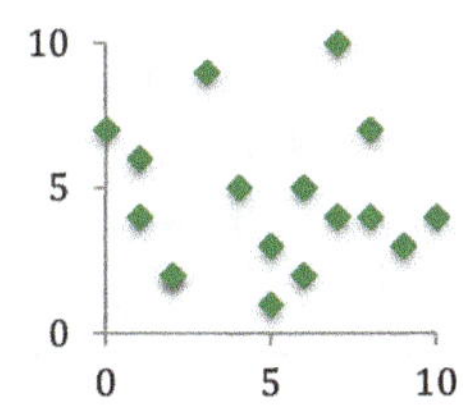

Weak

6.1.3 Finding the Slope and *y*-Intercept of the Regression Equation

When we review Section 1.1, we get a detailed look at the line and its makeup. We learned how to calculate the slope and took a peek at the slope-intercept form of the line. In simple linear regression, we explore these same concepts, but we focus on finding the slope and y-intercept using all of the data points and not just two points. The goal of linear regression becomes to find the best regression line (and its accompanying equation) that best fits or summarizes the trend of all bivariate data points. As mentioned earlier, this best line is known as the least-squares regression line and is given as $\hat{y} = mx + b$.

When we found the slope (m) in Section 1.1, we used the following formula: $m = (y_2 - y_1)/(x_2 - x_1)$, given that we had two data points: (x_1, y_1) and (x_2, y_2). In the current method, however, we note that we do not just have two data points to consider. In Table 6.1 or Figure 6.1, we see that we have five data points, each of which becomes equally important in figuring out what the slope is of this least-squares line. Hence, we must use a different formula when determining this slope, which takes into account *each* data point, which will be used for the regression line. We review the **slope** here:

Definition

In simple linear regression, we find the **slope** *of the regression equation by computing the following formula:*

$$m = \frac{n(\sum xy) - (\sum x)(\sum y)}{n(\sum x^2) - (\sum x)^2}, \qquad \textbf{Equation 6.1}$$

where n is the number of subjects for whom data are collected; other values are as follows:

> $\sum xy$ *is found by multiplying the x value with y value in each row and then adding each of the n products;*
> $\sum x$ *is found by adding all of the values in the explanatory (x) column;*
> $\sum y$ *is found by adding all of the values in the response (y) column;*
> $\sum x^2$ *is found by multiplying the x value by itself in each row and then adding each of the n products; and*
> $(\sum x)^2$ *is found by squaring the result we found for* $\sum x$.

We apply the previous definition in order to find the slope of the regression equation for the data in Table 6.1.

TABLE 6.2 Calculating the Values Needed for Slope

Credit Card Holder	Number of Credit Cards Owned (x)	Credit Score (y)	x^2	xy
Jessica	2	800	4	1600
Sunjay	6	590	36	3540
Thomas	4	570	16	2280
Lisa	0	780	0	0
Marge	1	600	1	600
Column totals	$\sum x = 13$	$\sum y = 3340$	$\sum x^2 = 57$	$\sum xy = 8020$

Using Equation 6.1, we substitute the appropriate values based on calculations in Table 6.2 as indicated below to find the slope (Note: Since we have information for five credit card holders, then $n = 5$):

$$\begin{aligned} m &= \frac{5(8020) - 13(3340)}{5(57) - (13)^2} \\ &= \frac{40100 - 43420}{285 - 169} \\ &= \frac{-3320}{116} \\ &= -28.621 \end{aligned}$$

So the value for the slope of the regression line is –28.621 (or $m = -28.621$). This becomes the value that we use to replace m in the regression equation ($\hat{y} = mx + b$). Once we find the ***y*-intercept**, we will then have the entire equation and can graph it along with the scatterplot.

We briefly mention the y-intercept in Section 6.1 as well, but we dedicate a little more time in this section regarding its calculation. In linear regression, we again consider the contribution of each data point when finding this value. We need to be guided by a separate equation that helps us find it.

Definition

In simple linear regression, we find the ***y-intercept (b)*** *of the regression equation by computing the following formula:*

$$b = \overline{y} - m\overline{x}, \qquad \textbf{Equation 6.2}$$

where $\overline{y}$ is the average of the values in the response (y) column; $\overline{x}$ is the average of the values in the explanatory (x) column; and m is the calculated slope of the linear regression equation.

For the data in Table 6.1, we note that $\overline{y} = \frac{\sum y}{n} = 3340/5 = 668$ and that $\overline{x} = \frac{\sum x}{n} = 13/5 = 2.6$. Earlier in this section, we found the slope (m) to be –28.621. Using these values, we calculate the y-intercept:

$$\begin{aligned} b &= 668 - (-28.621)(2.6) \\ &= 668 + (28.621)(2.6) \\ &= 668 + 74.412 \\ &= 742.41 \end{aligned}$$

The y-intercept becomes 742.41 (or $b = 742.41$). This becomes the value that we use to replace b in the regression equation.

When we consider both the slope and y-intercept values that we found, we determine that the least-squares regression equation for the bivariate credit card data are as follows:

$$\hat{y} = -28.621x + 742.41$$

When interpreting the slope in simple linear regression, we exploit what we already know about the role of the numerator and denominator for the slope in general. We remember that slope represents the ratio of the change in the y variable to the change in the x variable. Or we recall that:

$$\text{Slope} = \frac{\text{Rise}}{\text{Run}} = \frac{\Delta y}{\Delta x}.$$

Using this idea, we locate the slope in the equation and move forward with the interpretation, paying special attention to how we interpret Δx and Δy in the context of the problem.

We also recall that the y-intercept (b) is the location on the graph where the regression line crosses the y-axis. This point at which the line crosses the y-axis occurs when the corresponding x value is zero ($x = 0$). We have to use caution, however, when interpreting the y-intercept and use common sense in the situation when the x variable is zero. Further, if $x = 0$ is not within the range of observed values, then there is technically no practical interpretation of the y-intercept.

Example 6.2 We saw previously that the regression equation for predicting the cardholder's credit score using number of credit cards owned as the x variable is:

$$\hat{y} = -28.621x + 742.41$$

Provide the appropriate interpretation of the slope and the y-intercept in the context of this particular problem.

Solution 6.2 The slope of the regression equation is $m = -28.621 = \dfrac{-28.621}{1}$. This means that, on average, one's credit score decreases by 28.621 points for every 1 credit card that one owns. The y-intercept is (0, 742.41). Since $x = 0$ is included in the range of the x data (from 0 to 6 credit cards), we may proceed with the interpretation. Otherwise, we would not. This means that when one possesses no credit cards ($x = 0$), one's credit score is predicted to be around 742.

In the next section, we discuss how to superimpose the regression line atop the scatterplot. We also discuss why this line is the best-fit line for the data.

6.1.4 Drawing the Regression Line and Interpreting Results

We are now equipped to draw this regression line since we have its equation. One such method we could employ to plot the line is alluded to in Section 1.1.3. We can start by plotting the y-intercept and using our knowledge of the slope to achieve the second point.

Here, however, we use a different strategy to plot the line. Once we know the regression line, we may plot the line by choosing two arbitrary x values within the range of the given x values in the data and finding the corresponding y values. We then draw the line through these two sets of (x, y) points. We "ignore" dots that comprise the scatterplot itself and focus only on the prediction points that come from placing these two arbitrary x values in $\hat{y}$ when we construct the line.

For example, in our data, we choose two arbitrary x values within the range of our x values. When we take a look at Table 6.1, we see that the x values range from $x = 0$ to $x = 6$. We therefore choose any two x values within this range, say $x = 3$ and $x = 5$. Notice that we do not choose the point $x = 7$ because that value is outside of the given data range and would not lead to a reliable answer, although the answer may seem reasonable. In other words, we avoid the error of extrapolation when drawing the line, which means that we avoid offering a prediction for an x value that lies outside of the given x range. To offer a prediction value for an x value outside of the range is to assume that the trend outside of that given range continues to be linear, which is not always an accurate assumption in regression theory. We restrict our predictions and construct our regression line, then, by choosing two arbitrary points only within this given x range.

We predict the corresponding y values by placing the two x values ($x = 3$ and $x = 5$) into $\hat{y}$. We observe both computations:

$$\begin{aligned}\hat{y}(3) &= -28.621(3) + 742.41\\ &= -85.863 + 742.41\\ &= 656.547\end{aligned} \qquad \begin{aligned}\hat{y}(5) &= -28.621(5) + 742.41\\ &= -143.105 + 742.41\\ &= 599.305\end{aligned}$$

This means that we draw our regression line through the two points (3, 656.547) and (5, 599.305). This regression line represents the best line that fits the five scatterplot points for the credit card data. Figure 6.2 illustrates the drawing of the regression line using this technique:

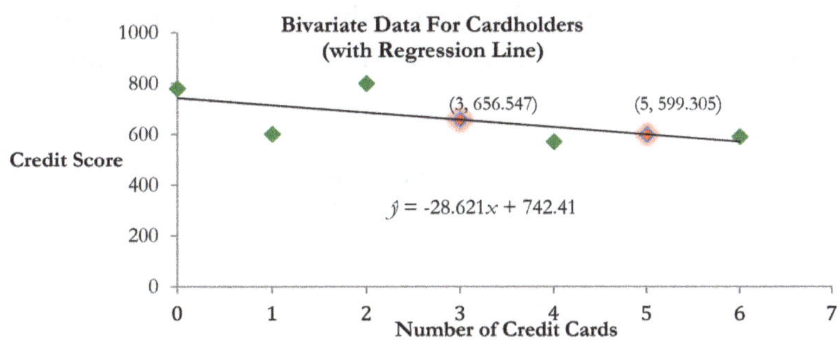

FIGURE 6.2 Scatterplot and Regression Line for Table 6.1

We note that the red values correspond to the two arbitrary x values and their associated y values (which we just found) that are used to plot the regression line. Once we determine these two (x, y) prediction values and plot them, we connect the dots through the red values to obtain the drawing of the regression line or $\hat{y}$. We generally only draw the line within the range of the given x values of our data. Hence, the regression line extends from $x = 0$ to $x = 6$. It is worth noting that we could have used any other arbitrary points within this same x data range (e.g., we could have used $x = 2$ or $x = 4$) and solved for their corresponding y values. Although we would have gotten two different points for these new arbitrary x values, we still would have plotted a line identical to the one already plotted. All (x, y) values would have landed on the same regression line that is drawn. We leave part of this confirmation as one of the exercises at the end of the asset.

In general, this best-fit, least-squares regression line minimizes the sum of the squared vertical distances from each of the scatterplot points to the regression line or trendline. We get a glimpse of this phenomenon by viewing Figure 6.3, which highlights these distances (called residuals) from the scatterplot to the found regression line. Again, in our credit card data, we square each of the five residual values (represented visually by dotted lines) and then add them together to arrive at this minimized sum.

If we were to compare this diagram of residuals to any other diagram of residuals for this same credit card data and go through the same squaring of vertical, dotted-line distances to the regression line and adding them together, the sum of squares we would get would always be more than the sum we would get from Figure 6.3, thus disqualifying the line from being the "best" line to fit the data. We take a look at Figure 6.4, which shows one such possible candidate vying for the status of "best" line.

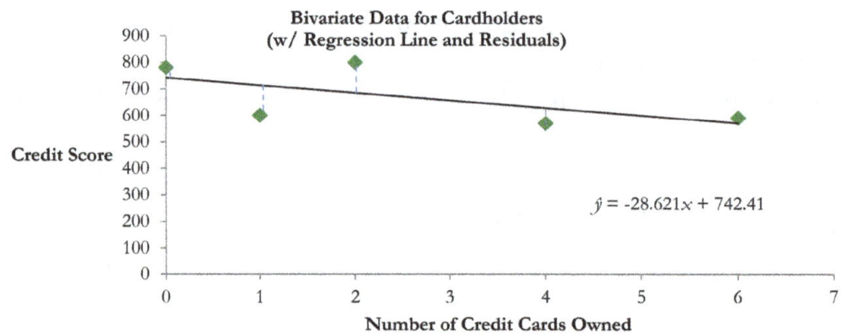

FIGURE 6.3 Visualizing the Meaning of "Best" Line for the Credit Card Data

Notice that we have the same scatterplot in both figures. The "regression" line in Figure 6.4, however, does not minimize the sum of the squared vertical distances of the dotted lines. When comparing both figures, we see that as a whole, the vertical distances from the dotted lines to the trendline are much shorter in Figure 6.3 than in Figure 6.4. The shorter the overall distance, the better the regression line.

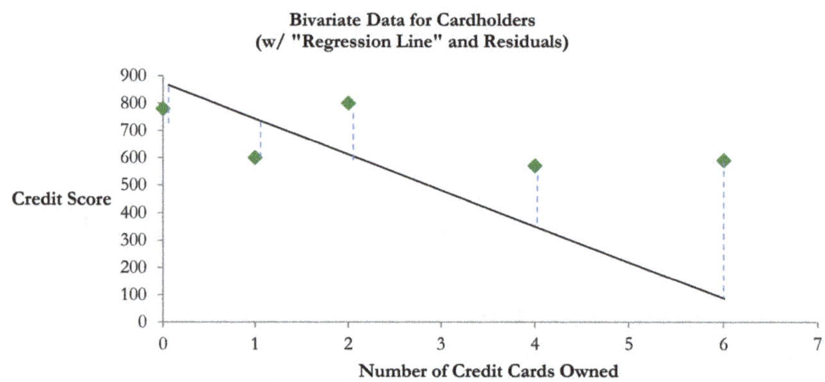

FIGURE 6.4 Another Line Attempting to Be the "Best" Line for Credit Card Data (Vertical Distances from Dotted Lines to Line Too Large)

In fact, after making slope and y-intercept calculations for this specific problem, it is determined that the regression line we find in Figure 6.3 will outperform any other line seeking to claim that it is the "best" regression line for summarizing our five credit card data points.

6.1.5 r and r^2

As witnessed in the previous section, we are always able to determine a least-squares regression equation from any scatterplot. We simply use the formulas for the slope and y-intercept to help us in that regard. We are also able to provide predictions of any x value within the given range using this equation. What we have yet to address, however, is how *reliable* or *strong* these y-valued predictions are that we get from using the prediction equation. This notion of quantifying strength within the regression process, mentioned in Section 6.1.2, is referred to as measuring **correlation**.

Definition

In simple linear regression, **correlation** *is a value that communicates how linear the relationship between the explanatory and response variables is. Denoted as* **r**, *the correlation coefficient is found by computing the following:*

$$r = \frac{n\left(\sum xy\right) - \left(\sum x\right)\left(\sum y\right)}{\sqrt{n\left(\sum x^2\right) - \left(\sum x\right)^2}\sqrt{n\left(\sum y^2\right) - \left(\sum y\right)^2}}, \qquad \textbf{Equation 6.3}$$

where

$\sum y^2$ *is found by multiplying the y value by itself in each row and then adding each of the n products;*

$\left(\sum y\right)^2$ *is found by squaring the result we found for* $\sum y$. *The other values are as defined in Equation 6.1.*

This measure of predictability (r) has a certain range and has a specific visual representation, depending on its value. Since the notion of strength deals with how certain scatterplot values congregate around the regression line, different values for r provide a sense of how close these scatterplot values converge toward the regression line. We investigate several examples below, highlighting varying values for r and how they translate visually. Note that as r approaches 0, the further the points tend to move away from the imaginary regression line. As r approaches 1 or –1, the closer the points tend to congregate toward the imaginary regression line.

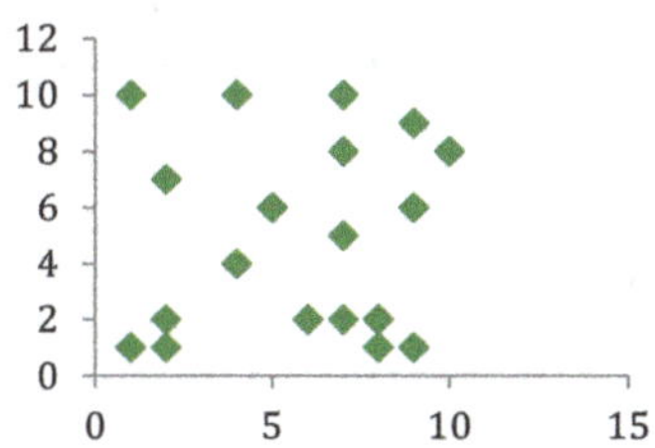

$r = 0$

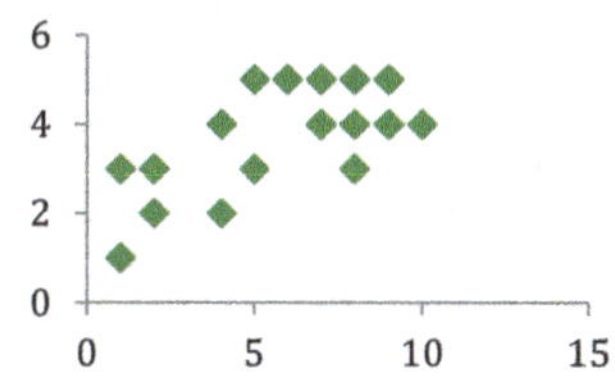

$r = 0.5$

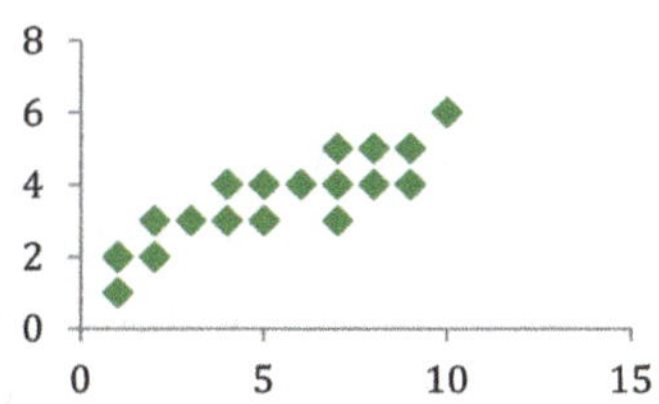

$r = 0.84$

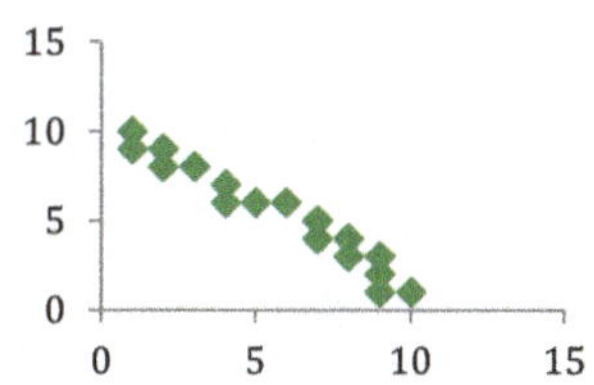

$r = -0.97$

Notice that if r is 1 or –1, all scatterplot points are touching the regression line, which means that the measure of predictability between the explanatory and response variables is perfect. We would feel very confident in these two cases when making a prediction of y from a given x value. When r is 0, we are not as confident when making a prediction of y since there is not a strong sense of linearity among scatterplot points.

Caveat

It becomes crucial to understand that strong correlation between variables does not imply strong causation between variables. In other words, one must not make the fallacy of assuming that, if two variables are such that r is 1 or -1, changes in the explanatory variable cause changes in the response variable. Strong correlation just suggests that a strong association exists between the two variables. Some other, unmeasured, underlying variable may very well be the source for the cause. For example, it may be that there is a strong negative correlation between the number of withdrawals a person makes (x) and how much money that person has in a savings account (y). But we may not say definitively that one has low savings *because* of too many withdrawals. First, we are not privy to how much money is withdrawn each time. Second, it may be that one's savings are low because of emergency financial situations that could have arisen. These unmeasured variables could very well contribute to the *whys* behind the y-variable phenomenon. Hence, we are not given the luxury of making causal inferences for y based on x.

We now list four key properties of correlation:

Properties of Correlation

Property 6.1 The correlation coefficient will always be -1, 1 or a value in between (or we say $-1 \leq r \leq 1$).

Property 6.2 Strong (or weak) correlation does not imply strong (or weak) causation. It only implies strong (or weak) association or relation.

Property 6.3 The correlation coefficient has no units. It is just a number.

Property 6.4 In simple linear regression, the correlation coefficient will always have the same sign as the slope of the regression line.

These properties only represent a few as we consider the importance of correlation and its impact on regression.

Example 6.3 Determine the value of r for the credit card data in Table 6.1. Discuss its meaning in the context of the data.

Solution 6.3 In the credit card data, we have that $r = -0.615$. We leave the details of this calculation as an exercise at the end of this asset. This means that as we look at the scatterplot points from left to right, there is an overall decreasing trend, resulting in a negative value for r (or a negative slope). As the value of r is closer to -1 than not, we conclude that the regression line, $\hat{y}$, is a relatively good predictor of one's credit score given the number of credit cards owned. There is a moderate negative linear relationship between the two variables.

In the study of regression, the correlation coefficient stands as a significant statistic, as mentioned earlier. Whereas the correlation coefficient provides the measure of predictability for the regression equation, another key statistic reveals how the variation in one variable is explained by the variation in another. We call this statistic the **coefficient of determination**.

Definition

The **coefficient of determination** *is an objective measure of the percentage of variation in the response variable (y) that is explained by the variation in the explanatory variable (x). Denoted as* $\boldsymbol{r^2}$*, this statistic is calculated by simply squaring the value of r, the correlation coefficient. The value is normally reported as a final percentage or* $\boldsymbol{100r^2}$.

This overall statistical value seeks to provide some insight into how successful the variation within one variable explains (not causes) the variation in another. Quite naturally, then, depending on how large this coefficient is, r^2 also relays how much of the variation in y is explained by the variation of other variables not included in the original regression equation or model. We find this particular variation of other variables by subtracting the reported percentage value of $100r^2$ from 100%. Since we square this r value, we lose information concerning *direction* when we speak of r^2. In other words, when we talk about the coefficient of determination, we have no information available to inform us of whether the relationship between x and y is positive or negative. We get that information from r. With r^2, we just retain information about the overall interplay between variation of both variables.

Example 6.4 Using the credit card data, determine the value of r^2 from Table 6.1. Discuss what this means within the context of the data.

Solution 6.4 We find that $r^2 = (-0.615)^2 = 0.378$. This means that 37.8% (or 100 × 0.378) of the variation in one's credit card score is explained by the variation in the number of credit cards that one owns. This means that 62.2% of the variation (or 100% – 37.8%) in one's credit card score is explained by the variation in factors other than how many credit cards one owns. Some of these factors could possibly be how many times bills were paid late per month, how much one saves each month, or the like.

It becomes advantageous for the student, especially the student of industry, to be adept at using a software program to perform regression. It is admirable to know how to calculate regression-related statistics by hand and even more praiseworthy when such statistics can be corroborated and verified by the software. In Figure 6.5, we use Excel to share regression results of our credit card data from Table 6.1. We highlight key regression values that we have found thus far.

	A	B	C	D	E
1	SUMMARY OUTPUT				
2					
3	*Regression Statistics*				
4	Multiple R	0.614789515			
5	R Square	0.377966148			
6	Adjusted R Square	0.170621531			
7	Standard Error	102.1042965			
8	Observations	5			
9					
10	ANOVA				
11		*df*	*SS*	*MS*	*F*
12	Regression	1	19,004.14	19,004.14	1.822889
13	Residual	3	31,275.86	10,425.29	
14	Total	4	50,280.00		
15					
16		*Coefficients*	*Standard Error*	*t Stat*	*P-value*
17	Intercept	742.41	71.5735322	10.37274	0.001912
18	Credit Cards Owned	-28.62	21.19825074	-1.35014	0.269798

FIGURE 6.5 **Partial Excel Regression Results Using Table 6.1 Data**

Using the Regression tool in the *Data Analysis Toolpak*, Excel provides several key statistics at the click of a button. Excel reports the following information without our going through the tedious calculations done earlier:

1. The coefficient (r) is reported as "Multiple R." Note that Excel reports only the absolute value of this statistic, which corresponds to the sums of the absolute differences of the actual credit scores and predicted credit scores $\left(\text{or} \sum|y - \hat{y}|\right)$. However, according to Property 6.4, we know that the correlation coefficient and the slope will always have the same sign. So as our slope is negative, so is our correlation coefficient ($r = -0.615$).
2. The coefficient of determination (r^2) is reported as "R Square" ($r^2 = 0.378$ or 37.8%).
3. The number of subjects that we have credit card information on is reported as "Observations" ($n = 5$).
4. Our y-intercept is logically reported in Excel as the value beside "Intercept" ($b = 742.41$).
5. Our slope is reported as the value beside the heading of our explanatory variable, which in our data is "Number of Credit Cards Owned" ($m = -28.621$).

We use Excel's *Data Analysis ToolPak* to process the data and analyze results without being bogged down with calculating values by hand. At the end of this asset, we provide a brief *ToolPak* tutorial and go through how to run a regression to obtain results in Figure 6.5.

6.2 Multiple Linear Regression

In Table 6.1, we use one explanatory variable (x) and one response variable (y) in the regression analysis. It is not all the time practical or sensible to only use one x variable in the analysis of y. In fact, real life demands sometimes that more than one x variable be considered in the analysis of the y variable when analyzing the relationship that streams from regression. For this strategy, we use a slight variation of simple linear regression called **multiple linear regression**, a phrase coined by Karl Pearson in 1907.

Definition

The method of **multiple linear regression** *explores and analyzes the relationship of multivariate data in which we have more than one explanatory variable used to predict the response variable.*

The overall mission of this form of regression is to the find the least-squares regression plane in the form of $\hat{y} = m_1x_1 + m_2x_2 + \cdots + m_kx_k + b$, *which illustrates the linkage between the set of explanatory variables and the response variable the best.*

In the multiple linear equation, we have that:

> $\hat{y}$ *is the predicted value given all explanatory values* $(x_1, x_2, \ldots, x_k)$;
> m_1 *is the slope of the regression equation with variable* x_1, *holding all other x's constant;*
> m_k *is the slope of the regression equation with variable* x_k, *holding all other x's constant; and*
> b *is the y-intercept of the regression equation.*

The major conceptual difference in using multiple linear regression is that there exists a number of explanatory variables that we use to predict the response variable. This reflects more of a more practical, real-world scenario because, often, more than one variable should be taken into account when predicting the outcome of a related variable. We revisit the previous credit card data but adjust it slightly so that we can glean a better understanding of this method. We take a look at the new data in Table 6.3.

TABLE 6.3 Credit Score, Number of Credit Cards Owned, and Amount Saved Monthly

Cardholder	Number of Credit Cards Owned (x_1)	Amount Saved Per Month (x_2)	Credit Score (y)
Jessica	2	$650	800
Sunjay	6	$180	590
Thomas	4	$35	570
Lisa	0	$450	780
Marge	1	$400	600

Notice that we are still predicting credit scores, but we have more than one explanatory variable that we will use in the model. In addition to using information on number of credit cards owned, we consider the variable per cardholder that has to do with how much money each has put away in savings per month. We now consider both of these variables in our regression equation when predicting credit score. Although in this example, the number of explanatory variables increases to two, we can have as many x variables that we would like when using the multiple regression technique.

6.2.1 A Modified Scatterplot

Geometrically, the scatterplot for the case of two explanatory variables plays out in the realm of multidimensional space. A situation in which we have two of these variables that predict a response variable is evident in three-dimensional space, in which the plotted points remain suspended in real space as opposed to on the flat surface of a two-dimensional Cartesian plane. In our case, the number of credit cards owned (x_1) and amount per month put away in savings (x_2) are the variables that we place on the bottom axes, and the credit score (y) becomes the height that we rise or fall for each pair of x data values. So the first threesome we plot is for Jessica in the form of (2, $650, 800). The next threesome is for Sanjay in the form of (6, $180, 590). We continue in this fashion for all cardholders. Figure 6.6 shows the final scatterplot for all cardholders for all three variables. As we see, all five points are suspended in mid-air, according to their location on the axes. Since the Excel software is unable to show diagrams having a multivariate flair, we use the JMP software (pronounced "jump") to assist us in showing our figure.

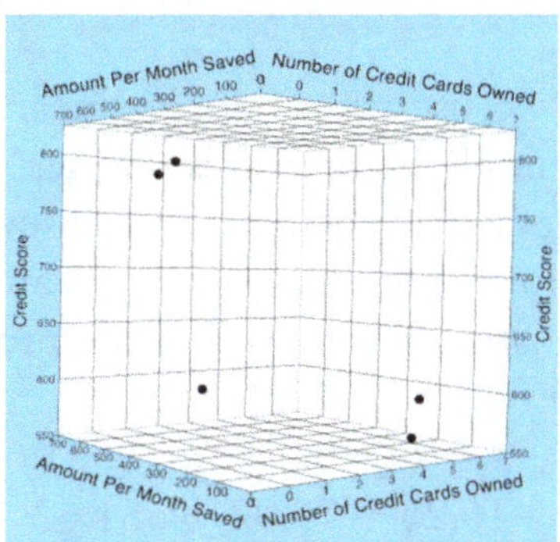

FIGURE 6.6 A Scatterplot of Table 6.3

6.2.2 Using the Regression Equation to Predict

Although equations can be used to solve for the coefficients in simple linear regression, in multiple regression the equations are more complex and a software package is most always used. Although many statistical software packages are available, we continue to use the *Data Analysis ToolPak*, which is the statistical analysis package offered in Excel. A partial Excel printout of the results for our example follows below in Figure 6.7:

	A	B	C	D	E
1	SUMMARY OUTPUT				
2					
3	*Regression Statistics*				
4	Multiple R	0.852935814			
5	R Square	0.727499503			
6	Adjusted R Square	0.454999007			
7	Standard Error	82.76872891			
8	Observations	5			
9					
10	ANOVA				
11		*df*	*SS*	*MS*	*F*
12	Regression	2	36,578.67503	18,289.34	2.669718
13	Residual	2	13,701.32497	6,850.662	
14	Total	4	50,280		
15					
16		*Coefficients*	*Standard Error*	*t Stat*	*P-value*
17	Intercept	551.62	132.4971244	4.163291	0.053137
18	Credit Cards Owned	-4.07	23.02770649	-0.17666	0.876047
19	Amount Per Month Saved	0.37	0.231085285	1.60168	0.250387

FIGURE 6.7 Partial Excel Regression Results for Table 6.3

We recall that the form of the regression equation in multiple linear regression is given by $\hat{y} = m_1x_1 + m_2x_2 + \cdots + m_kx_k + b$. Hence, once we identify the missing values for the variables, we will have the equation that we need to start predicting. We consider the values underneath "Coefficients" in the results to help us identify the specific regression equation using our two explanatory variables where we are predicting the credit score. From the printout, we observe that the value for the y-intercept is 551.62 (or $b = 551.62$). The first slope, reported as –4.07, has to do with the number of credit cards owned (or $m_1 = -4.07$). The second slope, reported as 0.37 has to do with the amount each cardholder saves each month (or $m_2 = 0.37$). We will address interpretations of these values later in this section.

Hence, for this specific example, our regression equation is expressed as follows:

$$\hat{y} = -4.07x_1 + 0.37x_2 + 551.62,$$

where $\hat{y}$ is the predicted credit score, x_1 is the number of credit cards owned, and x_2 is the amount of money put away in savings per month.

As with simple linear regression, we use the multiple linear regression equation to predict the response variable. The difference in multiple regression is that we predict y based on information provided for all of the explanatory variables in the equation. Suppose in our case, we wish to predict one's credit score when the cardholder has four credit cards ($x_1 = 4$) and saves \$216 per month ($x_2 = 216$).

We use the multiple regression equation above to find the prediction:

$$\begin{aligned}\hat{y} &= -4.07(4)+0.37(216)+551.62\\ &= -16.28 + 79.92 + 551.62\\ &= 615.26\end{aligned}$$

Hence, someone who owns four credit cards and who saves \$216 per month is predicted to have a credit score of 615.30 (approximately 615).

Example 6.5 Using the multiple regression equation, predict the credit score when the cardholder has three credit cards and saves \$700 per month.

Solution 6.5 Since the value of \$700 does not fall within the range of data points in the x_2 data column for monthly savings, we are not able to extrapolate or assume that the trend outside of this data range is still linear. *We thus are not able to provide a prediction for the final grade using the two given data values.* We draw this conclusion, even though the given value for the number of credit cards is rightly within the data range of the x_1 column ($0 < 3 < 6$).

6.2.3 A Geometric Visualization of this New Model

Visually, we may observe the idea of multiple linear regression and its utility in data analyses. When analyzing the variable of credit score in statistics based on observing the explanatory variables separately, we notice certain results concerning how well the model predicts using the reported coefficients of determination in separate cases. Using Excel, we first observe the effects of both independent variables *separately*.

Earlier in Figure 6.3, we presented the scatterplot showing the relationship between credit score and *only* the variable of number of credit cards owned. The figure also shows the line for the regression equation. We note that Excel overlays the regression line for this relationship and reports the coefficient of determination as $r^2 = 0.378$. Our simple linear regression equation, as noted on the plot, is:

$$\hat{y} = -28.621x + 742.41,$$

where x refers to the number of credit cards owned.

A second plot shows the simple linear regression relationship between credit score and *only* the variable referencing the amount of monthly savings. Again, Excel overlays the regression line for this relationship and reports the coefficient of determination as $r^2 = 0.72$. Our simple linear regression equation, as noted on the plot, is:

$$\hat{y} = 0.3973x + 531.73,$$

where x refers to the amount of savings put away per month. The plot, which ignores data concerning number of credit cards owned, is as follows:

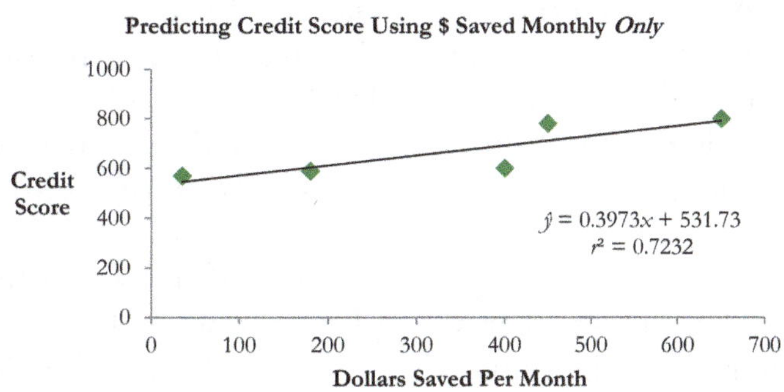

Geometrically, the idea of multiple linear regression plays out in the realm of multidimensional space. As discussed in Section 6.2.1, the plotted points remain suspended in three-dimensional space, and we plot a regression plane to summarize multivariate data in the multivariate regression scenario (instead of a regression line).

In our example, we migrate from analyzing the independent variables x_1 (number of credit cards owned) and x_2 (amount saved per month) *separately* to analyzing both variables *as a set* in order to predict the credit score. We recall that the multiple regression equation is the following:

$$\hat{y} = -4.07x_1 + 0.37x_2 + 551.62,$$

where x_1 is the variable for number of credit cards owned and x_2 is the variable for the amount saved per month.

When we observe plots of the relationship between credit score and both number of credit cards owned and money saved per month *as a set*, we note that our points occur in real space as the two explanatory variables are plotted on the x and y axes, while our response variable is plotted on the z (or vertical) axis. To visually represent how well these two explanatory variables are at predicting our response variable, we superimpose a regression plane and observe how far our multivariate points are from this prediction plane vertically. We again use JMP to assist in the visualization of the regression plane.

Figure 6.8 illustrates the scatterplot and this regression plane for our specific multiple regression:

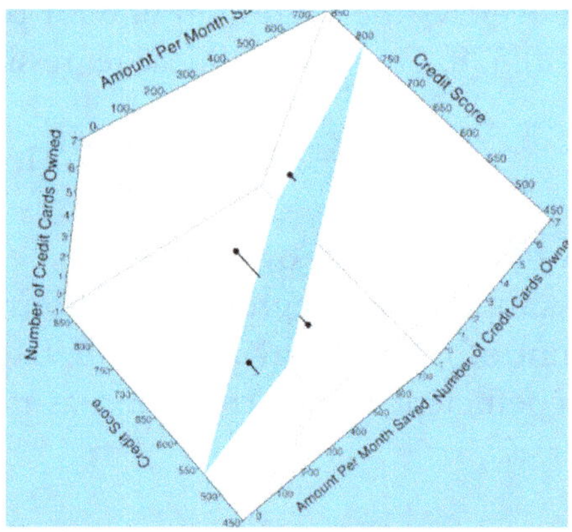

FIGURE 6.8 (Credit Score = −4.07 * Number of Owned Credit Cards + 0.37 * Amount Saved Per Month + 551.62)

We fit the best regression plane into the three-dimensional space, which best summarizes all five points. The fifth point is underneath the plane and is not visible from the particular perspective of Figure 6.8. We just show as many of the five points as possible that allow for a clear view of the plane. In fact, the flexibility of the JMP software allows us to rotate this image in Figure 6.8 so that we can view it from different angles. With easy maneuvers, we can adjust the orientation of the image and observe a better visual rendering of the mathematics that underlies the concept.

For example, one of the diagrams in Figure 6.9 allows us to see all five points but not a clear colored view of the plane. This multiple regression plane, as one might expect, based on the analog in simple linear regression, minimizes the sum of squared deviations of the *observed* credit score (actual

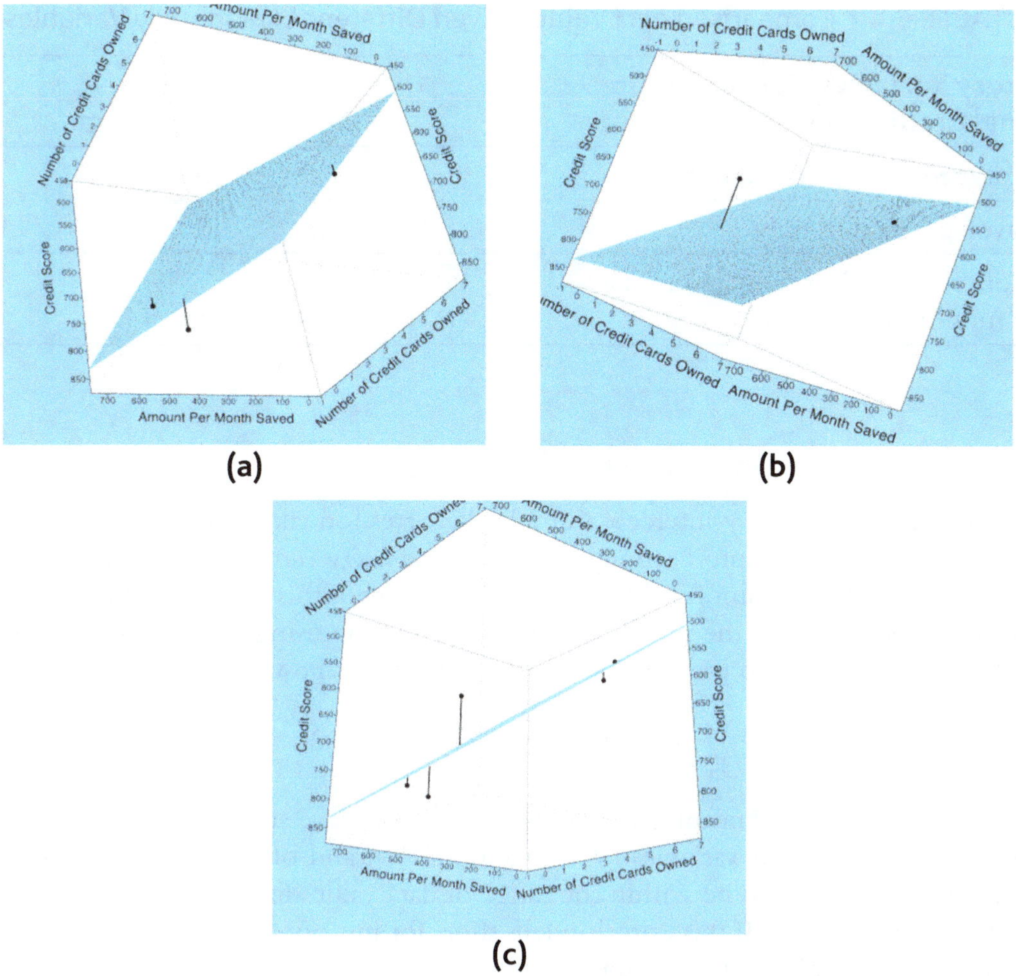

FIGURE 6.9 **More Visual Perspectives of Figure 6.8**

data in credit score column) and the *predicted* credit score (the set of solutions along the plane). We take a look at the various visual perspectives offered in Figure 6.9, also produced by JMP:

These surface plots represent the same visual plot as presented earlier but are viewed from varying angles. Plot (a) shows the first view, highlighting the three data points "below" the regression plane. Plot (b) shows the second view, highlighting the two data points "above" the regression plane. Plot (c) shows the regression plane from the vantage point of masquerading as a regular regression line. This perspective allows us to see all five data points and their near-vertical relation to the regression plane.

Again, we recall from Figure 6.7 that the coefficient of multiple determination, r^2, is 0.7275. The surface plots give a sense of how the two independent variables work together to predict the credit score. We see that we get a better model of predicting credit scores when we use number of credit cards owned together with amount saved per month. The larger r^2 value confirms this notion.

Table 6.4 illustrates this improvement of r^2 in both cases. We start with both explanatory variables singly and note how r^2 increases when we build to a multivariate model that includes both variables. We should note, however, that it is not always the case that r^2 increases when we analyze using all variables. It is possible that this value decreases, depending on the arrangement of variables considered. In Section 6.2.5, we discuss the meaning of r^2 of our data in this multivariate sense.

TABLE 6.4 Comparison of r^2 Values Given Different Explanatory Variables

Explanatory Variables Considered in Predicting Credit Score	r^2 as Percentage
Number of credit cards owned only	38%
Money saved per month only	72%
Number of credit cards owned and money saved per month	73%

6.2.4 Interpreting the *y*-Intercept and Slopes

Interpreting the meaning of the *y*-intercept in multiple regression takes on a similar flavor as in simple regression except that it takes into account *the set of explanatory variables* in its analysis. When interpreting the slopes, we also account for this interplay somehow of this set of variables. For example, we recall earlier in this section that the multiple regression equation using number of credit cards owned and amount saved per month to predict the credit score is the following:

$$\hat{y} = -4.07x_1 + 0.37x_2 + 551.62.$$

If we wish to interpret the meaning of the *y*-intercept here, we substitute the value of zero in the place of *all* of the independent variables ($x_1 = 0$ and $x_2 = 0$) and offer a logical explanation for the result. The values of zero should be within the range of data values for number of credit cards owned *and* for amount saved monthly. If this criterion falls short for just one of the independent variables, we forfeit a reliable interpretation for the *y*-intercept.

When substituting zero for both credit cards owned (x_1) and amount saved monthly (x_2), we have as follows:

$$\begin{aligned}\hat{y} &= -4.07(0) + 0.37(0) + 551.62\\ &= 551.62\end{aligned}$$

We note that $x_1 = 0$ falls within the data range for observed values for absences. This is fine. But we note that $x_2 = 0$ falls outside of the data range for observed values for amount saved per month. Since there is at least one value for which the substitution of zero for the explanatory variable falls outside of the data range of observed values, we conclude that the predicted credit score of 551.62 has no significant meaning in this context. Again, *the entire set* of explanatory variables in the multiple regression equation that is considered must pass this within-data-range test in order to provide a valid interpretation of the *y*-intercept.

When it comes to interpreting the slopes of the multiple linear regression equation, we must use careful consideration when doing so. The similarity in interpreting slopes in simple and multiple regression is that we use the same rise-over-run contextual phraseology. Depending on the slope we are interpreting, we use the denominator of the slope's coefficient to interpret change as it relates to that independent (x) variable, and we use the numerator of the slope's coefficient to interpret change as it relates to the dependent variable (y) that we are predicting. The difference in interpreting the slope in simple and multiple regression rests with the handling of other independent variables in the interpretation. We need not mention any role of other explanatory variables in the slope's interpretation for simple regression. As one might assume, we do not need to mention such a role because, outside of the independent variable in question, there are no other ones to consider in simple regression. This explanatory variable we consider is the only one in the equation that we analyze.

In multiple linear regression, however, when we analyze the slope of the explanatory variable in question, we must say a general word about the other independent variables that are not the focus of the question but still are present in the regression equation. For these peripheral variables, we attach a phrase, which suggests that we are reaching our results based on the assumption of *fixing the effect of the explanatory variables* that are not being asked for. Or put another way, we *hold constant any influence that any other explanatory variables* might have on the model when interpreting the specified slope.

We recall the multiple linear regression equation again:

$$\hat{y} = -4.07x_1 + 0.37x_2 + 551.62$$

If we wish to interpret the meaning of the slope associated with number of credit cards owned (m_1) with predicted credit score, we hold constant the effect of money saved monthly as it relates to the model and provide the appropriate explanation. Since the appropriate slope is –4.07 or −4.07/1, we essentially say that in this situation, for a fixed amount of money saved per month, as the number of credit cards owned increases by one, the mean change in the credit score is predicted to decrease by 4.07 points.

Example 6.6 Interpret the meaning of m_2 in the above example.

Solution 6.6 The slope, m_2, relates the amount saved monthly with credit score. Since that slope is 0.37 or 0.37/1, we say that for a given number of credit cards owned, for every $1 saved each month, the mean change in the credit score is predicted to increase by 0.37 points.

6.2.5 r^2 in Multiple Linear Regression

Extracting the key elements of the Excel printout in Figure 6.7 even further, we see that the Multiple R is now 0.85. This is quite a leap from the $R = 0.61$ we obtained in Figure 6.5, where we used only one explanatory variable, (number of credit cards owned). Using x_1, number of credit cards owned, and x_2, money saved per month, as a set of explanatory variables, we achieve a stronger correlation when compared to just using each one of those explanatory variables separately. This gives us a much better prediction of a student's credit score.

If the equation fits the data well, predictions made from the equation are more reliable. To determine this, r^2, **the coefficient of multiple determination**, is used.

Definition

The **coefficient of multiple determination** *is an objective measure of the percentage of variation in the response variable (y) that is explained by the variation in the set of explanatory variables. Still denoted as* $\boldsymbol{r^2}$*, this statistic is calculated by squaring r, the correlation coefficient. The value is normally reported as a final percentage or* ***100r²***.

In other words, with this statistic, we are able to analyze how well the explanatory variables in the model (i.e., number of credit cards owned and amount saved per month) relate collectively to the response variable. We use r^2 to determine how well the multiple regression equation fits the sample data. If the equation fits the data extremely well, the value of r^2 will be near 1.00 (or 100%). If the equation fits the data poorly, the value of r^2 will be near 0 (or 0%).

Investigating our results in Figure 6.7, we see that r^2 is 0.7275 (or 72.75%). In general, r^2 is often referred to as the measure of explained variation. In our case, this means that both variables, x_1, number of credit cards owned, and x_2, money saved monthly, are explaining 72.75% of the variation in y (credit score). Of course, this leaves 27.25% of the variation unexplained (100% – 72.75%). Such unexplained variables affecting credit score might be overall debt, income, and number of vacations taken each year.

6.2.6 Adjusted r^2

In the previous section, we compare r^2 from the multiple regression model with r^2 from two separate single regression models only to illustrate how that statistic can improve when single variables are analyzed together. In general, though, we do not compare r^2 values among models to determine which is best. We only use r^2 values to compare models when the following two criteria hold (Kahane 2008):

1. We are predicting the same response (y) variable in all comparisons.
2. We have the same number of explanatory (x) variables in the models that we are comparing.

If we are comparing models in which the number of independent variables is not the same for each model, then we do not use this r^2 value as our statistic to determine which model is the best. We now use the **adjusted r^2** statistic.

Definition

*The **adjusted r^2** statistic is used as the basis to compare regression models, which predict the same response (y) variable but have different number of explanatory (x) variables. It is defined as follows:*

$$r^2_{adj} = 1 - \left[\frac{(n-1)}{n-(k+1)}\left(1-r^2\right)\right], \qquad \textbf{Equation 6.4}$$

where n = sample size of the model; k = number of explanatory (x) variables in the model; and r^2 = the coefficient of determination.

We see that this adjusted r^2 value is greatly affected by the sample size (n), the number of explanatory variables measured (k), and the originally reported coefficient of (multiple) determination (r^2).

We recall our multiple regression example, in which we predict credit scores using number of credit cards owned and amount of money saved per month (Table 6.3). In this instance, our sample size is 5 ($n = 5$), the number of explanatory variables (number of credit cards owned and amount saved per month) in the model is 2 ($k = 2$), and our originally reported coefficient of multiple determination is 0.7275 ($r^2 = 0.7275$).

Hence, we find below the value for adjusted r^2 so that we may use it to compare with other models:

$$r^2_{adj} = 1 - \left[\frac{(5-1)}{5-(2+1)}(1-0.7275)\right]$$
$$= 0.455$$

Excel is wonderful because it shows all of the information we need to know. According to the printout shown in Figure 6.7, the adjusted r^2 statistic is reported beside "Adjusted R Square." The value matches the value we found after we substituted the appropriate values in the formula.

Problem 6.10 in the student exercises gives students experience applying this adjusted r^2 technique as it is used to compare multiple linear regression models. The solution for the problem is provided in the rear of the text, highlighting the different regression models and why we use this adjusted r^2 statistic instead of the regular r^2 statistic.

6.3 Regression Analysis in Excel

We can use Excel to assist us in performing simple and multiple linear regression.

Step 0 Click on the *Data* tab to see if you have the *Data Analysis ToolPak* (an Excel add-in program) loaded on your system. It should appear in the upper right-hand corner. If it appears, skip to **Step 1**. If it does not appear, you will have to load the *ToolPak* by following these instructions.

For PCs

a. Click the *File* tab, and then click *Options*.

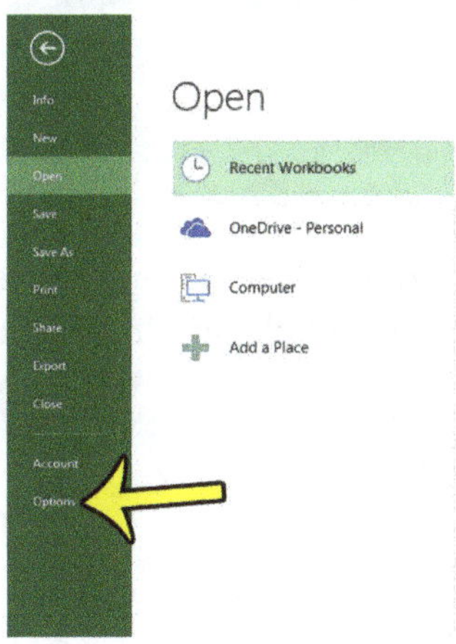

b. Click on *Add-Ins*, and then click on the *Analysis ToolPak* option in the list. Then click *Go* at the bottom.

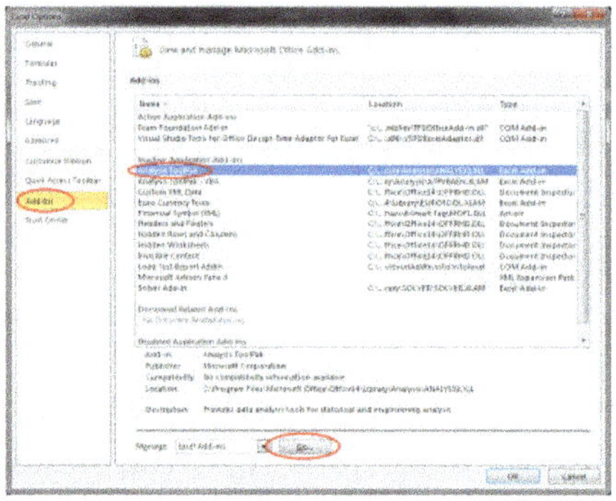

c. Select the *Analysis ToolPak* option, and click *OK*.

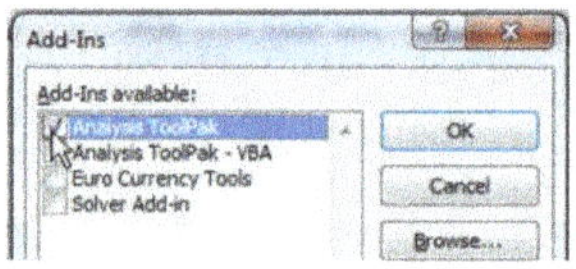

For Macs

To load the *ToolPak* on a Mac, click *Tools* on Excel's Toolbar and scroll to *Excel Add-ins*. Click *Analysis ToolPak* and then *OK*. Now, click on the *Data* tab in Excel and the *Data Analysis ToolPak* should be visible at the upper right.

After loading the *ToolPak*, you should be able to see the *Data Analysis* command (upper right) when you click on the *Data* tab. You may now proceed to **Step 1**.

Step 1 (Simple and Multiple Linear Regression) For simple and multiple linear regression, we begin by clicking the *Data Analysis* command, which appears after clicking the *Data* tab.

Step 2 (Simple and Multiple Linear Regression) For simple and multiple linear regression, when the Analysis Tools box appears, click on *Regression* and click *OK*.

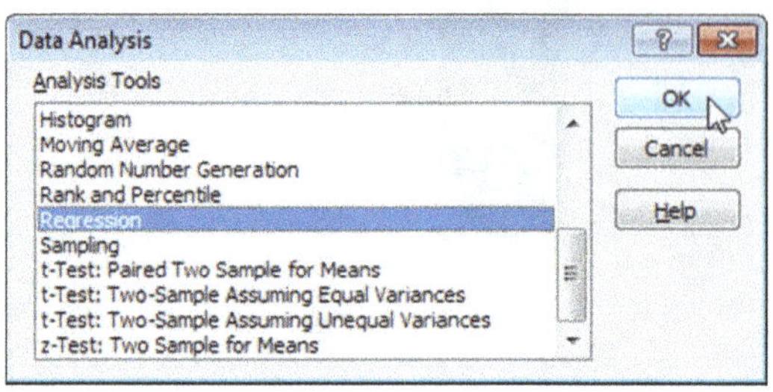

- For simple linear regression, proceed to **Step 3**.
- For multiple linear regression, proceed to **Step 4**.

Step 3 (Simple Linear Regression) Now, you are ready to place data from your independent variable column (x) and dependent variable column (y) into the appropriate fields. After clicking *OK*, the following screen should appear (without inserted values):

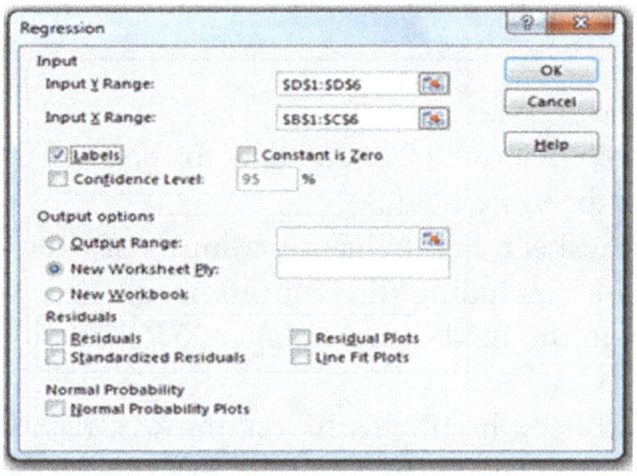

a. Once you see the screen above, place the cursor in the field that says *Input Y Range.*
b. In your Excel spreadsheet, highlight the column of cells for data values that correspond to your dependent (y) variable (including the column heading).
c. Now, place the cursor in the field that says *Input X Range.*
d. In your Excel spreadsheet, highlight the column of cells for data values that correspond to your independent (x) variable (including the column heading).
e. Click the box that says *Labels* since you included the headings in each column. Click *OK*. The results should be revealed on a new Excel spreadsheet. If you'd like, you can view your data by clicking on *Sheet 1* at the bottom of the Excel sheet.

For example, the snapshot below shows the column cells that should be highlighted for the independent variable in the simple regression model that we use in Table 6.1. We use number of credit cards owned as the independent variable in the model. We have filled in our Regression screen based on data below from Table 6.1. We highlight values in the C column for the *Y* range and those in the B column (as illustrated) for the *X* range.

	A	B	C
1	Cardholder	# of Credit Cards Owned	Credit Score
2	Jessica	2	800
3	Sunjay	6	590
4	Thomas	4	570
5	Lisa	0	780
6	Marge	1	600

Using information from Table 6.1, your printout results should resemble that of Figure 6.5.

Step 4 (Multiple Linear Regression) Now, you are ready to place data from your independent variable columns ($x_1, x_2, x_3, \ldots$) and dependent variable column (y) into the appropriate fields. After clicking *OK*, the following screen should appear (without inserted values):

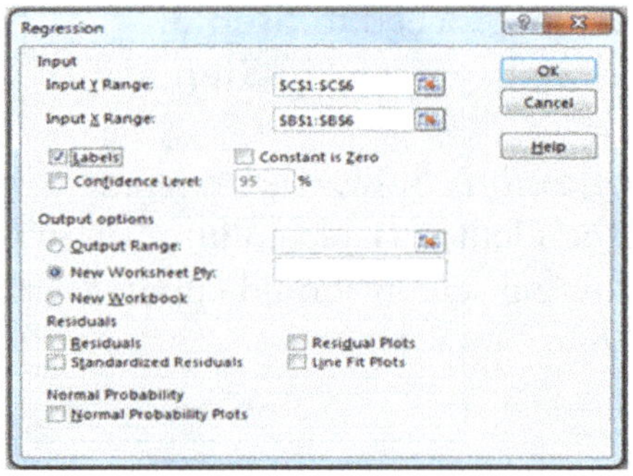

a. Once you see the screen above, clear any data in the field that says *Input Y Range* and allow the cursor to rest in the same field.

b. On your Excel spreadsheet, highlight the column of data values that correspond to your dependent (y) variable (including the column heading).

c. Now, clear any data in the field that says *Input X Range* and allow the cursor to rest in that same field.

d. In your Excel spreadsheet, highlight the columns of data values that correspond to your independent (x_1, x_2, x_3, …) variables (including the headings for each of the columns). Note that more than one column should be highlighted to account for all variables considered in the multiple regression model. For example, the snapshot below shows the column cells that should be highlighted for the independent variables in the multiple regression model that we use in Table 6.3. We use number of credit cards owned and amount saved monthly as independent variables in the model. We have filled in our Regression screen based on data below from Table 6.3. We highlight values in the C column for the *Y* range and those in the B and C columns (as illustrated) for the *X* range.

	A	B	C	D
1	Cardholder	# of Credit Cards Owned	Monthly $ Put in Savings	Credit Score
2	Jessica	2	$650	800
3	Sunjay	6	$180	590
4	Thomas	4	$35	570
5	Lisa	0	$450	780
6	Marge	1	$400	600
7				
8				

(Note that all the columns for the independent variables must be adjacent to one another. In other words, Excel requires that all of these columns be contiguous (touching); it will not perform the multiple regression if any gaps exist among this set of independent variables.)

e. Click the box that says *Labels* since you included the headings in each column. Click *OK*. The results should be revealed on a new Excel spreadsheet. If you would like, you can view your data by clicking on Sheet 1 at the bottom of the Excel sheet.

Your printout results should resemble that of Figure 6.7.

Money Talk

Me, Myself, and I: Combating Identity Theft

According to Investopedia, identity theft is defined as the "crime of obtaining the personal or financial information of another person for the sole purpose of assuming that person's name or identity in order to make transactions or purchases." The Federal Trade Commission (FTC) disclosed that, of the consumer complaints received in 2016, those related to identity theft were near the top of the list. Of the approximately 3.1 million complaints received that year, about 13% of them were related to identity theft (2017). Out of the top 30 categories into which the FTC sorts its complaints, Figure 6.10 highlights the top 5 complaints issued in 2016. The numbers reveal that identity theft ranks third among all categories, pushing a close second.

Here are a few weapons to use when waging war against the widespread pandemic of identity theft.

Weapon 1: As much as possible, use cash. This is more or less a proactive measure to avoid the likelihood of identity theft, especially around holiday seasons. Though it is advisable to use cards for large purchases for buyer protection, cash is king for small purchases like coffee and dinner. Decreasing card usage for small incidentals decreases the opportunity for thieves to swipe or skim debit/credit card information.

Weapon 2: Be sure that all debit/credit cards have fraud protection activated. This is another proactive measure and is free; this service promises to have banks call you when a transaction is attempted that is "out of the norm" of charges that you typically make. In rare events, the bank may fumble the ball and not call before transactions are attempted, but they have to honor their agreement of reimbursing questionable transactions if you have been proactive and put this protection in place.

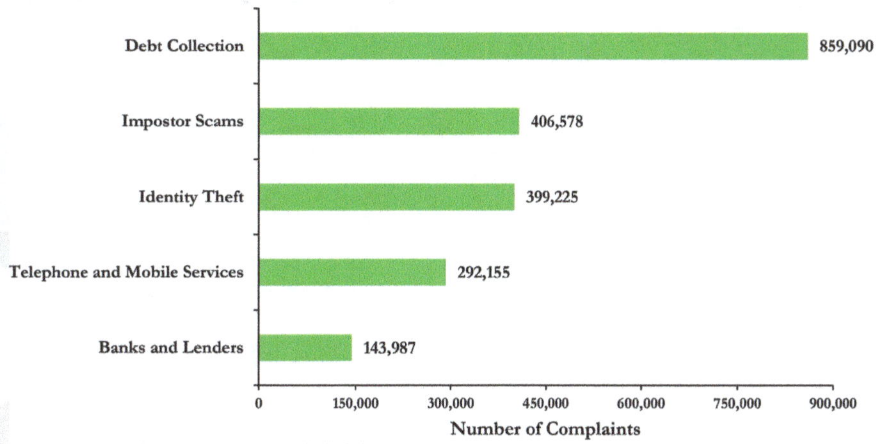

FIGURE 6.10 Top Five (out of 30) FTC Consumer Complaints in 2016

Weapon 3: Cancel compromised card immediately. You should have 1–800 numbers stored in your cell phone for all of your debit/credit cards. Thieves are shrewd in that they don't need the physical card to attempt to use information from it. If the card is in fact physically stolen, though, you do not want to lose precious seconds trying to locate lenders' contact information while others may still be trying to use the card again.

Weapon 4: File a police report immediately. Protocol requires you to file the report in the precinct nearest your resident, irrespective of where questionable purchases occur. Walking through a police precinct may be somewhat harrowing, but it is a necessary step to ensuring that you are protected. The detective and cops are only interested in helping you resolve the matter quickly. Once you receive the complaint report number from the precinct, give it to your bank so they can remain abreast of the process and reimburse your money quicker.

Weapon 5: Request credit reports and analyze thoroughly. Contact Experian **(www.experian.com)**, TransUnion **(www.transunion.com)**, and Equifax **(www.equifax.com)** to receive your credit reports. These agencies have gotten on board the online train and prefer to deliver your report to you online as opposed to using snail mail. You can download a PDF version of it and print right from your home or office. It is important to obtain reports from all three agencies and eyeball them closely to see if any inconsistencies on them exist. If so, start appropriate steps to address errors.

Through implementing these five weapons, you should be able to get back on the right financial track and ensure that your "me, myself, and I" only refer back to the same person—*you*!

Student Exercises: Linear Regression

6.1 The real estate agent at Century 21 was curious to see if there was a correlation between the asking price of a loft in Chelsea and the number of bedrooms in the loft. In this study, determine which variable is the explanatory variable and which is the response. Explain.

6.2 Consider the following set of data that shows the amount that Chic-fil-A's sales increased during the quarter along with how many times that quarter it offered its free-meal entrée plan for customers who dressed like a cow:

Store	Times Free-Meal Plan Offered for the Quarter (x)	Sales Increase for the Quarter (y)
Store one	6	$23,000
Store two	4	$14,784
Store three	10	$54,000
Store four	7	$43,896

a. Calculate the value of the slope (m) without using Excel.
b. Calculate the value of the y-intercept (b) without using Excel.
c. Verify your answers for m and b using Excel.

6.3 a. Using the data in 6.2, use Excel to construct the scatterplot for the bivariate data.
b. State the least-squares regression equation for the data using information in 6.2.
c. Using the equation, predict the sales increase for the quarter when the free-meal plan is offered (i) 5 times per quarter; and (ii) 9 times per quarter.
d. On the same scatterplot in a., use Excel to draw the least-squares regression line using the two values found in d.

6.4 In Section 6.1.4, we used the regression equation to plot the line using $x = 3$ and $x = 5$. We make the claim that we would have ended up with the same plot of the line if we would have used any other x values in the given range of explanatory values. Using any other two points in the x range, find the corresponding y values using the regression equation, and plot the regression line using these two new points. Do we in fact arrive at the same plot of the regression line as seen in Figure 6.2?

6.5 A conscientious student at Rice University decided to gather data on 230 students. The study involved finding out how much money students earned, on average, per month during the fall semester (x) and the students' GPA at the end of that semester (y). When the student ran a regression on the data, she discovered that the regression equation was as follows:

$$\hat{y} = -0.15x + 3.01$$

a. Interpret the slope in this equation as it relates to the actual scenario.
b. Interpret the y-intercept in this equation as it relates to the actual scenario. Assume the value of $x = 0$ is a bona fide value in the dataset (i.e., someone in the experiment really did earn $0 during the fall).

6.6 In Section 6.1.5, Solution 6.3 offered a correlation coefficient of –0.615 ($r = -0.6215$). Use Table 6.1 and Equation 6.3 to verify that this value of r is correct.

6.7 Ashley gathered some data from a few people who were willing to disclose their annual salary (y) and their current education level (x). She was hoping to use the sample to see what type of relationship existed between these two variables:

Salary (y)	Education (in years) 12: High School 14: Associate's Degree 16: Bachelor's Degree 18: Master's Degree (x)
$38,715	16
$40,320	17
$37,250	16
$34,135	12
$37,310	16
$36,985	14
$40,620	12
$39,200	18

a. Using Excel to assist, state the correlation coefficient (r) in Ashley's study. Interpret it in the context of this particular set of data.
b. Using Excel, state the coefficient of determination (r^2) in Ashley's study. Interpret it in the context of this particular set of data.

6.8 Ashley decided to expand her study, now considering more independent variables to conduct her study. In addition to years of education, she wanted to analyze how employees' salary depended on the length of employment and previous working experience. She now considered the following data, which summarizes information for each of the four variables.

Salary (y)	Length of Employment (in years) (x_1)	Previous Working Experience (in years) (x_2)	Education (in years) 12: High School 14: Associate's Degree 16: Bachelor's Degree 18: Master's Degree (x_3)
$38,715	8	8	16
$40,320	15	6	17
$37,250	4	6	16

Salary (y)	Length of Employment (in years) (x_1)	Previous Working Experience (in years) (x_2)	Education (in years) 12: High School 14: Associate's Degree 16: Bachelor's Degree 18: Master's Degree (x_3)
\$34,135	3	1	12
\$37,310	10	2	16
\$36,985	5	5	14
\$40,620	22	0	12
\$39,200	8	4	18

a. Using Excel, create three separate scatterplots of each independent variable separately with the dependent variable and decide which pairs of variables appear to have a strong linear correlation.
b. Use Excel to find a multiple regression equation that models the dataset.
c. Interpret the meaning of the coefficients of each term in the multiple regression equation (y-intercept and slopes).
d. Use the multiple regression equation to predict your future salary (based on your own length of employment, previous working experience, and education).

6.9 The Senate voted unanimously on May 19, 2009, to put new restrictions on the credit card industry, passing a bill where card companies will have to spell out their terms using "plain English" and treat customers more fairly. In response to the prospect of lost revenue and what some companies see as a watchdog government, banks are expected to consider reviving annual fees, stopping cash-back and other reward programs, and charging interest immediately on a purchase instead of allowing the usual grace period. Over the years, these interest rates have been pushed down for many consumers, but they soared for riskier cardholders, who became a significant course of revenue for the industry. The recent economic downturn challenged that formula, and banks now began dumping the most perilous customers and reducing credit limits as the recession accelerated. Consumers who pay their bills every month are now complaining about shortened grace periods, new hidden fees, and higher interest rates (Stout 2009).

In fact, the number of consumers paying their credit cards off each month has decreased considerably. Financial experts have investigated the interplay of several variables that associate themselves with the amount of credit card debt incurred by consumers in 2010 (y). Experts reported the increase in salary for the year per consumer (x_1), the number of times in 2010 consumers paid more than the minimum payment (x_2), and how many frequent-flier miles consumers obtained from their credit cards during the year (x_3). The partial data, based on a sample of 13 consumers is shown below:

Consumer Credit Card Debt Incurred for the Year (y)	Increase in \$ per Consumer for the Year (x_1)	# of Times Paid More Than Minimum Payment (x_2)	Frequent Flier Miles Gained from Credit Cards (x_3)
\$6700	\$1443	4	8112
\$2142	\$1100	8	1139

Consumer Credit Card Debt Incurred for the Year (y)	Increase in \$ per Consumer for the Year (x_1)	# of Times Paid More Than Minimum Payment (x_2)	Frequent Flier Miles Gained from Credit Cards (x_3)
\$19,544	\$1700	0	7999
\$16,746	\$1554	0	11,990
\$4812	\$2442	2	0
\$28,388	\$2900	0	21,422
\$762	\$1000	11	0
\$9800	\$1100	1	9800
\$12,122	\$2300	2	9881
\$5466	\$1001	3	7229
\$3007	\$700	8	4500
\$1794	\$1100	5	3800
\$338	\$0	9	500

a. State the regression equation using *only* x_2 and x_3, and draw the scatterplot that illustrates the model using those two explanatory variables and the response variable. (*Hint: See Figure 6.6. Think of a cube, and place the 2 explanatory variables on the bottom axes and plot "y" as the height of the vertical axis*).
b. State the regression equation using all three independent variables.
c. Interpret the y-intercept for the regression equation in **b**.
d. Predict the credit card debt when consumers received a salary increase of \$1500, paid more than minimum payments four times, and gained 8500 frequent-flier miles.
e. Predict the credit card debt when consumers received a \$5000 salary increase, paid more than the minimum payment six times, and gained 20,000 frequent-flier miles.

6.10 Use the same set of data provided in **6.9**.

a. State the coefficient of multiple determination (r^2) in the Excel results. Interpret its meaning in the context of the given data.
b. State the combination of variables that provide the *best* prediction of consumer credit card debt. Use Excel, and assume that $k > 1$. (*Hint: You will have to consider different arrangements when $k = 2$ and $k = 3$ and compare the values for r^2_{adj}.*)
c. State the combination of variables that provide the *worst* prediction of consumer credit card debt. Use Excel, and assume that $k > 1$. (*Use same hint.*)

References

Federal Trade Commission. "FTC Releases Annual Summary of Consumer Complaints." March 3, 2017. Accessed March 10, 2017. https://goo.gl/cgczk6

Gibson, Henry R., and Bernard L. Dillard. 2016. *Elementary Statistics*. 4th ed. Dubuque, IA: Kendall-Hunt Publishing.

Kahane, Leo H. 2008. *Regression Basics*. 2nd ed. Thousand Oaks, CA: Sage Publications, Inc.

Stout, David. 2009. "Senate Passes Bill to Restrict Credit Card Practices." *The New York Times*, May 19, 2009. Accessed March 12, 2016. https://goo.gl/2dAAEa

Asset Seven

Stocks and Time Series

Chapter Outline

Acting was just another part of my life, as it still is today.
It's 1 of the 10 things I love doing. It's never just been my life.
As cheesy at it sounds, all my eggs were never in just one basket.
I had a thousand baskets going on.

Kelly Cuoco

7.1 Stocks and Shares and Bears ... Oh My!

In Asset Two, we briefly discussed savings accounts, bonds, and their role in helping a person save money. The advantage with saving with a regular savings account or bond is that there is a guarantee that the money invested will always earn interest and increase. The disadvantage of saving with these types of accounts is that the money invested often grows at a snail's pace. For example, it is reasonable that a zero-coupon bond purchased for \$100 may double in value to \$200 after a period of 20 years. This is a very long time to wait for funds to go from \$100 to \$200. What if this \$100 could reach \$200 in only a matter of a month? Or two weeks? In the world of finance, it is indeed possible for this to happen. People who choose the route of buying and investing in stocks are placing themselves in a position not only to earn interest on their money but also to do it at a quicker pace.

7.1.1 Stocks Simplified

Suppose your friend opened a small fashion boutique store in the Beverly Hills area, strategically located on Rodeo Drive. Through loans and modest savings, she was able to close on the deal and has been doing relatively well over the last two years. Recently, she learned a building in downtown Los Angeles has become available through foreclosure, and she wants to buy it in order to expand her brand and open another boutique. Since she is still paying the first loan off, she only wants to use bank loans sparingly and has access to \$15,000 in savings from earnings from the first boutique location.

The building is being sold for \$75,000. She wants to pay \$50,000 of this total from bank loans. This leaves a balance of \$25,000, but she has the mentioned \$15,000 saved. This leaves a balance of \$10,000. She thought to herself, *I know what I'll do. I'll ask a few of my friends and business associates to help me raise the \$10,000. And the money they invest will count toward part ownership of the new boutique.* This will be the part or percentage of the business that others can contribute to and profit from. Essentially, 13.3% of the second company $\left(\text{or } \$10{,}000\ /\ \$75{,}000\right)$ is available for others to own in a unique way. This unique way is referred to as **stock** ownership.

> **Definition**
>
> *A* **stock** *is a percentage ownership stake in a company. It is the general term used to describe the stake ownership for all of the companies that a person has invested in using this investment strategy.*

You decide to accept your friend's offer to buy ownership into her second boutique store. You are willing to support her vision and agree to invest \$800 into her business. When you give her the money, she gives you back the equivalence in **shares**.

Definition

A **share** *is simply a stock for a specific company that a person has invested in using the percentage ownership strategy.*

In general, a company's share price is loosely based on the share price of the company's competition and also on what the company expects to earn in the future. Mergers of one company with another company can also affect share pricing.

The first criterion used to determine a company's share pricing is less scientific. We simply look at how much a share is currently worth or its **price per share**.

Definition

The **price per share** *is the current value or worth of a share.*

Researching share prices for the competition is simple. Sites such as http://goo.gl/jlw4 or http://goo.gl/2kGs provide up-to-the-minute prices per share of any company that has stock options. There is no hard-and-fast rule for a company's setting its own share price based solely on the competition's. These sites simply provide a general idea of a legitimate range of share prices for companies similar to each other. For example, Table 7.1 shows the closing price per share for the following sportswear companies on a certain day.

TABLE 7.1 Sportswear Companies, Their Ticker Symbols, and Price Per Share

Sportswear Company (and Ticker Symbol)	Price Per Share (PPS)
Skechers U.S.A., Inc. (SKX)	$30.22
Lululemon Athletica, Inc. (LULU)	$60.89
Foot Locker, Inc. (FL)	$63.47
Finish Line, Inc. (FINL)	$19.07

Definition

A **ticker symbol** *or* **stock symbol** *is an abbreviation of a particular stock that is used to identify it in the stock trading market.*

If other companies were to attempt to compete with these sportswear companies and offer stocks to those who wanted to invest, they would probably do well to set their price somewhere between the range of $19.07 and $63.47, the maximum and minimum values shown in Table 7.1. This is more of a subjective way of setting the price of a company's share.

Example 7.1 Research online to find ticker symbols for the following stocks:

1. Facebook, Inc.
2. Apple, Inc.
3. Starbucks Corporation
4. American Airlines Group, Inc.

Solution 7.1 Ticker symbols for the mentioned stocks are as follows:

1. FB
2. AAPL
3. SBUX
4. AAL

The second aspect of setting the price of a share is more slippery. A company has to try to determine its future worth and value and estimate what it thinks its future earnings will be. It is quite difficult to assess this if the company is just starting. Once it gets established, it can analyze its earnings over the time it has existed and base future earnings on past earnings. This, however, is still not a surefire method of prediction. Just because a company's earnings increased one year does not necessarily mean it will have similar growth the following year. Since no one is able to predict the future precisely, this aspect of pricing a share requires a bit more analysis. Many accountants, financial analysts, and statisticians spend their careers doing exactly this, but they often are incorrect and cannot always forecast correctly. We discuss this more in Section 7.3.2.

7.1.2 Winning Some, Losing Some

In the case of your friend and her boutique store in Beverly Hills, we will just assume she has done her research and settled in on a price of \$50 per share as it relates to her company. Remember, you invested a total of \$800 as part owner of her business, which means that you now own a total of 16 shares $((\$800/1) \cdot (1\,\text{share}/\$50) = 16\,\text{shares})$. Note that in the calculation, we multiplied by $1\,\text{share}/\$50$. This is known as a *conversion rate*. Note that one share equals \$50 in this example. When you multiply the numerator by its equivalent value in the denominator, we are essentially multiplying by the value of one. After multiplying, the unit of dollars (\$) cancels out, and we are left with the units of "shares." Your \$800 is no longer in the form of money as you are used to seeing it. Your friend has delivered to you how your money has taken on the look and form of shares. You may receive in the mail something that partially resembles what is shown in Figure 7.1.

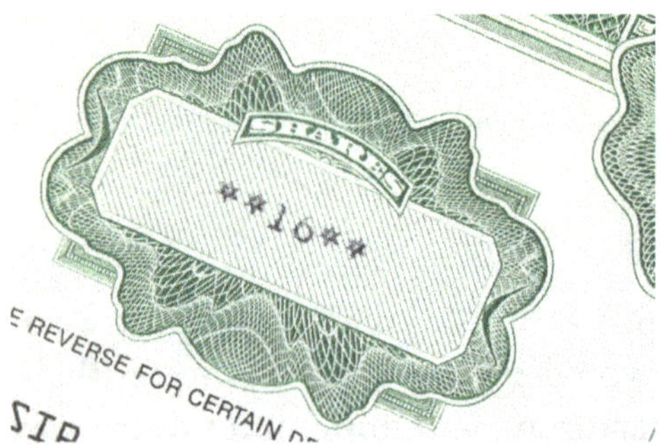

Tupungato/Shutterstock.com

FIGURE 7.1 Your Shares of Ownership in Your Friend's Boutique Reported on a Certificate

Example 7.2 Suppose Starbucks (SBUX) shares are currently priced at \$87.57. If you paid a total of \$1000 toward the purchase of SBUX shares, how many shares did you purchase?

Solution 7.2 We have: $\frac{\$1000}{1} \cdot \frac{1\,\text{share}}{\$87.57} = 11.419\,\text{shares}$. You purchased a total of 11.419 Starbucks shares.

Although it may seem a bit weird, the 16 shares you purchased from your friend's second boutique business are equivalent to the \$800 you invested, at least for now! As an investor in your friend's business, you are hoping that business starts booming. In fact, suppose you discover over the next year that the boutique business has started to do well and begins earning a profit. Its value and worth begins to increase as marked by the earnings it reports on its taxes at the end of the year. After reassessing its value as a company, your friend has determined that shares are no longer \$50 but are now \$65. This means that anyone who wishes to invest in her boutique business now must pay \$65 per share because the business is worth more now that when it originally started. But let's see what this means for you when it comes to the shares you purchased when the second boutique first opened.

After the first year, you decide that your friend's business is up and running well enough that it does not really need the \$800 you initially invested. You approach your friend with the certificate of 16 shares and inform her that you want to sell all of your shares and get your \$800 back. You did not mind helping her get the second business off of the ground, but you do not wish to have any ownership in her company anymore. When you return your shares to be sold, she gives you some great news!

Since the value of the company has increased and each share is now worth \$65, you receive more money back than you originally invested. Once you sell all of your shares, your friend hands you a check in the amount of \$1040. In one year's time, you have earned a profit that yielded more than you probably would have gotten if the money was placed in a regular savings account. We observe the calculations here, based on the share's new value:

$$\left(\frac{16\,\text{shares}}{1} \cdot \frac{\$65}{1\,\text{share}} = \$1040\right)$$

Example 7.3 How much profit did you make after the first year when you sold all of your shares from your friend's business?

Solution 7.3 To find the profit, we simply subtract your original investment from the amount yielded once the shares were sold. Your total profit is \$240

$$(\$1040 - \$800 = \$240)$$

This scenario is wonderful. Your friend's second boutique has done well and is thriving. Customers seem to have really taken to her brand well and seem to love her product. She seems to be cashing in on the American dream. The value of her business is increasing and all looks to be positive overall concerning her business ventures. Hence, shares in her business seem to be on an upward trend. In finance, a **bull market** reflects when stock prices seem to perform favorably for companies, indicating that the economy overall is strong.

Definition

A **bull market** *refers to a situation in which the economy is strong, as evidenced by rising or increasing stock prices.*

Note: Since the bull charges its enemies by taking its head and horns and thrusting upward, it has been used to symbolize the upward motion of stock prices.

Given how easily you earned a \$240 profit from investing in your friend's boutique, one wonders why everyone does not go the route of buying shares in a business and wait for the money to roll in. The truth is that things do *not* always work out financially the way they did for you and your investment in the boutique.

Imagine a different scenario. Suppose you invested the same \$800 into your friend's second boutique in Los Angeles, and suppose the business did not do as well as she had expected during that first year. Maybe it had to do with location. Perhaps the customer base in Los Angeles has different tastes overall for clothing than does that in Beverly Hills at the Rodeo Drive location. Perhaps customers in Beverly Hills do not mind the relatively high price tag for most of the items, or the L.A. customer may be more hesitant to pay the same prices. For whatever reason, business is slow and there seems to be no growth in sight for this particular boutique. As a result, your friend has determined that the price of a share has to decrease from \$50 to \$40.

For fear that the price of a share may fall even lower, suppose you decide to cash in your shares now. Since the value of the company has decreased and each share is now worth \$40, you will not be as happy as you were in the first scenario. Recall that you still have sixteen shares based on your initial purchase using your \$800. Once you cash in all of your shares this time, you observe that your investment did not pay off as you had intended. Your friend gives you a check this time in the amount of \$640. We observe the calculations here, based on the share's lowered value:

$$\left(\frac{16\text{ shares}}{1} \cdot \frac{\$40}{1\text{ share}} = \$640\right)$$

In this case, after the first year, you have incurred a loss from your initial investment.

Example 7.4 How much did you lose after the first year when you sold all of your shares from your friend's business in the second scenario?

Solution 7.4 To find the loss, we simply subtract your original investment from the amount yielded once the shares were sold. Your total loss is \$160 (\$640 − \$800 = −\$160).

It is unfortunate, but businesses encounter situations like this all of the time. Because of certain variables at play, sometimes businesses suffer and struggle, showing signs of minimal promise or growth. Investors who put money into a business have no way of knowing whether the price of shares or stock will increase or decrease. Since investments in stocks are not FDIC-insured, they may lose value. Even if investors do what they think is adequate research in the strength of a company, their best efforts are sometimes met with headaches and the loss of money from their investments. The truth is there is no surefire way to guard against a stock's poor performance. Factors outside of anyone's control can ultimately drag down a stock's value without notice. In finance, a **bear market** reflects when stock prices seem to perform poorly for companies, indicating that the economy overall is weak.

Definition

A **bear market** *refers to a situation in which the economy is weak, as evidenced by plummeting or decreasing stock prices.*

Note: Since the bear charges its enemies by using its hands to make downward swipes, it has been used to symbolize the downward motion of stock prices.

"We may not agree on the stock market, but we're both Chicago fans."

www.CartoonStock.com

This, then, becomes the tug-of-war that many people grapple with when it comes to trying to make their money grow. Do they stick with an investment like a savings account, CD, or bond, which yields minimum interest over time but does not lose money? Or do they invest in shares or stocks, knowing that they can gain a lot of interest quickly or can lose much of what they invested just as fast? Often, what determines how willing people are to lose or not lose money when trying to make it grow is their **risk tolerance**.

Definition

Risk tolerance *is the measure to which people feel comfortable with the notion that it is possible to lose some of the money that they invest.*

Some people cannot stomach the fact that they can lose one penny of their hard-earned money. Investing in stocks to them is too risky of a venture. Although it is possible to gain a lot of money investing in this way, they cannot fathom that losing money is just one hurdle in what can be a mountain of monetary gain. These people are said to have a *low* risk tolerance and are satisfied with placing their funds in savings accounts, CDs, and bonds. Although they will not earn much money on average when compared to those who have a *high* risk tolerance, their money is safe to them and they can sleep better at night. When it comes to losing money, those who have a high risk tolerance attempt to see the big picture in terms of their financial savings scenario. Often, those who have a high risk tolerance understand that, although they may lose money temporarily, they will generally gain it back and then some over the life of the investment.

7.2 Stocks as a Bridge to Retirement Wealth

We discussed in Asset Two, for example, the benefits of saving for a retirement. When it comes to saving money for one's retirement, especially for a 401(k) or 403(b), a decision one has to make is how the money that is being saved is allocated. In other words, many retirement companies would want to know how you would like to invest the money that you are saving. They would want to know if you would like for your money to be placed into accounts that cater to those with low risk tolerance or to those with high risk tolerance. Your decision would affect how quickly or how slowly your money grows in your retirement account.

7.2.1 Aggressive vs. Conservative Investing

Many financial analysts have encouraged those who are relatively young to invest their funds **aggressively** or in accounts showing a risk tolerance that is high. For those who are older or approaching their retirement age, analysts encourage people to invest their funds **conservatively** or in accounts showing a risk tolerance that is low.

Definition

Aggressive risk tolerance *describes the willingness of an investor to put herself in a position where her investments are poised for significant growth or significant loss.* **Conservative risk tolerance** *describes the willingness of an investor to put himself in a position where his investments are poised for modest growth or modest loss.*

The reasoning is that those who are young still have time for their accounts to recuperate from financial losses, whereas those who are older do not have as much time as their younger investor counterparts to rebound from any financial losses that may have occurred from investing so aggressively. Remember, investing aggressively (with stocks) could yield more money quickly but could also result in the loss of invested funds. The basic idea of investing for retirement implies that you are investing for the long haul as opposed to for a year or so. Arguably, investing most of one's funds in stocks typically helps funds grow quicker over a sustained period of time, despite a few bumps or losses along the way.

Consider the URL: https://goo.gl/iQDnUd. If we locate the figure titled "Growth of $10,000 from 1988 to 2008," we see an example comparing the performance of two actual accounts of $10,000, which grew over a 20-year period (1988–2008). One account had funds invested in equity funds (stocks) as indicated by S&P 500, which catalogues the growth of 500 large American companies and their stock strength. The other had funds invested in Barclays Capital US Aggregate Bond Index (bonds).

The top line of the graph shows the journey of the investor's money growth when the funds were invested in stocks (*high* risk tolerance). The bottom line of the graph shows the journey of the same $10,000 when the money was invested in bonds (*low* risk tolerance). Notice in the top line that the value of the funds sinks considerably between the years of 1999 and 2002 and also from 2007 and 2008. Nervous investors might not have felt as though their money was working in their favor if they just looked at their money growth between these years alone. When we observe the overall picture, however, we see that, although these dips occur during these years, the year-end value at the end of 2008 shows that money invested using stocks is approximately $50,000. The year-end value at the end of 2008 for bonds is approximately $40,000. This is a net difference of $10,000 when comparing both accounts. While the money growth with bonds steadily increases and never decreases, money growth using stocks still yielded a higher amount, even though the journey was more unpredictable.

Example 7.5 Consider the following URL: https://goo.gl/iQDnUd. Locate the figure with the title "Growth of $10,000 from 1988 to 2008." From 1999 to 2002, the stock investment decreases from $70,000 to $42,000. What percentage decrease is represented within this time frame?

Solution 7.5 To find the percentage increase or decrease, we solve the following ratio:

$$\frac{\text{Amount of increase or decrease}}{\text{Starting or base amount}} = \frac{\text{Percent}}{100}$$

The amount of decrease here is $70,000–$42,000, or $28,000. The starting or base amount for the period in question is $70,000. So we have:

$$\frac{\$28{,}000}{\$70{,}000} = \frac{x}{100}$$

$$\Rightarrow (\$28{,}000)(100) = \$70{,}000x$$

$$\Rightarrow \$2{,}800{,}000 = \$70{,}000x$$

$$\Rightarrow 40 = x$$

Hence, between 1999 and 2002, there is a 40% decrease in investment funds.

7.2.2 A Happy Medium

Although no one particular tolerance level for investment risk—aggressive or conservative—is necessarily better than the another, researchers have historically advised investors to follow certain recommended courses of action as they relate to planning for their financial future. One might conclude that it is always better to invest funds strictly in an aggressive fashion because of the potential quick gains, as stated earlier. However, the potential for quick gains is tempered by the potential for quick losses. Hence, a retired couple may not be as excited about visiting the shores of Honolulu when they know that their **retirement portfolio** has just taken a sharp hit, reducing the overall money pot.

Definition

A **retirement portfolio** *describes the details about how funds are allocated within the retirement account, providing insight into future cashflow needs. It provides a bird's eye view of the percentage of funds that are assigned to stocks, bonds, money market accounts, and savings, along with how much money overall is resting in the account.*

To guard against investors' possible financial disaster, financial advisors have often encouraged employees to not only automatically contribute to their retirement accounts each pay period, but advisors have also frequently recommended that the investment portfolio should not be strictly aggressive or strictly conservative. In other words, making sure that you contribute to the retirement account on a consistent basis is one thing. Determining how the funds grow is another. Recall that putting money into a retirement account is different than just making a deposit into a savings account, where you have no control over how it grows. The bank sets the interest rate for the savings account, and funds grow accordingly. With a retirement account, *you* must decide what kind of growth or interest rate to which your money will be subject. In this vein, advisors have continued to stress that one's retirement account should, among all things, show **diversification**.

Definition

Diversification *is an investment technique that minimizes risk in a portfolio by allocating funds across several risk-tolerance levels as opposed to allocating to just one.*

The idea behind diversification is that funds in a diversified portfolio would tend to be more protected or safeguarded, on average, when compared to a portfolio in which funds are strictly aggressively or strictly conservatively invested.

For example, when you were applying to college, your parents perhaps advised you not to "place all of your eggs in one basket." They hoped you would be wise enough not just to send an application only to one college or university. In the case that you were not accepted into your top college choice, they wanted to safeguard your chances of going to college *period* by having you attempt entry at a number of schools. Likewise, when it becomes time for you to determine the allocation percentages for your portfolio, you will need to decide whether you will funnel your money to grow in only one risk-tolerance category or in several. Regarding the egg-and-basket proverb, if the basket (degree of diversification) is too narrowly focused and all of your eggs (money) are in that basket, then your assets may either suffer great loss or grow at a snail's pace. This depends on which risk-tolerance class is the one in which your funds are invested. In general, if more eggs are distributed across investment category types, what happens in one category does not affect all of your money. Figure 7.2 illustrates this point, using the college application process as a vehicle for understanding the notion of diversification.

Roger Wohlner, in a poignant article (2013), showed the power of diversification in a portfolio. He assumed three separate scenarios in which the investor began with an investment of $100,000 and invested it from January 1, 2000 to December 31, 2009. Wohlner used actual data from the past (growth percentages) and simulated how much money would have been made in each of the three scenarios during that decade.

Strategy One shows money growth if all $100,000 was placed *only* in stocks (high risk tolerance). In this highly aggressive strategy, money was invested in a variety of stocks from the Vanguard 500 Index Fund. At the end of the decade, it was determined that the initial investment of $100,000 would have decreased to $90,165. Remember, stocks have the ability to cause sharp growth or loss in funds. In this case, the value of the investment decreased. This is the case of having all of your eggs in one basket, where 100% of your funds were placed in a high risk-tolerance level that is strictly high.

Strategy Two invests only 25% of your funds in the same Index Fund as in Strategy One. The remaining 75% was invested equally in three other fund types listed in the article. These three types of investment categories are not as aggressive as that in Strategy One alone. In this moderately aggressive case, the initial investment of $100,000 would have yielded a portfolio worth $137,511 at the end of that decade. In this case, your eggs were in four baskets, where 25% of your funds were placed in four separate investment account types.

Strategy Three, finally, invests 12.5% of your funds in each of eight separate categories. Four of the categories were those in Strategies One and Two. The other four were four different types of bonds. In this moderately conservative case, the initial investment of $100,000 would have yielded a portfolio worth $174,506 at the end of the decade. In this case, your eggs were in eight baskets. In other words, underperformance in one category was apparently offset by stellar performance in another.

Hence, we see in Wohlner's simulated study that spreading funds across several investment category types produces higher yields or more money. This does not necessarily guarantee that results would have been the same during another decade of scrutiny, but it just provides a general idea behind the strength of diversification when investing. Figure 7.3 provides a visual depiction for what we just explained with regard to diversifying funds.

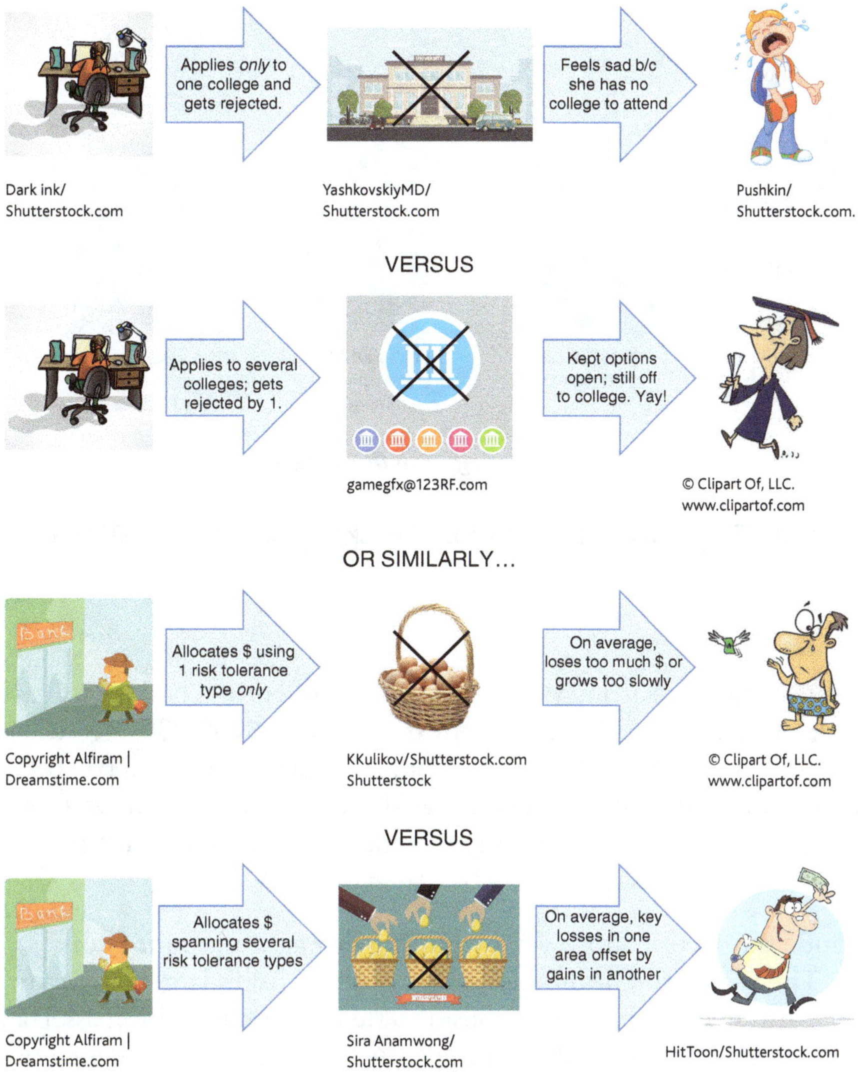

FIGURE 7.2 Diversification in Retirement: A College "Eggs-ample"

ulegundo/Shutterstock.com

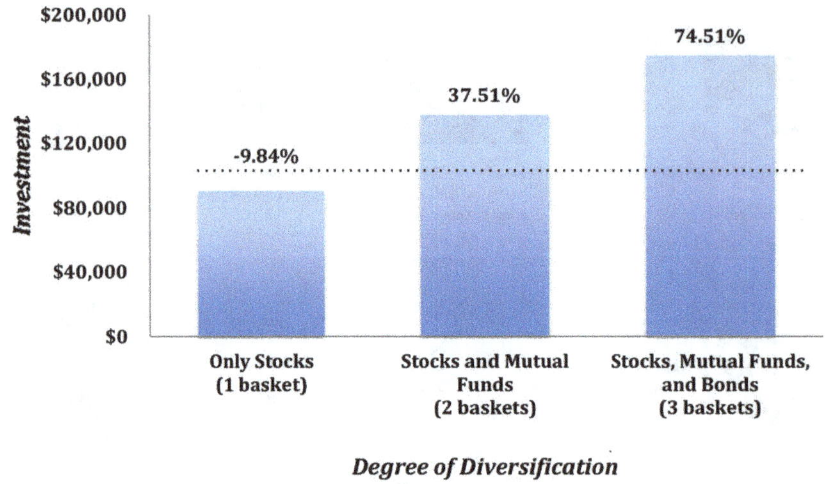

FIGURE 7.3 100,000 "Eggs" Invested in Various "Baskets": January 1, 2000–December 31, 2009

Note

The dotted line represents the starting value of $100,000 in all three "basket" scenarios. Percentages show the amount of increase or decrease from the original $100,000 investment for that particular diversification level over the 10-year period. For example, when $100,000 was invested in all stocks, the amount available in that account at the end of the decade was $90,165. This final amount represents a 9.84% decrease from the original investment amount.)

We must conclude this section, however, by putting diversification into context as it relates to the age of the investor. The Vanguard Group, Inc. is one of the world's largest investment firms. It is not necessarily the best company but does offer considerable advice concerning asset-allocation management (or risk management). Generally, the firm gives investors general guidance on how their retirement portfolio should look, depending on their age. This information should not be taken as absolute truth but should provide some idea for how an investor's allocations might appear. An example of allocation percentage recommendations follows. In general, they are listed under the firm's Target Retirement Funds page. Table 7.2 explains:

TABLE 7.2 Vanguard's Suggested Asset Allocation by Age

Age Range	% Invested in Stocks	% Invested in Bonds	% Invested in Short-Term Reserves
18–23	89.89	10.06	005
24–28	89.79	10.07	0.14
29–33	89.77	10.10	0.13
34–38	89.89	10.08	0.03
39–43	88.75	11.19	0.06
44–48	81.30	18.67	0.03

Age Range	% Invested in Stocks	% Invested in Bonds	% Invested in Short-Term Reserves
49–53	73.87	26.08	0.05
54–58	66.52	33.46	0.02
59–63	58.52	41.43	0.05
64–68	48.08	51.90	0.02
69–72	33.75	66.16	0.09

Note: Here, stocks refer to US and international stocks, mutual funds, and real-estate investment trusts (REITs). Bonds include US. and international bonds. Short-term reserves are those savings that may be used in less than a year or so without financial penalty. Examples include certificates of deposit (CDs), treasury bills, and cash deposits in banks.

The specific percentages in the table are not as important as observation of the overall trend in the data. What the table reveals and what most advisors suggest is that the closer one gets to the age of retirement, the more conservative the retirement portfolio becomes. At a young age, investors have time on their side to ride out any losses or financial bumps that may occur with their portfolio. The idea of investing suggests that money will stay in the account for the long haul. Investing aggressively at a young age, then, tends to make more sense. As one nears retirement, however, funds should be subject to less volatility. Hence, the larger percentage in the bond column becomes more logical. Most asset-allocation models champion this notion, although percentages vary within various models. The shift from aggressive allocation to more conservative allocation pervades in all models.

7.3 Choosing a Stock to Invest In: A Look at One Strategy

In the previous section, we addressed benefits and drawbacks of investing in stocks, especially in the case of retirement. We saw that in the case of the S&P 500, for example, the graph shows evidence of a bear and bull market over time. What's important to note is that the behavior displayed there is a summary of stock strength for all 500 companies that are affiliated with the S&P. We are not able to single out any one particular company to see how it is performing aside from the other 499. We are only afforded the opportunity to observe how the stocks as a whole perform on average over time.

It may be, however, that you as a consumer would like to choose which individual stock in which you would like to invest. Investment clubs all over the country have taken to finding, monitoring, and investing in stocks that they have researched on their own through strategies they have developed among themselves. More and more business schools are hosting investment competitions in which they invite students from junior high schools and high schools to build their own portfolio with virtual money to see how students are able to work together and choose stocks that they think will appreciate the best over time. Whether the money is real or virtual, learning how to select an individual stock can be invaluable.

7.3.1 Earnings Per Share

In Table 7.1, we took a look at certain sportswear companies, their ticker symbols, and their prices per share. In the table, the stock with the lowest price per share is Finish Line, Inc. (FINL) at a share price of $19.07. The proverbial advice regarding the purchase of stocks has always been to "buy low and sell high." In other words, the idea is to buy shares at a low price and then cash in once the share's price reaches a value that one considers to be high. So buying shares in FINL would seem to be the obvious choice out of the four sportswear companies since it is the cheapest, right?

Note

At this point, **Finish Line, Inc. (FINL)** appears to be the best stock to buy of the four in Table 7.1 since it has the lowest price per share ($19.07).

Well, before discussing this "obvious" choice, we proceed by posing an interesting scenario. This is a situation similar to one that aired on the popular TV series called *Shark Tank*, where business owners seek partnerships and investments from millionaires in the hopes of forging business dreams. In this particular case, the business owner who was seeking an investment from the sharks was an eighth-grader, a CEO of a company that makes stickers for cardboard boxes, turning them into airplanes, race cars, and fire trucks. His MBA-wielding father, who wished he had pursued his own dreams as a youngster, accompanied him on the show. The teen CEO explained that he was seeking $35,000 for a 25% stake in his business. He received offers from three of the sharks. The offers were as follows:

1. Shark One offered $35,000 for a 50% stake plus an option of selling the cardboard box.
2. Shark Two offered $35,000 for a 50% stake.
3. Shark Three offered $35,000 for a 35% stake plus an option for making the product more girl-friendly and an option of selling the cardboard box.

After mulling over the decision, the eighth-grader, without the help of his father, decided to go with the offer from Shark One. Flabbergasted, everyone believed the teen had been bamboozled and could not see straight. Surely, he had not seen through Shark One's schemes and wiles. Looking at just the numbers alone, this was arguably the worst offer out of the three. The owner was relinquishing half of the worth of his company to a greedy shark. Completely shocked, one of the sharks asked the teen to explain the rationale behind his decision. Without hesitating, the teen replied that the shark he chose to invest with "has a ton of background in the toy industry. He's got all of the background we need for this company." These were pearls of wisdom coming from the mind of someone well ahead of his years.

In the past, Shark One had done a $4 billion deal with Mattel, one of the leading toy companies and had inroads into great commercial printing facilities. This meant in theory, all things being equal, that the CEO would possibly see more money pouring into his business even though Shark One owned half of his company. Since Shark One had the expertise in that particular field, the business could conceivably push more inventory, thus raking in more dough.

Example 7.6 Suppose at the end of the first fiscal year, we were privy to how much the teen CEO would have made had he gone with each of the three different sharks. Suppose he would have grossed $1 million with Shark One, $500,000 with Shark Two, and

$375,000 with Shark Three. Determine how much profit the business would have made in each of the three circumstances. (We do not factor in the initial seed into the business of $35,000.)

Solution 7.6 In each case, we take the total gross amount and subtract the partner's percentage of it. So we have:

$$\begin{aligned} \text{Shark One:}\quad \text{Gross} &= \$1,000,000 - 0.50(\$1,000,000) \\ &= \$1,000,000 - \$500,000 \\ &= \$500,000 \end{aligned}$$

$$\begin{aligned} \text{Shark Two:}\quad \text{Gross} &= \$500,000 - 0.50(\$500,000) \\ &= \$500,000 - \$250,000 \\ &= \$250,000 \end{aligned}$$

$$\begin{aligned} \text{Shark Three:}\ \text{Gross} &= \$375,000 - 0.35(\$375,000) \\ &= \$375,000 - \$131,250 \\ &= \$243,750 \end{aligned}$$

We clearly see who had the last laugh … the teen! Even though Shark One had more equity in the company, his specific background in the toy industry helped to catapult the business into some significant money.

What the teen CEO considered was not just what the sharks' deals were in terms of percentages and amount to be invested in his business, but he also took into consideration how significant the shark's background would factor into the company's future. This notion is referred to as **growth capacity**.

> **Definition**
>
> **Growth capacity** *is the specific ability of a financial instrument to increase in quality and quantity over an extended period of time.*

That said, we now begin to focus on what the teen CEO's situation has to do with stocks and a strategy for choosing which ones to invest in. What we address shortly should in no way serve as official financial advice that one should use in purchasing shares. There is no guarantee that the technique or strategy will always produce the best results as they relate to stock investment. Since the stock market is volatile, it may go up and down, sometimes faking out the best of those who sit and analyze stocks all day.

In Table 7.3, we take a look a version of Table 7.1 again but with more data included in additional columns.

TABLE 7.3 Sportswear Companies, Share Prices, and Other Relevant Data (March 24, 2016)

Sportswear Company (and Ticker Symbol)	Price per Share (PPS)	Earnings per Share (EPS)	P/E Ratio
Skechers U.S.A., Inc. (SKX)	\$30.22	\$1.50	20.15
Lululemon Athletica, Inc. (LULU)	\$60.89	\$1.84	33.18
Foot Locker, Inc. (FL)	\$63.47	\$3.84	16.53
Finish Line, Inc. (FINL)	\$19.07	\$1.27	15.02

The first of the two new columns provides information on **earnings per share (EPS)**.

> **Definition**
>
> **Earnings per share (EPS)** *refers to how much a particular company has made per share over the past 12 months, generally.*

It is a summary piece of data, reflecting the net income for the company per how many shares is invested in it (after paying out necessary dividends to its investors). So if we look backward for a given year, a company could have amassed net earnings of \$500,000 and paid out \$75,000 in dividends, which leaves it with \$425,000 in net earnings (or \$500,000–\$75,000). If it is currently the case that the company's customers have purchased a total of 170,000 shares, then the EPS for that company is \$2.50 per share (or \$425,000/170,000 shares). In Table 7.3, Skechers for example, shows an EPS of \$1.50.

7.3.2 Price-to-Earnings Ratio

We further attempt to get at a true sense of the stock's value by using how much the stock costs per share and its EPS to arrive at what is called the **price-to-earnings (P/E) ratio**, which is information provided in the next new column in Table 7.3.

> **Definition**
>
> *The* **price-to-earnings (P/E) ratio** *conveys the sense of a stock's value by dividing the stock's current price per share with its past earnings per share, generally calculated from over the last 12-month period.*

By simply dividing the price for each share and the earnings per share, we get a better sense of the stock's worth. It's not enough just to look at the cost of each stock. But we look at the cost in relation to how much was actually earned per stock bought. For all the stocks in Table 7.3, we are given this P/E ratio. Its calculation is no more than dividing the price per share by the EPS. In the case of Skechers, we see that the P/E ratio of 20.15 comes from dividing the price per share of \$30.22 by the EPS of \$1.50. Note that there are no units for the P/E ratio. It is not \$20.15. It is simply 20.15 or written as 20.15x. In other words, the investor is paying \$20.15 for every \$1 of Skechers' earnings or profit. Or, we say:

$$\begin{aligned}\frac{P}{E}\text{ratio} &= \frac{\$30.22}{1\,\text{share}} \div \frac{\$1.50}{1\,\text{share}}\\ &= \frac{\$30.22}{1\,\text{share}} \times \frac{1\,\text{share}}{\$1.50}\\ &= 20.15\,(\text{units cancel out})\end{aligned}$$

This P/E ratio is what analysts used for years to determine which stock's value was really better than other stocks. A low P/E ratio suggested that, when compared to other companies in the same category, perhaps the stock was undervalued and was ripe for the customer's picking for purchase. Or on the other hand, perhaps it was a dud, offering no promise of real growth for the future. The shortcoming of using the P/E ratio was, in fact, this uncertainty of knowing whether the stock was really a gem as witnessed by its undervalued state. Of the four stocks in Table 7.3, the best stock to buy now, using our knowledge of the P/E ratio, still appears to be FINL, which has the lowest P/E ratio at 15.02.

Note

At this point, **Finish Line, Inc. (FINL)** still appears to be the best stock to buy of the four in Table 7.3 since it has the lowest P/E ratio (15.02x).

Many analysts, however, realized that choosing a stock strictly using the P/E ratio was limited and misleading. Remember, one of the values used to calculate this ratio is the EPS. By nature and definition, this piece of data always looked backward to assess earnings in the past. It constantly looked in the company's 12-month rearview mirror and offered no information by way of a stock's projected future performance. Somehow, analysts had to do what the teen CEO of the toy company did: find a way to factor in some value that accounts for the company's capacity for growth. You thought I forgot … LOL!

7.3.3 Price-to-Earnings-Growth Ratio

In order to account for a stock's capacity for growth, we add another variable to the P/E ratio equation. When we include information concerning earnings-per-share growth, we are now considering as part of the stock-value equation how well the stock is projected to perform in the future. When we look at the previous P/E ratio in relation to the earnings per share growth, we are left with a value known as the **price-to-earnings-to-growth (PEG) ratio**.

Definition

The **price-to-earnings-to-growth (PEG) ratio** helps to assess the value of a stock by comparing similar companies that have different P/E ratios and different growth rates. We calculate the PEG ratio by dividing the company's P/E ratio by its earnings growth rate.

The earnings growth rate is provided generally as a projection 12 months into the future. It is reported as an expected percentage growth that many analysts struggle to find. Even so, there is no guarantee that what analysts project will actually be what the earnings will indeed be. Stock behavior, as noted, is unpredictable, so this growth rate percentage is a rough guesstimate on the part of analysts to predict how a company will perform in the near future.

TABLE 7.4 P/E Ratio, Earnings Growth Per Share, and PEG Ratio for Sportswear Companies

Sportswear Company (and Ticker Symbol)	P/E Ratio	Earnings Growth per Share (%)	PEG Ratio
Skechers U.S.A., Inc. (SKX)	20.15	27.60	0.73
Lululemon Athletica, Inc. (LULU)	33.18	15.95	2.08
Foot Locker, Inc. (FL)	16.53	13.89	1.19
Finish Line, Inc. (FINL)	15.02	14.30	1.05

This earning growth percentage may be found on some sites that track stock statistics but not all of them. On the NASDAQ site (http://goo.gl/jlw4), the general percentage growth can be found by clicking at the bottom right on the Earnings Growth link on the page where basic stock information is found. One should be sure to use the percentage that reflects one year ahead of the current year being studied. Even if one cannot find this percentage, this is fine. All we need to locate is the PEG ratio, which is explicitly given for each stock by scrolling to the very bottom of the page and observing the value for **PEG Ratio** in the *Analyst Info* box. Table 7.4 shows the P/E ratio, estimated earnings growth percentage per share for our sportswear companies, and the PEG ratio. Essentially, the PEG ratio is preferable to the P/E ratio because, unlike the P/E ratio, the PEG ratio accounts for the history of the stock as well as projected future capacity for growth. Essentially, this one number provides relevant information about a stock's *past* performance, *present* value, and *future* growth potential.

We have just summed up the value of the stock into one number, the PEG ratio. In general, we are now able to make an apples-to-apples comparison of similar stocks and make an assessment of the stock's worth, assuming all other criteria for choosing a stock are equal. Table 7.5 provides general guidelines for interpreting the stock's PEG ratio as it relates to whether the stock is generally good to invest in or not at the moment.

TABLE 7.5 The PEG Ratio and Its Implications

Stock's PEG Ratio	General Recommendation
PEG < 0.5	This means that the stock is considerably undervalued and shows great promise for growth. Investors will probably get great returns by investing in these stocks.
0.5 ≤ PEG < 1	This means that the stock is undervalued and shows good promise for growth. Investors will probably get adequate returns by investing in these stocks.
PEG = 1	This means that the stock is priced fairly equal to its anticipated growth. Investors will probably experience slight gains or slight losses by investing in these stocks.
PEG > 1	This means that the stock is overvalued and shows no real promise for growth. Investors will probably lose money by investing in these stocks.

Source: Adapted from: http://goo.gl/guhafH.

Out of the four sportswear companies, it looks now as though Skechers is arguably the stock that is the best to invest in with a PEG ratio of 0.73. According to this value, its stock is undervalued and shows good promise for growth. So we have to remember not just to look at the basic price of a stock or its P/E ratio. Looking at the PEG ratio gives a better overall sense of the stock's value in relation to its overall capacity for growth.

Note

At this point, **Skechers U.S.A., Inc. (SKX)** appears to be the best stock to buy of the four in Table 7.4 since it has the lowest PEG ratio (0.73).

We summarize which stocks from Table 7.1 are the best to buy when we *strictly* consider the three criteria discussed previously.

1. When only considering the price per share, **FINL** is the best of the four stocks to buy since it is the cheapest. The price per share only provides *present* information about a stock.
2. When only considering the P/E ratio, **FINL** is the best of the four stocks to buy since it has the lowest P/E ratio. The P/E ratio provides *present* and *past* information about a stock.
3. When only considering the PEG ratio, **Skechers U.S.A., Inc.** is the best of the four stocks to buy since it has the lowest PEG ratio. The PEG ratio provides *present*, *past*, and *future* information about a stock.

We finally reiterate that there are a number of factors to consider when it comes to purchasing a stock. The PEG ratio is but one factor out of many that one should consider when determining which is the best stock to buy. A few other factors are: (i) the company's total debt; (ii) the company's leadership and management; (iii) the economic condition of the country (as indicated by the gross domestic product), and others. All in all, the PEG ratio remains an important data value to consider when attempting to choose a stock.

Example 7.7 Consider the following values for Facebook, Inc. (FB):

Price Per Share: $113.05 EPS: $1.29 Earnings Growth Per Share: 78.25%

Find the PEG ratio for the FB stock. Does it appear to be a stock worth investing in if you were just considering its PEG ratio?

Solution 7.7 We first find the P/E ratio:

$$\frac{P}{E} = \frac{\text{Price per Share}}{\text{EPS}} = \frac{\$113.05}{\$1.29} = 87.64$$

Now, we find the PEG ratio:

$$\text{PEG ratio} = \frac{P/E\text{ ratio}}{\text{Earnings growth per share}} = \frac{87.64}{78.25\%} = 1.12$$

Notice that we do not turn the percent into a decimal. We divide in the form of the percent that is given. Hence, the PEG ratio for FB is 1.12 on March 24, 2016. Since $PEG > 1$, the stock seems to be overvalued and shows no real promise for growth, according to the guidelines referenced in Table 7.5.

7.4 Smoothing and Predicting Stocks with Time Series

One of the most notable ways in which data are presented in the field of statistics, especially as it relates to viewing stock behavior, is as a time series. Simply, a **time series** is a sequence of numerical observations over a specific time frame. Observations of the time series may typically be made annually, quarterly, monthly, daily, or even hourly.

Definition

A **time series** *is a sequence of numerical observations taken over time.*

When we study time series, we are able to perform wonderful analyses on time-sensitive data by applying a number of statistical techniques. First, though, we discuss the universal manner in which time series are displayed or visualized.

7.4.1 Time Series Visualized

To understand better the notion of time series, we take a look at the stock activity for Wynn Resorts, Ltd. (ticker symbol: WYNN), based out of Las Vegas, Nevada. Founded in 2002, it owns and operates resorts in both Las Vegas and China. We consider the monthly closing stock prices for the company from October of 2002 to March of 2016. Data are given at roughly the beginning of each month. A partial list of all of the monthly data is revealed in Table 7.6, excluding weekends and holidays.

TABLE 7.6 Partial Monthly Stock Prices for Wynn Resorts, Ltd. (October, 2002–March, 2016)

Month/Year	Price	Month/Year	Price	Month/Year	Price
10/02	\$12.61	01/04	\$29.53	04/05	\$52.94
11/02	\$12.82	02/04	\$36.34	05/05	\$46.85
12/02	\$13.11	03/04	\$35.00	06/05	\$47.27
01/03	\$13.75	04/04	\$39.93	07/05	\$56.30
02/03	\$14.22	05/04	\$38.66	08/05	\$47.72

Month/Year	Price	Month/Year	Price	Month/Year	Price
03/03	$15.40	06/04	$38.63	09/05	$45.15
04/03	$17.00	07/04	$35.78	10/05	$46.63
05/03	$18.83	08/04	$38.60	11/05	$55.83
06/03	$17.74	09/04	$51.69	12/05	$54.85
07/03	$17.05	10/04	$58.15	01/06	$64.58
08/03	$16.65	11/04	$58.09	02/06	$66.45
09/03	$18.18	12/04	$66.92	03/06	$76.85
10/03	$20.16	01/05	$65.56	04/06	$76.11
11/03	$24.89	02/05	$71.57	05/06	$71.20
12/03	$28.01	03/05	$67.74	06/06	$73.30

⋮

Month/Year	Price	Month/Year	Price	Month/Year	Price
07/12	$93.75	10/13	$166.25	01/15	$147.95
08/12	$103.17	11/13	$165.87	02/15	$142.50
09/12	$115.44	12/13	$194.21	03/15	$125.88
10/12	$121.06	01/14	$217.42	04/15	$111.07
11/12	$112.40	02/14	$242.49	05/15	$100.69
12/12	$217.42	03/14	$222.15	06/15	$98.67
01/13	$125.22	04/14	$203.89	07/15	$103.23
02/13	$116.90	05/14	$214.97	08/15	$75.05
03/13	$125.16	06/14	$207.56	09/15	$53.12
04/13	$137.30	07/14	$213.20	10/15	$69.95
05/13	$135.89	08/14	$192.88	11/15	$62.77
06/13	$127.97	09/14	$187.08	12/15	$69.19
07/13	$133.13	10/14	$190.01	01/16	$67.34
08/13	$141.04	11/14	$178.61	02/16	$82.48
09/13	$158.01	12/14	$148.76	03/16	$92.74

Source: http://goo.gl/G9Vuq5.

As we observe, listing all data in table form could take up a lot of space, especially if there is a lot of data to be analyzed. We omitted some of the data in Table 7.6 and still manage to fill up a little over a page when we show the monthly prices for WYNN stock. As an alternative, we generally tend to present such data spanning over a substantial period of time in visual form as a time series plot. Figure 7.4 presents the same stock data for Wynn Resorts, Ltd., but since we are showing the data as a visual plot, it becomes easy for us to show all of the data, not just some of it.

FIGURE 7.4 Plot of Closing Stock Prices for Wynn Resorts, Ltd.

The figure shows that stock prices for Wynn Resorts, Ltd., were expensive during some months and not so expensive during others. The overall pattern seems to mimic the highs and lows of a roller-coaster ride as you eyeball from left to right. We focus on certain aspects of this roller-coaster effect soon.

7.4.2 Four Crucial Components

Viewing the data as seen in Figure 7.4 allows us get a quick feel for the data over time and allows us to investigate several key components of the data, which we explore here. In most business circles, we generally work with the classical multiplicative model of a time series. Generally, four major factors or components are instrumental in influencing this time series model. It is important to identify and isolate each of these components so that we can understand the time series a little better. These four key components help one to understand the **classical multiplicative time series**. In real life, it is rare for one time series to show evidence of all four components at the same time.

Definition

The **classical multiplicative time series** *is given by:*

$$Y_t = T_t \times C_t \times S_t \times R_t,$$

where

Y_t *is the actual value of the time series at time t;*
T_t *is the value of the* **trend component** *of the time series at time t;*
C_t *is the value of the* **cyclical component** *of the time series at time t;*
S_t *is the value of the* **seasonal component** *of the time series at time t; and,*
R_t *is the value of the* **random component** *of the time series at time t.*

The **trend component** provides information concerning the overall increasing or decreasing movement of the time series, as the series goes from left to right. In Figure 7.4, we observe that as the series goes from left to right, stock prices for Wynn Resorts, Ltd. increase overall over the roughly 14-year period. Hence, we say that WYNN stocks are showing an upward trend.

In addition to the trend component, time series are also influenced by the **cyclical component**. This component refers to the up-and-down movements around a given trend throughout the series. Cycles typically span more than a year and are indicated by the successive highs and lows above and below the trend line. The length of the cycle depends on the actual time series, and there is no guarantee that a series will always present a cycle that is clearly defined. Hence, the fluctuations occur within a period of time that is *not fixed*. Sometimes, for this reason, cycles are difficult to locate and analyze. Cycles tend to surface with stock data especially because a stock's vibrance and value often mirror how the economy is fairing. If the economy is vibrant, then the stock's value tends to soar. If the economy is suffering, then the stock value often plummets. For certain stocks, we can generally observe telltale signs of a recession. When one considers stocks like those for luxury brands or high-end restaurants, it makes sense that a stock's value would tend to vacillate more than others. When the economy is thriving, we would assume that people would be more apt to splurge and partake in luxurious things. If the economy suffers, we do not expect for the average person to eat in fancy restaurants. So cycles would be more noticeable for stocks that fit into these types of categories.

Of course, we have established that Wynn Resorts, Ltd., is one of those luxury brands. When we look again at the series, we can identify cyclical behavior that is present. Figure 7.5 shows the time series again for Wynn Resorts, Ltd., but is displayed through the lens of identifying cycles in the data. In the figure, we see that the first cycle goes from 2002 to 2009, and the second cycle goes from 2009 to 2015. Note that both cycles show repeating behavior, starting relatively at low values, increasing to a certain maximum point and then mellowing out at the end of the cycle. The cycle itself, as stated earlier, spans for more than one year. The fluctuations in each cycle are not fixed; the first cycle occurs in about six years, while the second cycle occurs in about seven years. Even though the second cycle is at a "higher" level than the first cycle in terms of stock prices overall, both cycles basically have the same shape.

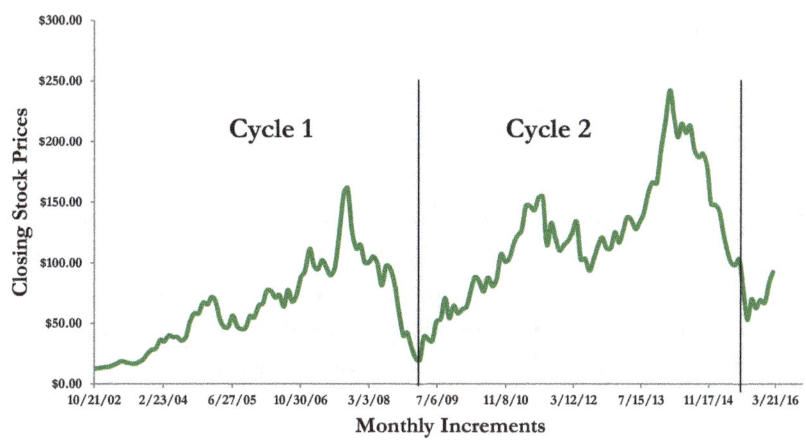

FIGURE 7.5 WYNN Stock and the Cyclical Component

The **seasonal component** of a series reflects observable and predictable fluctuations that occur within a *fixed* time period. Although the component is called seasonal, it does not mean that what we focus on has to be one of the four seasons of the year. It just means that we have to identify a unique and, often, recurring pattern (which could be the quarter, the month, the week, or the day) within the known period. Figure 7.6 zooms in on a seven-month span of the Wynn Resorts, Ltd., data. We make a statement concerning the seasonality component that is evident within that particular subset of the data.

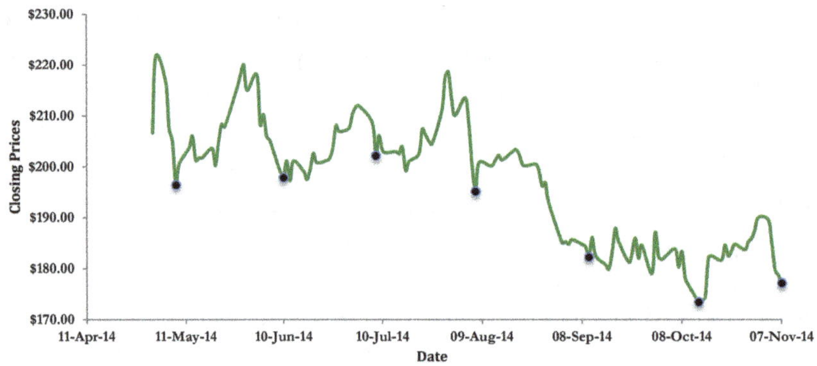

FIGURE 7.6 WYNN Closing Stock Prices

In the seven-month span, we observe that around the same time each month, there is a decrease in stock price for WYNN. Indicated by the dots in the Figure 7.6, these localized dips signify a predictable drop in prices. The dates corresponding to these dips are around the same time: May 8, June 10, July 8, August 7, September 10, October 13, and November 7. Hence, within this seven-month fixed time span, this notion of seasonality prevails, as we observe the same price decrease around the same time each month. Time series in general do not attempt to explain why the seasonal footprint is what it is. We just describe it and may offer an educated guess about factors that may underlie it.

Finally, the **random (or irregular) component** of a time series is the "wild child" of the series. It is the representation of the series that is unlikely to be repeated. Functioning much like an outlier, the random component is the one that cannot be explained by trend, cyclical, or seasonal fluctuations. There are no apparent random components noticeable in the WYNN data.

Example 7.8 Describe a real-life situation in which the plot of a time series could show a random component.

Solution 7.8 Suppose we were plotting daily ridership of passengers on a subway or train. If subway workers decided to strike, the ridership on days of the strike would fall to zero (no ridership). So the series would show a certain steady ridership (with some mild variation) and then all of a sudden drop to zero. Since zero ridership reflects something unpredictable (the strike), it would be the random component on the plot.

7.4.3 Smoothing with a Simple Moving Average

Now, we consider a different stock whose behavior varies from that of the WYNN stock we have been investigating up to this point. Remember, we observed an upward trend for the WYNN stock, as evidenced by Figure 7.4. Sometimes, however, we are not easily able to determine what the trend is for a given set of data. We take a look at a case in point.

Figure 7.7 shows a time series plot for daily closing stock prices for Google, Inc. (GOOG) from July 29, 2014 through September 15, 2014.

FIGURE 7.7 GOOG Closing Stock Prices

Source: http://goo.gl/EKI4lY

For example, the closing price for Google on July 29, 2014, was $585.61. Unlike the WYNN time series, where we are able to get a sense of the upward trend upon first glance, the GOOG time series does not reveal a sense of trend immediately. Sometimes, it is in fact the case where the overall trend in the series is not as apparent. In these instances, we rely on any of two **smoothing** techniques to assist us in discovering what the overall trend is.

Definition

To **smooth** *a time series is to reduce the effect of random variation (noise) in the data, revealing more clearly the underlying trend.*

The technique using the **simple moving average (SMA)** is one of the key techniques used to smooth a series and is the most basic. It involves determining a set window or span of data values in the series, adding specific values in the window, and dividing by the number of values in the window. Once we find the "first" average, we shift (or "move") the window to the next set of values of the same window size and find the "second" average. We continue "moving" the window and finding averages until there are no more data points left in the time series.

Definition

The smoothing technique using the **simple moving average (SMA)** *calculates indicator averages over a period of time and plots results as its own time series. For a fixed window size S, we compute a sequence of averages so that each average is calculated for a series of S observed values. We denote the moving averages by SMA(S).*

A smaller window size S tends to respond quickly to changes in the data, while larger values for S respond slower to changes in the data. The value for S will typically be given in a problem, but the analyst would have to determine his or her own value in real life, depending on what the goals of the analysis are.

To illustrate, we consider the Google data. Suppose we wish to impose a five-day moving average to the series. We are simply stating that the size of our window is five ($S = 5$). So we are tasked with performing an SMA(5). We present partial Google data in table form to show the SMA technique in action. Table 7.7 shows the first few closing stock prices for Google and the last few, excluding weekends and holidays.

TABLE 7.7 Partial Daily Stock Prices for Google, Inc. (July 29, 2014–September 15, 2014)

Date	Price
07/29	\$585.61
07/30	\$587.42
07/31	\$571.60
08/01	\$566.07
08/04	\$573.15
08/05	\$565.07
08/06	\$566.37

⋮

Date	Price
09/05	\$586.08
09/08	\$589.72
09/09	\$581.01
09/10	\$583.10
09/11	\$581.35
09/12	\$575.62
09/15	\$573.10

Since we have that $S = 5$, these moving averages require that the sequence of means comes from averaging the sequence of five consecutive daily values. First, we calculate the average that comes from taking the mean of the first five daily values in our Google data from the table:

$$\text{SMA}(5) = \frac{585.61 + 587.42 + 571.60 + 566.07 + 573.15}{5} = 576.77$$

Keeping the size of the window the same ($S = 5$), we slide or "move" the window down one position (or one day). This now means we find the average of five more daily values, the first four of which are the same values from the first average we found. As a general rule, we will use two decimal places. We now have:

$$\text{SMA}(5) = \frac{587.42 + 571.60 + 566.07 + 573.15 + 565.07}{5} = 572.66$$

Continuing the pattern, we next have:

$$\text{SMA}(5) = \frac{571.60 + 566.07 + 573.15 + 565.07 + 566.37}{5} = 568.45$$

We continue the process, moving the same-sized window down one data point at a time and recording the new average we get from the five appropriate daily data values. At the end of the entire SMA procedure, our final average, which comes from using the last five data values (September 9, 10, 11, 12, and 15), would be:

$$\text{SMA}(5) = \frac{581.01 + 583.10 + 581.35 + 575.62 + 573.10}{5} = 578.84$$

Since our window size is an odd number, we are prohibited from calculating moving averages for the first $(S - 1)/2$ days or the last $(S - 1)/2$ days. Since $S = 5$, we have that $(5 - 1)/2 = 2$. For this particular problem, this means we are not able to make calculations for the first two days (July 29 and 30) or the last two days (September 12 and 15) of the Google data.

More specifically, when we plot the SMA values that we calculated, we plot each value in a place that corresponds to the middle time point used to compute it. In other words, for the first SMA value, we took the averages of GOOG closing prices for the first five days: July 29, 30, 31, August 1, and 4. When we plot our first SMA value, which is \$576.77, we place its value in the SMA column of values in the middle of the time points used to calculate it, which is July 31. For the values that have no data in the SMA column, we use the placeholder of #N/A. This is the syntax that Excel understands when making the plot of the SMA column.

In fact, although we can do calculations by hand, as shown earlier, we generally use Excel to compute these moving averages as well as to plot the new series using moving averages. Figure 7.8 shows

	Date	GOOG Stock Price	SMA(5)
2	29-Jul-14	\$585.61	#N/A
3	30-Jul-14	\$587.42	#N/A
4	31-Jul-14	\$571.60	\$576.77
5	1-Aug-14	\$566.07	\$572.66
6	4-Aug-14	\$573.15	\$568.45
7	5-Aug-14	\$565.07	\$566.80
8	6-Aug-14	\$566.37	\$567.34
9	7-Aug-14	\$563.36	\$566.29
10	8-Aug-14	\$568.77	\$565.82
11	11-Aug-14	\$567.88	\$567.50
12	12-Aug-14	\$562.73	\$569.76
13	13-Aug-14	\$574.78	\$570.70
14	14-Aug-14	\$574.65	\$573.56
15	15-Aug-14	\$573.48	\$578.39
16	18-Aug-14	\$582.16	\$580.33
17	19-Aug-14	\$586.86	\$582.07
18	20-Aug-14	\$584.49	\$583.89
19	21-Aug-14	\$583.37	\$583.50
20	22-Aug-14	\$582.56	\$581.70
21	25-Aug-14	\$580.20	\$579.00
22	26-Aug-14	\$577.86	\$576.16
23	27-Aug-14	\$571.00	\$573.97
24	28-Aug-14	\$569.20	\$573.40
25	29-Aug-14	\$571.60	\$573.41
26	2-Sep-14	\$577.33	\$575.61
27	3-Sep-14	\$577.94	\$578.99
28	4-Sep-14	\$581.98	\$582.61
29	5-Sep-14	\$586.08	\$583.35
30	8-Sep-14	\$589.72	\$584.38
31	9-Sep-14	\$581.01	\$584.25
32	10-Sep-14	\$583.10	\$582.16
33	11-Sep-14	\$581.35	\$578.84
34	12-Sep-14	\$575.62	#N/A
35	15-Sep-14	\$573.10	#N/A

FIGURE 7.8 GOOG Data, SMA(5), and Time Series Plots

the original Google stock data, the new data using simple moving averages with $S = 5$, and plots of both series. At the end of this section, we discuss how to use Excel to produce the plots.

When we observe Figure 7.8, we note that the dotted line, which represents the SMA(5) plot, has no value plotted for the dates of July 29 and 30. As mentioned, this represents the fact that we begin plotting an SMA(5) in the middle time point in the window, the first of which occurs at July 31. This is why the first point of the smoothed series is plotted there. Similarly, the last point of the SMA(5) plot occurs two time points before the end or on September 11.

We also take note, as stated earlier, that the main purpose of using the SMA(5) is to reduce the effects of random variation or noise in the original data to give us a better sense of overall trend. Strictly looking at the original plot of the Google data in Figure 7.7, it is somewhat difficult to visualize what the overall trend is. Upon first glance, it seems as though there is an overall downward trend. The first data point of \$585.61 for July 29 and the last data point of \$573.10 for September 15 could suggest that the overall series is decreasing for the most part.

When we take a look at the plot of the SMA(5), however, the plot suggests a different conclusion. Contrary to what the last data point suggests, the overall trend using simple moving averages shows that the overall trend in the series is upward. The dotted lines give an overall sense of increasing as one observes from left to right. Such is the beauty of using techniques using simple moving averages. This technique serves as a magnifying glass for the original series and helps to determine information about trend that may not be as obvious when simply observing the original series by itself. Next, we discuss another technique, which is an adaptation of moving averages.

7.4.4 Smoothing with an Exponentially Weighted Moving Average

We can also smooth the series using the technique referred to as **exponentially weighted moving averages (EWMA)**, which is a unique spin on the SMA technique. In the EWMA technique, we assign decreasing weights to the values such that the higher weight is assigned to the most recent value and the lower weight to the older value. As the EWMA technique progresses, the contribution each data value has on the newest smoothed value decreases *exponentially*.

A major difference between the EWMA procedure and the SMA technique is that the EWMA technique analyzes data from the original series as well as previously smoothed EWMA values. This means that the contributions of old data are always in the mix when using the EWMA technique, whereas information from old data points is lost in the SMA technique once the moving window shifts. We speak more about that shortly. At this point, we supply an official definition of the EWMA procedure for smoothing series.

Definition

The smoothing technique using the **exponentially weighted moving average (EWMA)** *calculates weighted indicator averages from current values in the original series and from previously exponentially smoothed values. To find the exponentially smoothed series, we use the following algorithm:*

$$\text{EWMA}_0 = Y_0 \qquad \textbf{Equation 7.1}$$
$$\text{EWMA}_t = \lambda Y_t + (1 - \lambda)\text{EWMA}_{t-1} \quad t = 1, 2, 3 \ldots$$

where

$EWMA_t$ = *the exponentially smoothed value calculated at time t;*
$EWMA_{t-1}$ = *the exponentially smoothed valued calculated at time (t − 1);*
Y_t = *value of the original series at time t; and,*
λ = *assigned weight or smoothing coefficient (0 < λ < 1).*

The smoothing coefficient, λ (pronounced lambda), is the eleventh letter of the Greek alphabet. As stated in the definition, it is a value between zero and one and is the weight assigned to the values to be smoothed. This smoothing coefficient is somewhat subjective and depends on the goal of the analysis. Larger values for λ suggest that short-term, quick changes in the data will be more apparent in the analysis, while smaller values tend to highlight long-term changes in the data. In more business applications, many statisticians tend to choose values for λ that are less than or equal to 0.5 ($\lambda \leq 0.5$).

We illustrate how to smooth our Google stock data using the EWMA technique. Unlike the SMA technique, we do not need to specify the size of our window for the EWMA technique. The window size for this technique will always be a size of two. As indicated in Equation 7.1, we are only concerned with two pieces of data: one from the original series and one from the exponentially smoothed series. These two pieces of data are those that contribute to the window size of two. In this instance, we arbitrarily choose a λ value of 0.6. Hence, our task is to smooth or discover the trend in our data by performing an EWMA(λ = 0.6).

First, Equation 7.1 states that, in order to smooth using this technique, we must apply the following:

$$\text{EWMA}_0 = Y_0.$$

This means that the first smoothed data value that we are to use in the exponentially smoothed series is the first data value provided in the original Google series. The zeroes in the formula refer to when the time is zero ($t = 0$). When we apply this our GOOG data, this translates into finding:

$$\text{EWMA}_{\text{July 29}} = Y_{\text{July 29}}.$$

In other words, for our GOOG data, $t = 0$ translates into observing the data value corresponding to when zero time has passed, which is for the closing stock price for July 29. This gives us a value of 585.61, or:

$$\text{EWMA}_{\text{July 29}} = Y_{\text{July 29}} = 585.61.$$

This will always be the case for the EWMA technique. The first value in the exponentially smoothed series will *always* be the first value in the original series.

To understand the other part of Equation 7.1, we take a look at the original GOOG series (Y_t) alongside the exponentially smoothed series (EWMA_t) that we are calculating since we need both for this technique. We leave room to calculate the next three values in the latter series. Table 7.8 shows partial data of both of our series. Remember, the data for Y_t is the original GOOG data series from Table 7.7. We also recall that our smoothing parameter is 0.6. In the exponentially smoothed series, we fill in the first value that we just noted ($585.61). Finally, we insert an extra column to clarify which moment in time on which we are focusing in the data.

TABLE 7.8 Partial 2014 GOOG Data and Exponentially Smoothed Data (t = 0)

Date	Time	Y_t	EWMA(λ = 0.6)
July 29	$t = 0$	585.61	585.61
July 30	$t = 1$	587.42	–
July 31	$t = 2$	571.60	–
August 1	$t = 3$	566.07	–

To find the next value in the exponentially smoothed series, we focus on the second part of Equation 7.1, which states:

$$\text{EWMA}_t = \lambda Y_t + (1 - \lambda)\text{EWMA}_{t-1}.$$

For the first time period (t = 1), we find the exponentially smoothed value, which corresponds to the closing stock price for Google for July 30. Placing t = 1 into the formula for Equation 7.1, we have:

$$\begin{aligned} &\text{EWMA}_1 = \lambda Y_1 + (1 - \lambda)\text{EWMA}_{1-1} \\ \Rightarrow\ &\text{EWMA}_1 = \lambda Y_1 + (1 - \lambda)\text{EWMA}_0 \end{aligned}.$$

We can now substitute the specific date from our data into Equation 7.1 that corresponds to the appropriate t level that it represents. So, we have the following:

$$\text{EWMA}_{\text{July 30}} = \lambda Y_{\text{July 30}} + (1 - \lambda)\text{EWMA}_{\text{July 29}}$$

Since we have established that λ = 0.6, we find the exponentially smoothed value for July 30 as follows:

$$\begin{aligned} \text{EWMA}_{\text{July 30}} &= \lambda Y_{\text{July 30}} + (1 - \lambda)\text{EWMA}_{\text{July 29}} \\ &= (0.6)(587.42) + (1 - 0.6)(585.61) \\ &= 352.452 + (0.4)(585.61) \\ &= 352.452 + 234.244 \\ &= 586.70 \end{aligned}$$

So we fill in this value as the next exponentially smoothed value in Table 7.8 to reveal Table 7.9.

TABLE 7.9 Updated Partial 2014 GOOG Data and Exponentially Smoothed Data (t = 0, 1)

Date	Time	Y_t	EWMA(λ = 0.6)
July 29	$t = 0$	\$585.61	\$585.61
July 30	$t = 1$	\$587.42	\$586.70
July 31	$t = 2$	\$571.60	–
August 1	$t = 3$	\$566.07	–

To find the exponentially smoothed value for GOOG's closing stock price for July 31, we use Equation 7.1 but now for the second time period ($t = 2$). Notice that in order to find this new value, we have to use as part of the equation the value we just calculated and inserted into Table 7.9. Placing $t = 2$ into the formula for Equation 7.1, we have:

$$\begin{aligned} \text{EWMA}_2 &= \lambda Y_2 + (1 - \lambda)\text{EWMA}_{2-1} \\ \Rightarrow \text{EWMA}_2 &= \lambda Y_2 + (1 - \lambda)\text{EWMA}_1 \end{aligned}$$

Substituting the appropriate marking for the specific date into the equation that corresponds to the appropriate t level that it represents, we have the following:

$$\text{EWMA}_{\text{July 31}} = \lambda Y_{\text{July 31}} + (1 - \lambda)\text{EWMA}_{\text{July 30}}$$

Now, we find the exponentially smoothed value for July 31 as follows, remembering that the smoothing coefficient (λ) is still 0.6:

$$\begin{aligned} \text{EWMA}_{\text{July 31}} &= \lambda Y_{\text{July 31}} + (1 - \lambda)\text{EWMA}_{\text{July 30}} \\ &= (0.6)(571.60) + (0.4)(586.70) \\ &= 352.452 + (0.4)(585.61) \\ &= 342.96 + 234.68 \\ &= 577.64 \end{aligned}$$

So we fill in this value as the next exponentially smoothed value in Table 7.9 to reveal Table 7.10.

TABLE 7.10 Updated Partial 2014 GOOG Data and Exponentially Smoothed Data ($t = 0, 1, 2$)

Date	Time	Y_t	EWMA($\lambda = 0.6$)
July 29	$t = 0$	\$585.61	\$585.61
July 30	$t = 1$	\$587.42	\$586.70
July 31	$t = 2$	\$571.60	\$577.64
August 1	$t = 3$	\$566.07	–

Example 7.9 Using information from Table 7.10, find $\text{EWMA}_{\text{August 1}}$.

Solution 7.9 So we have:

$$\begin{aligned} \text{EWMA}_{\text{August 1}} &= \lambda Y_{\text{August 1}} + (1 - \lambda)\text{EWMA}_{\text{July 31}} \\ &= (0.6)(566.07) + (0.4)(577.64) \\ &= 339.642 + 231.056 \\ &= 570.70 \end{aligned}$$

Hence, the exponentially smoothed value for August 1 is \$570.70.

We can use Excel again to compute these exponentially smoothed averages as well as to plot the new series using exponentially weighted moving averages. Figure 7.9 shows the original GOOG data, the SMA(5), and the EWMA ($\lambda = 0.6$). At the end of this chapter, we provide further details on how to construct the entire EWMA-smoothed series. We remind that in the EWMA series, we do not place #N/A in any of the cells because there is no need to begin plotting in the middle of the moving-average window.

The three series in Figure 7.9 look a bit cluttered, but vital information is revealed in their plots, especially in the EWMA plot. We notice how the EWMA technique pinpoints when there is a particularly high or low GOOG stock value. For example, for August 4 and 19, the EWMA plot rises quickly above plot values of the SMA plot from the day before. This shows that the EWMA technique responds almost immediately to the sharp rise in the GOOG data on the preceding day. Likewise, for August 28, it falls sharply below SMA plot values from the day before. These indicate that the EWMA technique alerts quickly when there is an abrupt and immediate increase or decrease in the data. Finally, we see that the EWMA technique helps establish the trend for the GOOG data. Clearly, we see that the EWMA line suggests an overall upward trend in the data, which we may not have known by strictly observing the GOOG data alone.

	A	B	C	D
1	Date	GOOG Stock Price	SMA(5)	EWMA(λ=0.6)
2	29-Jul-14	$585.61	#N/A	$585.61
3	30-Jul-14	$587.42	#N/A	$586.70
4	31-Jul-14	$571.60	$576.77	$577.64
5	1-Aug-14	$566.07	$572.66	$570.70
6	4-Aug-14	$573.15	$568.45	$572.17
7	5-Aug-14	$565.07	$566.80	$567.91
8	6-Aug-14	$566.37	$567.34	$566.99
9	7-Aug-14	$563.36	$566.29	$564.81
10	8-Aug-14	$568.77	$565.82	$567.19
11	11-Aug-14	$567.88	$567.50	$567.60
12	12-Aug-14	$562.73	$569.76	$564.68
13	13-Aug-14	$574.78	$570.70	$570.74
14	14-Aug-14	$574.65	$573.56	$573.09
15	15-Aug-14	$573.48	$578.39	$573.32
16	18-Aug-14	$582.16	$580.33	$578.62
17	19-Aug-14	$586.86	$582.07	$583.57
18	20-Aug-14	$584.49	$583.89	$584.12
19	21-Aug-14	$583.37	$583.50	$583.67
20	22-Aug-14	$582.36	$581.70	$583.00
21	25-Aug-14	$580.20	$579.00	$581.32
22	26-Aug-14	$577.86	$576.16	$579.24
23	27-Aug-14	$571.00	$573.97	$574.30
24	28-Aug-14	$569.20	$573.40	$571.24
25	29-Aug-14	$571.60	$573.41	$571.46
26	2-Sep-14	$577.33	$575.61	$574.98
27	3-Sep-14	$577.94	$578.99	$576.76
28	4-Sep-14	$581.98	$582.61	$579.89
29	5-Sep-14	$586.08	$583.35	$583.60
30	8-Sep-14	$589.72	$584.38	$587.27
31	9-Sep-14	$581.01	$584.23	$583.52
32	10-Sep-14	$583.10	$582.16	$583.27
33	11-Sep-14	$581.35	$578.64	$582.12
34	12-Sep-14	$575.62	#N/A	$578.22
35	15-Sep-14	$573.10	#N/A	$575.15

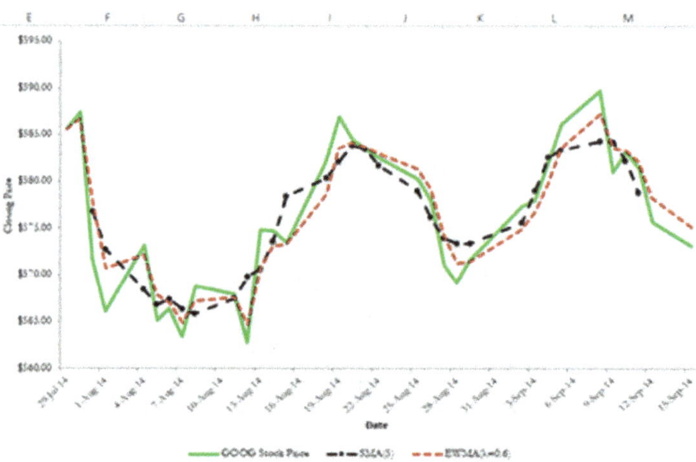

FIGURE 7.9 GOOG Data, SMA(5), and EWMA ($\lambda = 0.6$), and Their Plots

7.4.5 Forecasting Stock Prices with EWMA

In addition to smoothing, we are equally as interested in forecasting time series using special statistical techniques. Forecasting is the lifeblood of much of what statisticians do, especially if the data that is used in the analysis concerns a key topic (like the economy or health). For example, marketers forecast sales; financial analysts predict stock prices; and those who work for life insurance companies forecast deaths (uh oh!). No matter what the field, using statistical methods to forecast is a vital component of what makes industries succeed. Of course, no forecast is perfect, as there will always be situations that occur that are beyond companies' control. However, some measure of reliability is possible when predictions are based on history. We investigate two forecasting techniques in particular that are often used when predicting future values for time series. We first look at a slightly adjusted form of the exponential smoothing technique that we just learned. Then, we consider forecasting using a slightly adjusted form of regression techniques that we have also encountered already.

We have seen in the previous section how we use exponential smoothing to smooth a series or make more apparent the trend in a series. We are also able to use the same technique, with slight adjustment, in order to forecast or predict. We recall that we used Equation 7.1 to guide us in our quest to smooth a time series. In order to forecast into the next time period (or the *[t+1]*st time period), we tweak the second part of the equation slightly as follows:

$$\hat{Y}_{t+1} = \text{EWMA}_t$$

This means that, in order to forecast for one time period outside of our smoothed series, we substitute the value of $\hat{Y}_{t+1}$ everywhere that we have $EWMA_t$ and see what the new equation looks like. If data are given in days, we are able to predict data for the next day; if given in months, we are able to predict data for the next month. So we start with the equation with that which we are familiar, make the substitution, and see what results occur:

$$\begin{aligned} \text{EWMA}_t &= \lambda Y_t + (1-\lambda)\text{EWMA}_{t-1} \\ \Rightarrow \hat{Y}_{t+1} &= \lambda Y_t + (1-\lambda)\hat{Y}_{t+1-1} \left(\text{substitute EWMA}_t \text{ with } \hat{Y}_{t+1}\right) \\ \Rightarrow \hat{Y}_{t+1} &= \lambda Y_t + (1-\lambda)\hat{Y}_t \quad (\text{simplify}) \end{aligned}$$

This essentially says that the **forecasted value** is equal to the smoothing coefficient times the most recent data value plus the damping factor (discussed in the Excel section at the end of this Asset) times the most recently smoothed value. This most recently smoothed value simultaneously serves as the current forecasted value in the EWMA series. We state this formally in a definition and then apply to our Google data.

Definition

To ***forecast using EWMA****, we calculate the predicted value by using the most recent value in the original series and the most recently forecasted exponentially smoothed value. To find this forecasted value, we use the following:*

$$\hat{Y}_{t+1} = \lambda Y_t + (1-\lambda)\hat{Y}_t, \qquad \textbf{Equation 7.2}$$

where

$\hat{Y}_t$ = *the most recently EWMA-smoothed value (current forecast); and,*

$\hat{Y}_{t+1}$ = *the forecast for one time period outside of the given time series.*

If we consider the EWMA-smoothed series for the GOOG stock prices in Figure 7.9, we can use Equation 7.2 to predict the GOOG stock price for the day after the given data range. We see from Figure 7.9 that the most recent stock price for the GOOG data is recorded on September 15. On this day, the Google stock price is \$573.10. On this same day, the smoothed EWMA value is \$575.15.

Since the original data are given in days, we are able to predict the Google stock price for the day that logically comes next, which would be September 16. In order to predict the Google stock price for September 16, we apply Equation 7.2 using these previous values.

$$\begin{aligned} \hat{Y}_{t+1} &= \lambda Y_t + (1-\lambda)\hat{Y}_t \\ \Rightarrow \hat{Y}_{(\text{Sept }15)+1} &= \lambda Y_{\text{Sept }15} + (1-\lambda)\hat{Y}_{\text{Sept }15} \\ \Rightarrow \hat{Y}_{\text{Sept }16} &= \lambda Y_{\text{Sept }15} + (1-\lambda)\hat{Y}_{\text{Sept }15} \end{aligned}$$

Remember that t refers to time in the context of this problem, which is in increments of days. So $(t + 1)$ in this case means we are adding one increment to the most recent day that we are observing. If data were presented for each month, for example, and we were analyzing data that ended with the month of April, then $(t + 1)$ would mean we are adding one increment to the most recent month, which would be May. Hence, in that case, we would interpret $(t + 1)$ as (April + 1), which would be May. Now, we can follow through with our prediction, still using $\lambda = 0.6$, the two values for September 15 from Figure 7.9, and Equation 7.2:

$$\begin{aligned} \hat{Y}_{\text{Sept }16} &= \lambda Y_{\text{Sept }15} + (1-\lambda)\hat{Y}_{\text{Sept }15} \\ \Rightarrow \hat{Y}_{\text{Sept }16} &= (0.6)(573.10) + (0.4)(575.15) \\ \Rightarrow \hat{Y}_{\text{Sept }16} &= 343.86 + 230.06 \\ \Rightarrow \hat{Y}_{\text{Sept }16} &= 573.92 \end{aligned}$$

Hence, using the exponential smoothing method, we predict that the stock price for Google would be $573.92 for September 16.

7.4.6 Forecasting Stock Prices with Regression

Not only can we predict using the EWMA technique. We can also use a variation of the notion of regression to assist our efforts in forecasting the next time point in a time series. Equation 7.3 gives us the simple linear regression equation that we use to help us predict the value at one time point outside of our original series, which should look rather familiar to the formula discussed in Asset 6:

$$\hat{y} = mx + b \qquad \textbf{Equation 7.3}$$

We remember that in regression analysis, we calculate the value of the slope, m, and the y-intercept, b, to identify the particular regression equation we need in order to predict $\hat{y}$. We discover that we have to make a slight change as it relates to using the regression equation when forecasting a value in time series.

The main difference conceptually with a regular bivariate data set and a time series is that a bivariate set of data has no sense of time associated with it. For example, the x variable in a bivariate set of data could be number of hours studied. When analyzing this x variable, we use the numerical data as presented to analyze this variable in the grand scheme of things in regression. With time series, however, the x variable is always presented as some aspect of time (days, months, years, etc.). Since this is the case, we have to find a fair way of doing calculations on this new presentation of the x variable.

If data were presented in terms of months, for example, we are not able to put "June" into the equation and do calculations on it. We need to find a crafty way of transforming "June" into something that makes sense as it relates to Equation 7.3.

As a result, the solution to running a regression on a time series is to transform the x column in a special way to compensate for the fact that it should gauge the notion of time. Before we forecast, we come up with the best linear regression line that fits the time series by assigning an "alias" value of $x = 0$ for the first value of the time series. Irrespective of how the time series data is presented (days, months, etc.), we assign this initial value to the first point. After this, for every subsequent data value, we assign an "alias" value which increases by 1 from the initial value. Table 7.11 shows the x value, the transformed "alias" values for these x values, and the y values we need to find the regression line for the series (excluding holidays and weekends).

TABLE 7.11 Partial 2014 GOOG Time Series with Alias Values Inserted

Date	Alias Date Counter	Stock Price
July 29	0	$585.61
July 30	1	$587.42
July 1	2	$571.60
August 1	3	$566.07
August 4	4	$573.15
⋮	⋮	⋮
September 9	29	$581.01
September 10	30	$583.10
September 11	31	$581.35
September 12	32	$575.62
September 15	33	$573.10

We use the *Data Analysis ToolPak* in Excel to conduct our simple linear regression analysis. But the difference here is that we must use the Alias Date Counter column as our x column instead of the regular Date column. This helps to codify our original data into the form needed to perform the regression analysis. As expected, we continue to use the closing prices for Google as our y column. When we run the regression analysis, we get the partial Excel results shown in Figure 7.10. We discuss in the Excel Excitement section at the end of this chapter how we obtain these results.

	A	B	C	D	E	F
1	SUMMARY OUTPUT					
2						
3	*Regression Statistics*					
4	Multiple R	0.36504101				
5	R Square	0.13325494				
6	Adjusted R Square	0.10616915				
7	Standard Error	7.17432283				
8	Observations	34				
9						
10	ANOVA					
11		*df*	*SS*	*MS*	*F*	*Significance F*
12	Regression	1	253.2233458	253.2233	4.919737	0.033771285
13	Residual	32	1647.069057	51.47091		
14	Total	33	1900.292403			
15						
16		*Coefficients*	*Standard Error*	*t Stat*	*P-value*	*Lower 95%*
17	Intercept	571.8	2.407464177	237.514	1.59E-53	566.9025089
18	Alias Date Counter	0.278	0.125412576	2.218048	0.033771	0.022714066

FIGURE 7.10 **Partial Regression Results for GOOG Stock Prices**

From the Excel results, we observe our regression coefficients and obtain our least-squares regression equation, which becomes the forecasting equation that we will use to predict one time point into the future:

$$\hat{y} = 0.278x + 571.8 \qquad \textbf{Equation 7.4}$$

Before discussing how we forecast, we clarify the meaning of the slope and y-intercept in the context of time series. We recall in Asset 6 that we rendered specific interpretations for the meanings of these coefficients in a normal regression scenario. With respect to time series, however, we have to adapt what these coefficients mean in light of our GOOG data.

The slope in our forecasting equation is 0.278 ($m = 0.278 = 0.278 / 1$). We recall that the number in the denominator references information regarding the change in x, which is time in this case. The number in the numerator references information regarding the change in y, which is the price of Google stock. Hence, our interpretation of the slope is that, on average, the price of Google stock is predicted to increase by $0.28 every 1 day (since data are presented in days).

Our y-intercept is 571.8 ($b = 571.8$). We recall that our y-intercept occurs when $x = 0$. In our data, $x = 0$ always occurs when our alias value equals zero. In the GOOG data, this occurs during the first day that information is presented in our data, which is July 29. So the appropriate interpretation of our y-intercept is that the closing stock price for Google is predicted to be $571.80 for July 29.

Example 7.10 Suppose we have quarterly data beginning the first quarter of 2018. If x represents this quarterly notion of time and y represents closing stock prices for Facebook (FB), provide interpretations for the slope and y-intercept if the forecasting equation is:

$$\hat{y} = 99x + 226.$$

Solution 7.10 The slope is 99 ($m = 99 = 99 / 1$). Our interpretation of this slope is that FB stock prices are predicted to increase by \$99 every 1 quarter. The y-intercept is 226 ($b = 226$). Our interpretation of this y-intercept is that FB closing stock prices are predicted to be \$226 for the first quarter of 2018.

Our final task is to use our regression equation to assist us in predicting one day in the future for our data. We notice that our final data value given in our time series is for September 15. So our forecast using regression, as it was with predicting with EWMA, will be for predicting the Google closing stock price for September 16. In Table 7.11, we have shown partial Google data but with alias values to help normalize our data in some sense. The alias value for the last value is $x = 33$, according to the table, which corresponds to Google stock prices for September 15. This means that the value we wish to predict, Google stock prices for September 16, would naturally have an alias value of $x = 34$. In order to forecast Google stock prices for this day, we simply insert this alias value of $x = 34$ into Equation 7.4 from Excel and solve for $\hat{y}$.

$$\begin{aligned} \hat{y}(34) &= 0.278(34) + 571.8 \\ &= 581.25 \end{aligned}$$

Hence, using the least-squares forecasting equation, Google stock prices are predicted to be \$581.25 for September 16.

We note from the results in Figure 7.10 that we have a coefficient of determination value of 0.133 ($r^2 = 0.13$). At 13%, this statistic basically provides a sense of how well the regression line predicts Google stock prices. In this case, this percentage is not particularly comforting since it is notably less than 100%. Hence, this forecast of \$581.25 is not as reliable as one might hope since the percentage of variation in Google stock prices that is explained by the overall trend is terribly low. Nonetheless, we are able to use the forecasting equation to render a prediction because we have a forecasting equation and the appropriate alias x value.

Figure 7.11 illustrates our original GOOG time series with the forecasting (regression) line superimposed atop it. We place the forecasting equation, along with r^2, on the plot as well. Note that data points in the time series are spread pretty far away from the forecasting line. This contributes to why the r^2 value is so small at about 13%.

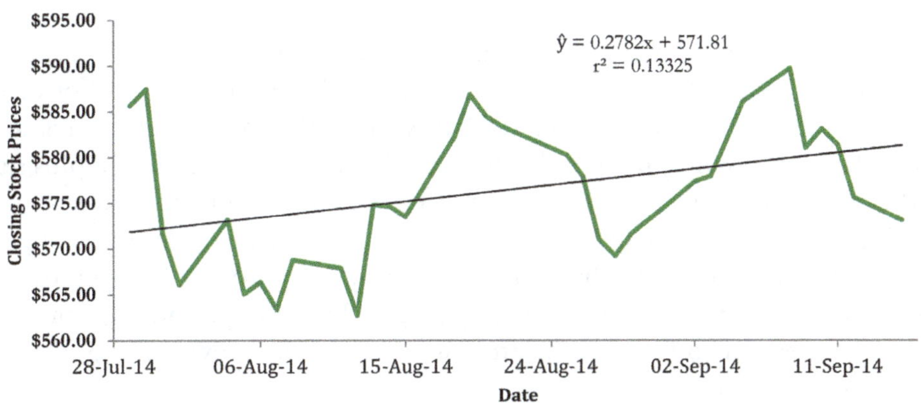

FIGURE 7.11 GOOG Time Series and Forecasting (Regression) Line

Example 7.11 Suppose we have quarterly data beginning the first quarter of 2018 and ends at the end of the year (four data values included in series). If x represents this quarterly notion of time and y represents Facebook (FB) closing stock prices, provide the predicted FB closing stock price for the first quarter of 2019 if the forecasting equation is: $\hat{y} = 99x + 226$.

Solution 7.11 For our data, our alias values go from $x = 0$ through $x = 3$, which correspond to the first quarter of 2018 through the fourth quarter of 2018. Since we are being asked to predict the FB closing stock price for the first quarter of 2019, we should solve the forecasting equation using the next alias value in sequence ($x = 4$).

$$\begin{aligned}\hat{y}(4) &= 99(4) + 226 \\ &= 622\end{aligned}$$

For the first quarter of 2019, we predict that the FB closing stock price will be \$622.

7.5 Time Series Analysis in Excel

7.5.1 Basic Time Series Plots

To illustrate a basic time series plot, we simply:

1. Arrange our data in column form with our time variable (x) placed in the left column and the observed value of the study (y) in the right column, along with their labels.
2. Next, we highlight all data, including labels.
3. At the top of the menu bar, click the *Insert* tab and then click the line graph icon, which is the icon above the pie chart:

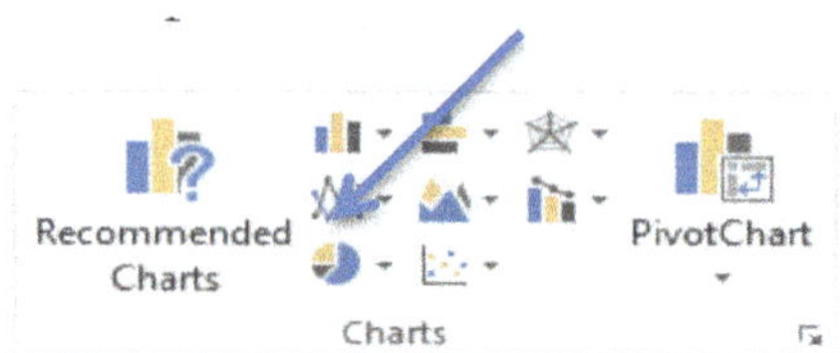

4. Click *More Line Charts*. Maneuver over the graph choices and select the graph that illustrates the time series to your liking, with or without dots. Choose *OK* at the bottom right.
5. In order to include horizontal and vertical axes, chart title, and legend, click anywhere in the diagram. A few icons will appear to the right of the diagram, including a plus sign. After clicking on the plus sign, a few chart elements will appear. Once you check boxes for *Axis Titles* and *Chart Titles*, you should manually enter the axis labels and chart title in the appropriate section of the figure. You can place the chart legend where you desire by checking the *Legend* box and then by clicking the arrow that appears to its right. This will provide options as to where you would like the legend to be placed. After tweaking to your own liking, the diagram should result in something close to Figure 7.4.

Sometimes, we want to have more than one time series to overlap each other, as seen in Figures 7.8 and 7.9. To produce such figures, we do the following:

1. Enter data as shown in Figures 7.8 and 7.9, having the time variable in the leftmost column and other columns to the right of it.
2. We simply highlight all data again, including labels.
3. We now follow instructions from number 3 in the previous section, in which we only have one time series to plot.

Finally, we can change the color, type, and thickness of the line that we would like in our figure. Excel has its own default, which shows the different lines as different colors. If we wish to change the details of line displayed, we do the following:

1. On the figure, click on the line whose physical properties are to be changed. The line should indicate that it is ready to be changed (often by the awakening of the dots on the line itself).
2. Right-click the line and choose *Format Data Series* from the menu that appears. The following menu will appear to the far right that looks as follows:

3. Click on the *Fill and Line* icon, which looks like a can of paint spilling its contents.
4. Scroll down and change the color, dash type, and width of the line by clicking the appropriate arrow next to the formatting description in which you are interested. Change to your liking.

7.5.2 Simple Moving Average

We can use the *Data Analysis ToolPak* to illustrate the smoothing technique using the simple moving average. If the *ToolPak* is missing from the Excel tool bar menu, follow instructions in Section 6.3 to load it. For SMA, we demonstrate how to create the SMA(5) column using the data for stock prices for Google from Figure 7.8 as our focal point:

1. Enter **Date** and **GOOG Stock Price** data labels in A1 and B1, respectively, along with the time and stock data in the appropriate columns.
2. Enter the **SMA(5)** label in C1.
3. After clicking on the *Data Analysis* tab, scroll down and click on the *Moving Average* option. Click *OK*.

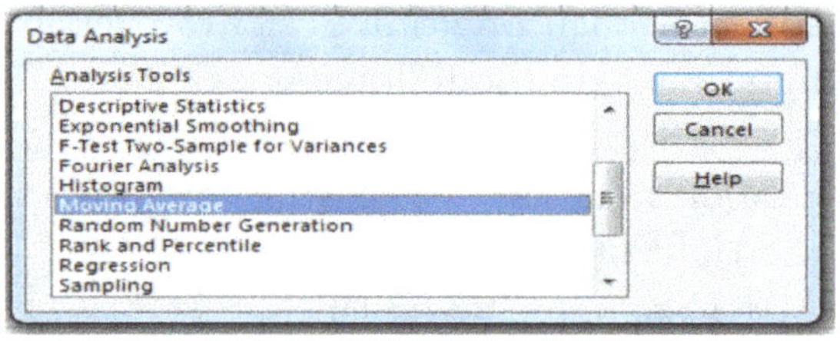

4. From here, we highlight cells containing the data for Google's stock prices (including the label) in for *Input Range*. Since we are including the heading with the data, we must check the box that says *Labels in First Row*. Since the size of our moving window is five time periods long, we place the number 5 in for *Interval*. If the size of the window were three time periods long, we would insert 3. While the cursor is in the field for *Output Range*, we click on cell C2. All values will immediately fall in line in appropriate cells beneath that one.

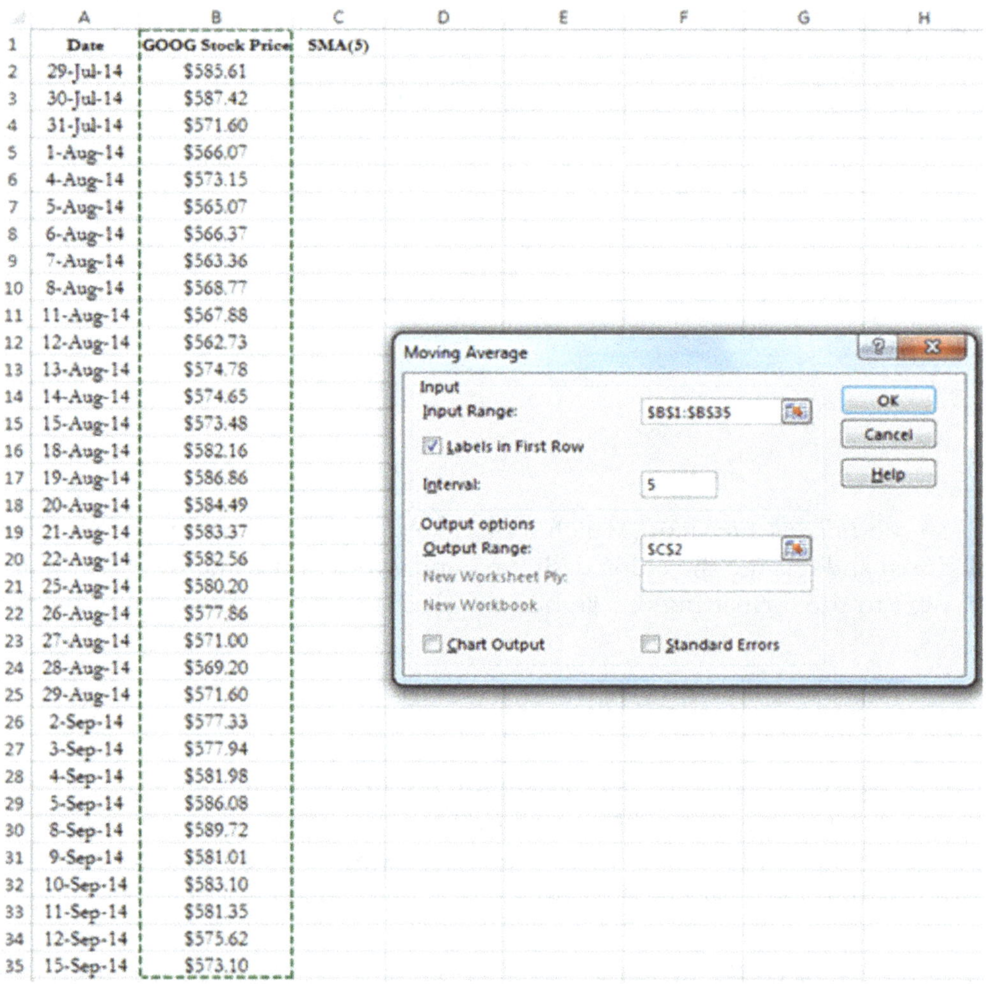

	A	B	C
1	Date	GOOG Stock Price	SMA(5)
2	29-Jul-14	$585.61	
3	30-Jul-14	$587.42	
4	31-Jul-14	$571.60	
5	1-Aug-14	$566.07	
6	4-Aug-14	$573.15	
7	5-Aug-14	$565.07	
8	6-Aug-14	$566.37	
9	7-Aug-14	$563.36	
10	8-Aug-14	$568.77	
11	11-Aug-14	$567.88	
12	12-Aug-14	$562.73	
13	13-Aug-14	$574.78	
14	14-Aug-14	$574.65	
15	15-Aug-14	$573.48	
16	18-Aug-14	$582.16	
17	19-Aug-14	$586.86	
18	20-Aug-14	$584.49	
19	21-Aug-14	$583.37	
20	22-Aug-14	$582.56	
21	25-Aug-14	$580.20	
22	26-Aug-14	$577.86	
23	27-Aug-14	$571.00	
24	28-Aug-14	$569.20	
25	29-Aug-14	$571.60	
26	2-Sep-14	$577.33	
27	3-Sep-14	$577.94	
28	4-Sep-14	$581.98	
29	5-Sep-14	$586.08	
30	8-Sep-14	$589.72	
31	9-Sep-14	$581.01	
32	10-Sep-14	$583.10	
33	11-Sep-14	$581.35	
34	12-Sep-14	$575.62	
35	15-Sep-14	$573.10	

Note that Excel places all four #N/A values in consecutive cells (B2 through B5). Hence, Excel provides results by placing SMA values in the last (fifth) position of the moving window, whereas we placed our values in the middle of the moving window when we did it by hand. So the SMA(5) results look like this at first:

	A	B	C
1	Date	GOOG Stock Price	SMA(5)
2	29-Jul-14	$585.61	#N/A
3	30-Jul-14	$587.42	#N/A
4	31-Jul-14	$571.60	#N/A
5	1-Aug-14	$566.07	#N/A
6	4-Aug-14	$573.15	$576.77
7	5-Aug-14	$565.07	$572.66
8	6-Aug-14	$566.37	$568.45
9	7-Aug-14	$563.36	$566.80
10	8-Aug-14	$568.77	$567.34
11	11-Aug-14	$567.88	$566.29
12	12-Aug-14	$562.73	$565.82
13	13-Aug-14	$574.78	$567.50
14	14-Aug-14	$574.65	$569.76
15	15-Aug-14	$573.48	$570.70
16	18-Aug-14	$582.16	$573.56
17	19-Aug-14	$586.86	$578.39
18	20-Aug-14	$584.49	$580.33
19	21-Aug-14	$583.37	$582.07
20	22-Aug-14	$582.56	$583.89
21	25-Aug-14	$580.20	$583.50
22	26-Aug-14	$577.86	$581.70
23	27-Aug-14	$571.00	$579.00
24	28-Aug-14	$569.20	$576.16
25	29-Aug-14	$571.60	$573.97
26	2-Sep-14	$577.33	$573.40
27	3-Sep-14	$577.94	$573.41
28	4-Sep-14	$581.98	$575.61
29	5-Sep-14	$586.08	$578.99
30	8-Sep-14	$589.72	$582.61
31	9-Sep-14	$581.01	$583.35
32	10-Sep-14	$583.10	$584.38
33	11-Sep-14	$581.35	$584.25
34	12-Sep-14	$575.62	$582.16
35	15-Sep-14	$573.10	$578.84

All this means is that we will have to manually remove two of the #N/A values from the top of the column and shift all SMA(5) values up two cells. We then transfer the last two #N/A values to the last two cells in the column. Essentially, we keep the #N/A values in the first two cells of the SMA(5) column (B2 and B3) and move the other two #N/A values to the last two cells since $S = 5$ (B34 and B35) to reveal the following:

	A	B	C
1	Date	GOOG Stock Price	SMA(5)
2	29-Jul-14	$585.61	#N/A
3	30-Jul-14	$587.42	#N/A
4	31-Jul-14	$571.60	$576.77
5	1-Aug-14	$566.07	$572.66
6	4-Aug-14	$573.15	$568.45
7	5-Aug-14	$565.07	$566.80
8	6-Aug-14	$566.37	$567.34
9	7-Aug-14	$563.36	$566.29
10	8-Aug-14	$568.77	$565.82
11	11-Aug-14	$567.88	$567.50
12	12-Aug-14	$562.73	$569.76
13	13-Aug-14	$574.78	$570.70
14	14-Aug-14	$574.65	$573.56
15	15-Aug-14	$573.48	$578.39
16	18-Aug-14	$582.16	$580.33
17	19-Aug-14	$586.86	$582.07
18	20-Aug-14	$584.49	$583.89
19	21-Aug-14	$583.37	$583.50
20	22-Aug-14	$582.56	$581.70
21	25-Aug-14	$580.20	$579.00
22	26-Aug-14	$577.86	$576.16
23	27-Aug-14	$571.00	$573.97
24	28-Aug-14	$569.20	$573.40
25	29-Aug-14	$571.60	$573.41
26	2-Sep-14	$577.33	$575.61
27	3-Sep-14	$577.94	$578.99
28	4-Sep-14	$581.98	$582.61
29	5-Sep-14	$586.08	$583.35
30	8-Sep-14	$589.72	$584.38
31	9-Sep-14	$581.01	$584.25
32	10-Sep-14	$583.10	$582.16
33	11-Sep-14	$581.35	$578.84
34	12-Sep-14	$575.62	#N/A
35	15-Sep-14	$573.10	#N/A

To perform this data shift, we delete the first two #N/A values, which provides room for the shift. We then highlight the rest of the data (including the #N/A values). We move the cursor atop the highlighted border until it changes form to look like a black cross instead of a white plus sign (different from the black cross that appears when we want to use the fill handle). From this point, click and drag so that all values move up two cells at the same time. Once we make that change, our final columns should look like the SMA(5) column in Figure 7.8.

Of course, we can create the plot itself using instructions stated in Section 7.5.1 or by clicking the box in the lower left that says *Chart Output*.

7.5.3 Exponentially Weighted Moving Average

For EWMA, to use the *ToolPak* would be somewhat counterproductive based on our explanation of the concept in this chapter. In our discussion, our first EWMA value is the same as our first Y value $(\text{EWMA}_0 = Y_0)$. However, when using the *ToolPak*, Excel assumes that $\text{EWMA}_1 = Y_0$. This assumption shifts results by one time position. Hence, there is one less final smoothed result presented using the *ToolPak* than when done in the manner presented in the text. To be consistent, we approach the EWMA technique in Excel using our own programming skills as opposed to using the *ToolPak*.

Using the *ToolPak*, however, is quite simple if you would like to explore. After clicking *Data Analysis*, choose *Exponential Smoothing* in the menu. Choose the original data as *Input Range*. For damping factor, be sure to put in the value of $1 - \alpha$ in for the damping factor. In the case of our GOOG stock data, we would put in the value of 0.4 for this value since our lambda is 0.6. Proceed as you normally would to see the results.

For our purposes, we follow these instructions to find our EWMA results:

1. We place **EWMA (λ=0.6)** as our label in cell D1.
2. In cell D2, we type the following: **=B2**
   This automatically assigns the same value in the EWMA column as the original Google data $(\text{EWMA}_0 = Y_0)$.
3. In cell D3, we type the formula as seen in the Excel sheet: **= 0.6 * B3 + 0.4 * D2**.
   This assigns a weight of 0.6 to the current Y value and a weight of 0.4 (or 1–0.6) to the EWMA value from the time period before.

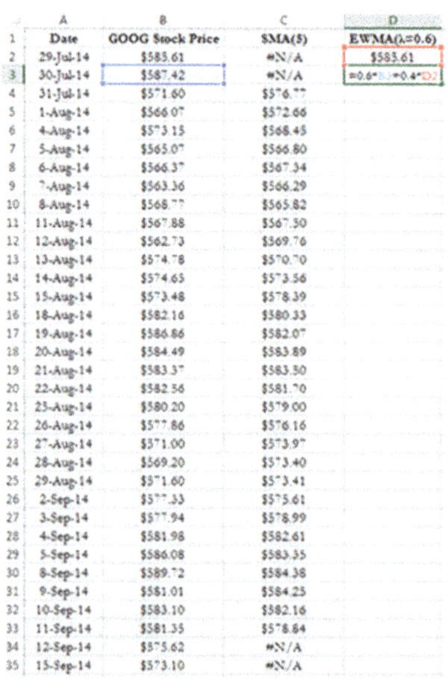

[illegible]	A	B	C	D
1	Date	GOOG Stock Price	SMA(5)	EWMA(λ=0.6)
2	29-Jul-14	$585.61	#N/A	$585.61
3	30-Jul-14	$587.42	#N/A	=0.6*[illegible]+0.4*D2
4	31-Jul-14	$571.60	$576.77	
5	1-Aug-14	$566.07	$572.66	
6	4-Aug-14	$573.15	$568.45	
7	5-Aug-14	$565.07	$566.80	
8	6-Aug-14	$566.37	$567.34	
9	7-Aug-14	$563.36	$566.29	
10	8-Aug-14	$568.77	$565.82	
11	11-Aug-14	$567.88	$567.50	
12	12-Aug-14	$562.73	$569.76	
13	13-Aug-14	$574.78	$570.70	
14	14-Aug-14	$574.65	$573.56	
15	15-Aug-14	$573.48	$578.39	
16	18-Aug-14	$582.16	$580.33	
17	19-Aug-14	$586.86	$582.07	
18	20-Aug-14	$584.49	$583.89	
19	21-Aug-14	$583.37	$583.50	
20	22-Aug-14	$582.56	$581.70	
21	25-Aug-14	$580.20	$579.00	
22	26-Aug-14	$577.86	$576.16	
23	27-Aug-14	$571.00	$573.97	
24	28-Aug-14	$569.20	$573.40	
25	29-Aug-14	$571.60	$573.41	
26	2-Sep-14	$577.33	$575.61	
27	3-Sep-14	$577.94	$578.99	
28	4-Sep-14	$581.98	$582.61	
29	5-Sep-14	$586.08	$583.35	
30	8-Sep-14	$589.72	$584.38	
31	9-Sep-14	$581.01	$584.25	
32	10-Sep-14	$583.10	$582.16	
33	11-Sep-14	$581.35	$578.84	
34	12-Sep-14	$575.62	#N/A	
35	15-Sep-14	$573.10	#N/A	

4. Once we press Enter, we have the correct EWMA value in that cell. Once we grab the fill handle and scroll to cell D35, we now have all smoothed EWMA values. We should see all values that are presented in Figure 7.9. We can create the plot itself using instructions stated in Section 7.5.1.

7.5.4 Forecasting Techniques

EWMA Methods

To forecast with exponential smoothing, remember that we use the original data value and the exponentially smoothed value for the current year. In Excel, this is an easy, one-step task. Using the basic information in Figure 7.9, we enter **16-Sep-14** in cell A37. This becomes the time point for which we wish to predict. In cell D37, we enter the following prediction formula using the previous lambda values and the two values for 15-Sep-14: **= 0.6 * B35 + 0.4 * D35**. Once we press Enter, we obtain the EWMA prediction given in Section 7.4.5 in the text (573.92).

	A	B	C	D
1	Date	GOOG Stock Price	SMA(5)	EWMA(λ=0.6)
2	29-Jul-14	$585.61	#N/A	$585.61
3	30-Jul-14	$587.42	#N/A	$586.70
4	31-Jul-14	$571.60	$576.77	$577.64
5	1-Aug-14	$566.07	$572.66	$570.70
6	4-Aug-14	$573.15	$568.45	$572.17
7	5-Aug-14	$565.07	$566.80	$567.91
8	6-Aug-14	$566.37	$567.34	$566.99
9	7-Aug-14	$563.36	$566.29	$564.81
10	8-Aug-14	$568.77	$565.82	$567.19
11	11-Aug-14	$567.88	$567.50	$567.60
12	12-Aug-14	$562.73	$569.76	$564.68
13	13-Aug-14	$574.78	$570.70	$570.74
14	14-Aug-14	$574.65	$573.56	$573.09
15	15-Aug-14	$573.48	$578.39	$573.32
16	18-Aug-14	$582.16	$580.33	$578.62
17	19-Aug-14	$586.86	$582.07	$583.57
18	20-Aug-14	$584.49	$583.89	$584.12
19	21-Aug-14	$583.37	$583.50	$583.67
20	22-Aug-14	$582.56	$581.70	$583.00
21	25-Aug-14	$580.20	$579.00	$581.32
22	26-Aug-14	$577.86	$576.16	$579.24
23	27-Aug-14	$571.00	$573.97	$574.30
24	28-Aug-14	$569.20	$573.40	$571.24
25	29-Aug-14	$571.60	$573.41	$571.46
26	2-Sep-14	$577.33	$575.61	$574.98
27	3-Sep-14	$577.94	$578.99	$576.76
28	4-Sep-14	$581.98	$582.61	$579.89
29	5-Sep-14	$586.08	$583.35	$583.60
30	8-Sep-14	$589.72	$584.38	$587.27
31	9-Sep-14	$581.01	$584.25	$583.52
32	10-Sep-14	$583.10	$582.16	$583.27
33	11-Sep-14	$581.35	$578.84	$582.12
34	12-Sep-14	$575.62	#N/A	$578.22
35	15-Sep-14	$573.10	#N/A	$575.15
36				
37	16-Sep-14			=0.6*B35+0.4*D35

Regression Methods

To forecast using linear trend forecasting, we revisit our procedures for obtaining the Excel results in Figure 7.10.

1. Enter the following GOOG data as shown. Note that an additional column labeled **Alias Date Counter** has been inserted between the dates and Google stock prices. Recall that this is necessary so that we can quantify the notion of time as it is presented in terms of days in this case.

	A	B	C
1	**Date**	**Alias Date Counter**	**GOOG Stock Price**
2	29-Jul-14	0	$585.61
3	30-Jul-14	1	$587.42
4	31-Jul-14	2	$571.60
5	1-Aug-14	3	$566.07
6	4-Aug-14	4	$573.15
7	5-Aug-14	5	$565.07
8	6-Aug-14	6	$566.37
9	7-Aug-14	7	$563.36
10	8-Aug-14	8	$568.77
11	11-Aug-14	9	$567.88
12	12-Aug-14	10	$562.73
13	13-Aug-14	11	$574.78
14	14-Aug-14	12	$574.65
15	15-Aug-14	13	$573.48
16	18-Aug-14	14	$582.16
17	19-Aug-14	15	$586.86
18	20-Aug-14	16	$584.49
19	21-Aug-14	17	$583.37
20	22-Aug-14	18	$582.56
21	25-Aug-14	19	$580.20
22	26-Aug-14	20	$577.86
23	27-Aug-14	21	$571.00
24	28-Aug-14	22	$569.20
25	29-Aug-14	23	$571.60
26	2-Sep-14	24	$577.33
27	3-Sep-14	25	$577.94
28	4-Sep-14	26	$581.98
29	5-Sep-14	27	$586.08
30	8-Sep-14	28	$589.72
31	9-Sep-14	29	$581.01
32	10-Sep-14	30	$583.10
33	11-Sep-14	31	$581.35
34	12-Sep-14	32	$575.62
35	15-Sep-14	33	$573.10

2. After clicking on the *Data Analysis* tab, scroll down and click on the *Regression* option. Click *OK*.

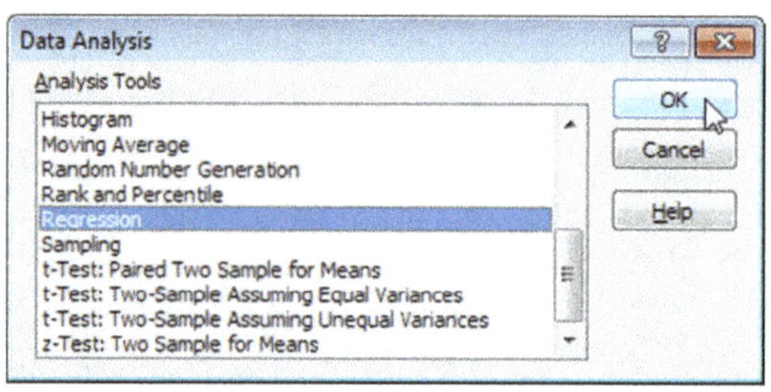

3. Now, you are ready to place data from your **Alias Date Counter** column (x) and **GOOG Stock Price** column (y) into the appropriate fields. After clicking *OK*, the following screen should appear:

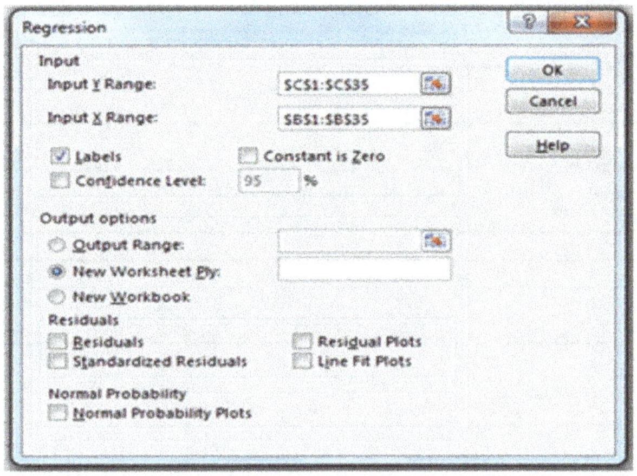

   a. Once you see the screen above, place the cursor in the field that says *Input Y Range.*
   b. In your Excel spreadsheet, highlight the column of cells for data values that correspond to your dependent (y) variable (including the column heading). In this case, it would be the **GOOG Stock Price** column.
   c. Now, place the cursor in the field that says *Input X Range.*
   d. In your Excel spreadsheet, highlight the column of cells for the newly created **Alias Date Counter** column, which corresponds to your independent (x) variable (including the column heading).
   e. Click the box that says *Labels* since you included the headings in each column. Click *OK.* The results should be revealed on a new Excel spreadsheet. If you'd like, you can view your data by clicking on *Sheet 1* at the bottom of the Excel sheet. In this case, your results should look like that in Figure 7.10.

4. To predict, we choose any arbitrary cell, say A21, and type the formula for the regression equation $\left(\hat{y} = mx + b\right)$ in Excel with the appropriate value of x entered to reflect the next time point. In this case, we type the following formula:

   = B18 * 34 + B17

   The value for B18 corresponds to the slope (m). The value for B17 corresponds to the y-intercept. Note that the x value we use in our prediction will *always* be one more than the value given for the intersection of the **Total** row and the **Df** column in the Excel results (Figure 7.10). In our case, this value corresponds to 34 (33 + 1), which is one time period in the future for the original data series.

	A	B	C	D	E	F
1	SUMMARY OUTPUT					
2						
3	*Regression Statistics*					
4	Multiple R	0.365041008				
5	R Square	0.133254938				
6	Adjusted R Square	0.106169155				
7	Standard Error	7.174322828				
8	Observations	34				
9						
10	ANOVA					
11		*df*	*SS*	*MS*	*F*	*Significance F*
12	Regression	1	253.2233458	253.2233	4.919737	0.033771285
13	Residual	32	1647.069057	51.47091		
14	Total	33	1900.292403			
15						
16		*Coefficients*	*Standard Error*	*t Stat*	*P-value*	*Lower 95%*
17	Intercept	571.8	2.407464177	237.514	1.59E-53	566.9025089
18	Alias Date Counter	0.278	0.125412576	2.218048	0.033771	0.022714066
19						
20						
21	=B18*34+B17					

Once we press Enter, we obtain the regression prediction given in Section 7.4.6 in the text (581.25).

Money Talk

Do You Have a Will or a Won't?

Although the topic of having a will is an emotional and touchy subject, you would have to consider what would happen to your assets if there are no specific details about who receives them once you pass away. It would be a sad sight for you to have planned for retirement all of your life and made sure your portfolio was diverse over the years, only for the end result to be that your assets are divvied up according to state law.

A *DailyFinance* contributor found that younger people (18–34) are more likely to be concerned about maintaining their weight than protecting their financial assets (Nance-Nash 2011). And young people are not the only ones neglecting such important financial matters as indicated earlier. The reasons most people admit to not preparing for or planning a will vary. As reported by Rocket Lawyer, a website that offers reasonably priced legal services, several of the reasons include (Eisenberg 2014):

- Some felt as though making a will was not urgent.
- A few didn't think they needed a will.
- Some didn't have a will because they didn't like thinking about death.

The truth of the matter is that life continues to march on whether you acknowledge it or not. A few moments of being uncomfortable as related to estate planning outweigh a lifetime of pain that comes with neglecting such a responsibility of planning the direction your possessions will go. When preparing a will, then, you should consider two of many types, which you should put in writing and have notarized: a living will and an attested will.

A living will, signed by the owner, informs doctors and health staff how you should be treated in the event that you become incapacitated from unfortunate events. Families often struggle with this type of scenario—where the family member unconsciously lies on life support. Tension often builds because some family members want to "pull the plug" while others do not, believing a miracle of God may occur. If you specify that you would prefer a do-not-resuscitate (DNR) order, you remove the pressure and guilt from family members as it relates to your wishes in that regard and give hospitals the go-ahead to remove you from life support. Or if you prefer not to have a DNR order, then medical staff knows that as well. In a nutshell, writing and communicating your desires in this vein will only serve to help the situation in the event that things in your life go awry.

The attested will is the most common and arguably the most important. This, the more traditional will, must be signed by the owner as well as by at least one witness. This will expresses how one's property should be dispersed after one's passing. Details may be included for something as "trivial" as a picture hanging on the wall to the vintage Cadillac to the mansion on the hill. This will can be as specific as the owner wishes. In fact, the more detailed, the better. As a part of a new age of information, you are encouraged more and more to consider how you will account for and distribute your digital estate. We're not just talking about your Facebook and Twitter accounts and passwords associated with them; but more people nowadays have accounts that are strictly online. Without the owner's foresight to leave such information known (website URLs, usernames, passwords, etc.) via a will, no one will know how to access them or even know they exist. You should write down websites for all accounts and their access information, decide how assets therein (cash, shares, etc.) should be distributed, and make them a part of your official will.

Finally, establishing a will is not as daunting as you might expect. Sure, if you use the services of a lawyer, you may expect to pay a pretty penny (between $300 and $1200). For those who have very basic assets and beneficiaries, however, it is possible to devise a will without an attorney. Those who have modest incomes can gain legal assistance in this regard free or at no cost through local legal groups or student-run efforts at law schools. The American Bar Association (http://goo.gl/pX9Gs) provides further details concerning such services in your own particular region. In addition, several businesses offer affordable estate-planning services online at very little cost. For example, you can complete a short form for your will for less than $10 online at LegalDocs (http://goo.gl/xH9YrW).

Wills should be kept with an attorney, and the will's owner should inform a family member as to the name of the attorney with whom the will is retained. This should make the execution of the will somewhat seamless, as far as it pertains to logistics concerning obtaining the official version of it. Following these steps should help with producing the will and getting to a place where it may be executed.

So, here's to hoping you live well into your 100s! If not, however, at least you will have the comfort and reassurance in knowing that your assets will go to the right persons or charities that you have requested.

Refrain from having a "won't." Get a will.

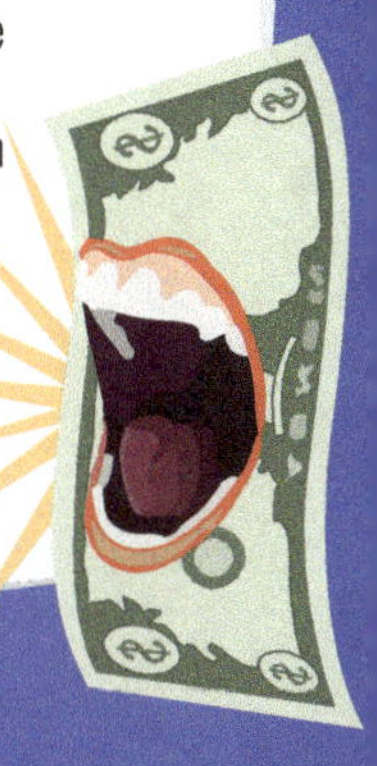

Student Exercises: Stocks and Time Series

7.1 Consider the following and solve:

a. Assume that the Microsoft (MSFT) stock had a closing price of $48.03 per share. If you ended up with a total of 24 shares, how much did you pay altogether to acquire those shares (assume there were no other fees or commissions)?

b. Assume you have $775 to invest in Hershey (HSY) stock. If the cost of the stock is $39 per share, how many shares do you acquire if you use all of your money to purchase shares?

7.2 Consider the URL: https://goo.gl/iQDnUd. Locate the figure titled "Growth of $10,000 from 1988 to 2008," and answer the following.

a. Which time period indicates a bear market? There may be more than one.

b. Which time period indicates a bull market? There may be more than one.

7.3 Consider the following and solve:

a. Melody's retirement portfolio was valued at $109,000. If it decreased by 5.7%, what was the new value of her portfolio?

b. A stock's price grew from $38.12 to $48.27. What percent increase is represented by this growth?

7.4 Cosmo, a 30-year-old manager at Bvlgari, has $29,000 on hand to invest right now for his retirement. Using Table 7.2, determine how much of his money would fund each of the three investment categories, according to Vanguard's suggested asset-allocation model.

a. Dollar amount to be invested in stocks

b. Dollar amount to be invested in bonds

c. Dollar amount to be invested in short-term reserves

7.5 Partial data are given below for daily sales for a popular shoe brand, along with a five-day simple moving average:

Day	Shoe Sales	SMA(5)
Monday	$7388	#N/A
Tuesday	$9344	#N/A
Wednesday	$4887	?
Thursday	$7190	$9921.33
Friday	$11,987	#N/A
Saturday	?	#N/A

a. Determine the SMA(5) value for Wednesday.

b. Determine shoe sales for Saturday. (Hint: We solve by working backward to find specific values in the shoe sales column using the average of certain values in the SMA(5) column.)

7.6 Go to http://goo.gl/jlw4. Decide on a date for which you will complete this problem. Answers need to come from the same date so that the PPS is comparable. You will only be able to solve this problem with data on the actual day you visit the website (after 4:00 pm). You will need to observe stock behavior for three stocks on one specific current date.

(i) Tiffany & Co. (TIF)
(ii) Chipotle Mexican Grill, Inc. (CMG)
(iii) The New York Times Co. (NYT)

a. Complete the following table for each of the three stocks:

Stock	Closing Price per Share (PPS)	Earnings per Share (EPS)	P/E Ratio
TIF	–	–	–
CMG	–	–	–
NYT	–	–	–

b. Explain how the three values for each stock are related to each other. Verify your answer using the Chipotle stock. In other words, calculate the value in one column based on values from other columns.
c. Based only on the information provided in the chart, which of the three stocks is the best one to purchase? Why?
d. Complete the following table for each of the three stocks:

Stock	PEG Ratio
TIF	–
CMG	–
NYT	–

e. Based only on the information provided in the new chart, which of the three stocks is the best one to purchase? Why?

7.7 Despite the economic and financial challenges young adults have braved since the recession, the millennial generation represented the largest share of recent buyers, according to the *2015 National Association of Realtors Home Buyer and Seller Generational Trends* study, which evaluates the generational differences of recent buyers and sellers. The survey additionally found that an overwhelming majority of buyers search for homes online and then purchase through a real estate agent, with millennials using agents the most.

For the second consecutive year, NAR's study found that the largest group of recent buyers was the millennial generation, those 34 and younger, who composed 32% of all buyers (31% in 2013). Generation X, ages 35–49, was closely behind with a 27% share. Millennial buyers represented more than double the amount of younger boomer (ages 50–59) and older boomer (60–68) buyers (at 31%). The Silent Generation (ages 69–89) made up 10% of buyers in the past year.

With millennials entering the peak buying period and expected to soon surpass boomers in total population, Lawrence Yun, NAR chief economist, believes the share of millennial purchases would be higher if not for the numerous obstacles that have slowed their journey to homeownership. "Many millennials have endured underemployment and subpar wage growth, and rising rents and repaying student debt have made it very difficult to save for a down payment. For some, even forming households of their own has been a challenge" (*National Association of Realtors* 2015).

The following data show the total number of houses sold in the United States from 1963 to 2015. Data are provided in thousands. Hence, the 1963 value of 560 means that 560,000 homes were sold during that year. Data were retrieved from the US Census Bureau at https://goo.gl/r9rmf7.

Year	Homes Sold	Year	Homes Sold	Year	Homes Sold	Year	Homes Sold
1964	565	1977	819	1990	534	2003	1086
1965	575	1978	817	1991	509	2004	1203
1966	461	1979	709	1992	610	2005	1283
1967	487	1980	545	1993	666	2006	1051
1968	490	1981	436	1994	670	2007	776
1969	448	1982	412	1995	667	2008	485
1970	485	1983	623	1996	757	2009	375
1971	656	1984	639	1997	804	2010	323
1972	718	1985	688	1998	886	2011	306
1973	634	1986	750	1999	880	2012	368
1974	519	1987	671	2000	877	2013	429
1975	549	1988	676	2001	908	2014	437
1976	646	1989	650	2002	973	2015	501

a. Perform an EWMA($\lambda = 0.8$) using the housing data, showing the appropriate column of results.
b. Show plots of the original housing data and the EWMA($\lambda = 0.8$).
c. Discuss what the EWMA($\lambda = 0.8$) reveals about the trend in the housing data.

7.8 Enjoying those prices at the pump? You might not want to get used to them, especially if you're on a tight budget. A former top oil executive says the price of gas at the pump could double by the end of 2015. In an interview with CNBC, former Shell Oil President John Hofmeister predicts that US oil could skyrocket from the currently levels under \$48 a barrel to \$80 by this fall, just as consumers are getting used to the windfall from lower gas prices. That would force gas prices to double. The reason, he says, is the oil companies are masters of the simple economics of supply and demand. He predicts gas prices could pass the \$3-a-gallon range in September and October (of 2015). By December and next January, he says, gas prices will be nearing $4 a gallon. Looking further into the future, the former oil executive sees prices rising to "$5 gasoline in the United States as we approach the end of the decade. Whoever is the next president must look at the needs of the nation 20–30 years down the road," he added. He says that unless the United States reduces oil consumption, "we will face inevitable and perpetual volatility in oil, especially as we approach the end of the decade" (Gillies 2015).

The following data show average retail fuel prices (approximately 3 months leading up to reported month) in the United States from July 3, 2007 to January 1, 2016. Data were retrieved from the Alternative Fuel Data Center of the Department of Energy (http://goo.gl/UtkFP).

Month/ Year	Gas Price	Month/ Year	Gas Price	Month/Year	Gas Price
10/2008	\$3.04	04/2011	\$3.69	10/2013	\$3.45
01/2009	\$1.86	07/2011	\$3.68	01/2014	\$3.34
04/2009	\$2.02	09/2011	\$3.46	04/2014	\$3.65
07/2009	\$2.44	01/2012	\$3.37	07/2014	\$3.70
10/2009	\$2.64	03/2012	\$3.89	10/2014	\$3.34
01/2010	\$2.65	07/2012	\$3.52	01/2015	\$2.30
04/2010	\$2.84	09/2012	\$3.82	04/2015	\$2.42
07/2010	\$2.71	01/2013	\$3.29	07/2015	\$2.82
10/2010	\$2.78	03/2013	\$3.59	10/2015	\$2.35
01/2011	\$3.08	07/2013	\$3.65	01/2016	\$1.98

a. With or without Excel, perform an SMA(3) using the pricing data, showing the appropriate column of results. Be sure to place the right number of #N/A values in the correct locations.
b. With or without Excel, perform an EWMA($\lambda = 0.7$) using the fuel data, showing the appropriate column of results.
c. Show time series plots of the original fuel data, the SMA(3), and the EWMA($\lambda = 0.7$).
d. Between the SMA(3) and the EWMA($\lambda = 0.7$), which of the two smoothers seems to respond quicker to sharp increases or decreases in the original pricing data? Explain with specific information in the data.

7.9 Partial data are given for the number of customers who visited the Museum of American Finance one day. Visits were recorded on an hourly basis. Shown too is an EWMA-smoothed column with $\lambda = 0.4$.

Time	Museum Visitors	$EWMA_t(0.4)$
2:00pm–3:00pm	25	25
3:00pm–4:00pm	24	?

Time	Museum Visitors	$EWMA_t(0.4)$
4:00pm–5:00pm	36	29.16
5:00pm–6:00pm	?	33.90
6:00pm–7:00pm	12	25.14
7:00pm–8:00pm	–	?

a. From the data provided, determine the EWMA value for the number of museum visitors between 3:00pm and 4:00pm.
b. From the data provided, determine the approximate number of museum visitors from 5:00pm to 6:00pm. Round to the nearest visitor.
c. Forecast the approximate number of museum visitors from 7:00pm to 8:00pm using EWMA techniques. Round to the nearest visitor.

7.10 Suppose you were hired to analyze the number of tweets that occurred per minute for the car seat gap filler product during a television segment on QVC. Data collection of sales started from 9:00pm and ended at 9:30pm (i.e., 9:00 to 9:01, 9:01 to 9:02, etc.). After viewing the data, you ran a regression on it and found the following regression equation:

$$\hat{y} = 938x + 5710$$

a. State the slope in the regression equation and discuss what it means in the context of the QVC data.
b. State the y-intercept in the regression equation and discuss what it means in the context of the QVC data.
c. Using regression techniques, forecast the number of tweets expected to occur from 9:30pm to 9:31pm.

7.11 The Goldman Sachs Group, Inc. is a leading global investment banking, securities, and investment management firm that provides a wide range of financial services to a substantial and diversified client base that includes corporations, financial institutions, governments, and high-net-worth individuals. Founded in 1869, the firm is headquartered in New York and maintains offices in all major financial centers around the world.

The following data show the evolution of closing stock prices of Goldman Sachs from 2004 to 2014 as of year end, as quoted on the NASDAQ Stock Exchange. Data were retrieved from Statista: The Statistics Portal (http://goo.gl/BUenFB).

Year	Closing Price
2004	$104.04
2005	$127.71
2006	$199.35
2007	$215.05

Year	Closing Price
2008	$84.39
2009	$168.84
2010	$168.16
2011	$90.43
2012	$127.56
2013	$177.26
2014	$193.83
2015	$180.23
2016	$239.45

a. Perform an EWMA($\lambda = 0.3$) using the Goldman Sachs data, showing the appropriate column of results.
b. Forecast the Goldman Sachs closing price for 2017 using EWMA techniques (same λ value).
c. Perform a regression on the Goldman Sachs data, and state the forecasting equation.
d. Using regression techniques, forecast the Goldman Sachs closing price for 2017.
e. State the coefficient of determination (r^2), and state its interpretation in the context of the Goldman Sachs data.

References

Eisenberg, Richard. "Americans' Ostrich Approach to Estate Planning." *Next Avenue*, April 8, 2014. Accessed May 22, 2015. http://goo.gl/7PlxKj.

Gillies, T. "Here Today, Up Tomorrow: Why Gas Prices May Be on the Rise." *CNBC: On the Money*, February 1, 2015. Accessed April 7, 2015. http://goo.gl/XU0iBX.

Nance-Nash, Sheryl. "Why More Than Half of Americans Don't Have Wills." *DailyFinance*, August 26, 2011. Accessed May 22, 2015. http://goo.gl/JfVqK.

National Association of Realtors. *NAR Generational Survey: Millennials Lead All Buyers, Most Likely to Use Real Estate Agent* [News Release], 2015. http://goo.gl/bKR1XK.

Wohlner, R. "Investment Diversification—A Look at the Basics." *The Chicago Financial Planner*, March 13, 2013. Accessed May 16, 2015. http://goo.gl/n99bWS.

Solutions to Odd-Numbered Student Exercises

Asset One

1.1 **a.** $-\frac{7}{8}+\frac{5}{6}=-\frac{21}{24}+\frac{20}{24}=-\frac{1}{24}$

b. $-7\times 9\frac{1}{3}=-\frac{7}{1}\times\frac{28}{3}=-\frac{196}{3}=-65\frac{1}{3}$

c. $-3.11-(-4.6)=-3.11+4.6=1.49$

d. $\frac{4}{5}\div\frac{3}{10}=\frac{4}{5}\times\frac{10}{3}=\frac{4}{1}\times\frac{2}{3}=\frac{8}{3}=2\frac{2}{3}$

1.3 **a.**

$$\begin{aligned} 4v-(v-2) &= 7-2(3v-4) \\ 4v-v+2 &= 7-6v+8 \\ 3v+2 &= 15-6v \\ 9v &= 13 \\ v &= \frac{13}{9} \text{ or } 1\frac{4}{9} \end{aligned}$$

b.

$$\begin{aligned} 5.5-3j &= j-3.5 \\ -4j &= -9 \\ j &= \frac{9}{4} \text{ or } 2\frac{1}{4} \end{aligned}$$

1.5 We prove that the points are not on the same line by showing that the slopes for each group of pairs are not equal.

(i) (2, 6) and (1, 1) $m = \dfrac{1-6}{1-2} = \dfrac{-5}{-1} = 5$

(ii) (1, 1) and (−4, 0) $m = \dfrac{0-1}{-4-1} = \dfrac{-1}{-5} = \dfrac{1}{5}$

(iii) (2, 6) and (−4, 0) $m = \dfrac{0-6}{-4-2} = \dfrac{-6}{-6} = 1$

Since the slopes are different for all possible pairs of points, we conclude that the points are not on the same line.

1.7 **a.** $c = 5$ and $a = 4$

b. $c = \dfrac{1}{2}$ and $a = 3$

c. $c = 1$ and $a = \dfrac{2}{3}$

d. $y = 4^x \times 6^x = 24^x$ so, $c = 1$ and $a = 24$

1.9 **a.** Without Excel, we use the strategy of graphing the line by plotting the y-intercept first and using the slope to move to the second point. In the first case, we plot $(0, -4)$ first. Our slope is $\dfrac{1}{2}\left(m = \dfrac{1}{2}\right)$, so from the y-intercept, we move two units to the right and then one unit up. This is where we plot the next point, which ends up at $(2, -3)$. In the second case, we plot $(0, 3)$ first. Our slope is $-4\left(m = -4 = \dfrac{-4}{1}\right)$, so from the y-intercept, we move one unit to the right and four units down. We end up at $(1, -1)$.

b. In Excel, we enter data in two columns, the x column and y column. We place any values of choice in the x column, normally −2, −1, 0, 1, and 2. In the y column beside the first x value, we enter the formula for our line. In the first case, for example, we enter in cell B2 the following formula, =1/2*A2−4, as shown. After pressing *Enter*, we grab the fill handle and scroll down so that values automatically fill in based on the same formula:

From here, we highlight all values in the x and y columns, including the headings and click on the Insert tab. From here, we choose either of the line graphs underneath the *Scatter* command, shown here:

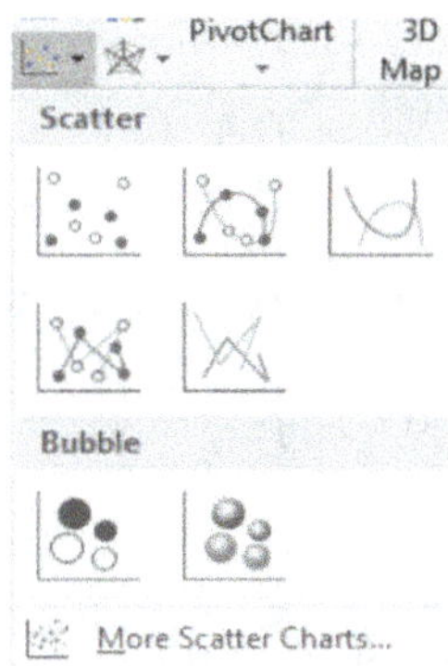

Once we click on the appropriate graph, we are able to see the graph of the line:

Graph of $y = \frac{1}{2}x - 4$

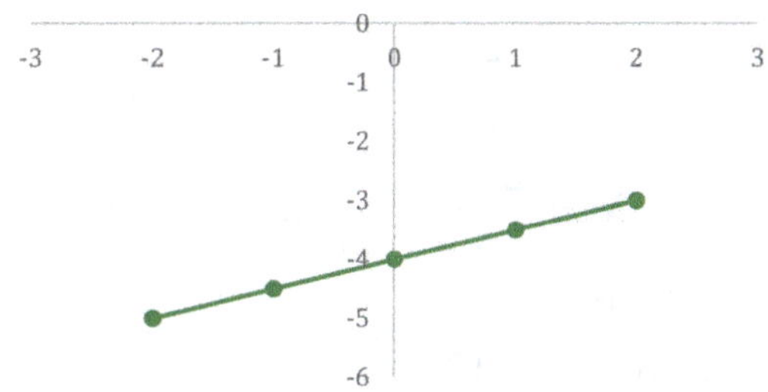

Following similar steps to get the graph above, we are able to obtain the graph of the second equation.

Graph of $y = -4x + 3$

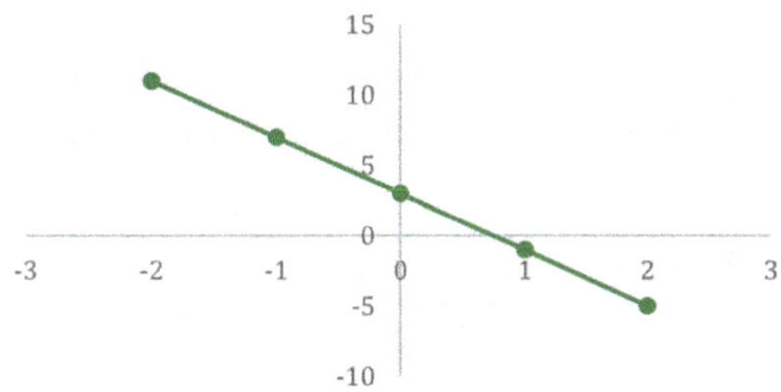

Asset Two

2.1 a. We solve for I in the interest formula:

$$\begin{aligned} I &= P \cdot r \cdot t \\ &= (2230)(0.0245)(3) \\ &= 163.91 \end{aligned}$$

Jill has earned a total interest of \$163.91.

b. We solve for A in the maturity value formula:

$$\begin{aligned} A &= P + I \\ &= 2230 + 163.91 \\ &= 2393.91 \end{aligned}$$

The maturity value for Jill's account is \$2393.91.

2.3 **a.** We solve for P in the maturity value formula:

$$\begin{aligned} A &= P + I \\ A &= P + P \cdot r \cdot t \\ A &= P(1 + r \cdot t) \\ 7700 &= P(1 + 0.0354 \cdot 4) \\ 7700 &= P(1.1416) \\ 6744.92 &= P \end{aligned}$$

Alvin's principal was \$6744.92.

2.5 We solve for t in the compound interest formula:

$$\begin{aligned} A &= P\left(1 + \frac{r}{c}\right)^{ct} \\ 2290 &= 1784\left(1 + \frac{0.0611}{52}\right)^{52t} \\ \frac{2290}{1784} &= (1.001175)^{52t} \\ \log\left(\frac{2290}{1784}\right) &= 52t \log(1.001175) \\ \frac{0.108440632}{52 \log(1.001175)} &= t \\ \frac{0.108440632}{0.026519816} &= t \\ 4.089 &= t \end{aligned}$$

It takes approximately four years and one month for such growth to occur.

2.7 We use the continuous compound formula and solve for P. We can only enter t in terms of years, but it is given as years and months. Time is given as four years and three months. So we convert the months to years:

$$\frac{3\text{ months}}{1} \times \frac{1\text{ year}}{12\text{ months}} = 0.25\text{ years}$$

Our total time in years is 4.25. So in our continuous compound formula, we use 4.25 as our t.

$$\begin{aligned} A &= Pe^{rt} \\ 3109 &= Pe^{0.0299(4.25)} \\ 3109 &= Pe^{0.127075} \\ \frac{3109}{e^{0.127075}} &= P \\ 2738 &= P \end{aligned}$$

Roberto would have to deposit \$2738.00.

2.9 **a.** Solve for A in the continuous compound formula. Derek would have \$3839.76 in his account at the end of seven years.

b. We use the answer that we obtained in **a.** and solve for P.

$$3839.76 = Pe^{0.06(7)}$$
$$\frac{3839.76}{e^{0.06(7)}} = P$$
$$2522.90 = P$$

Derek would have to deposit $2522.90 for his account to reach this new amount.

2.11 a. We use the simple interest equation in Excel: $A = P + P \cdot r \cdot t$

In Excel, we set up the table, placing time in years in the rows and interest rates in columns. We enter the *simple interest formula*, referencing values for P, r, and t, respectively. We solve for A. For the principal (P), we click on the appropriate cell and fix it as an absolute reference in the formula since that value remains constant throughout the chart. We do this by inserting dollar signs in front of the column and row references. For the time in years (t) and interest rates (r), we use mixed references, placing dollar signs in appropriate locations in the formula. The initial chart and formula follows:

	A	B	C	D	E	F	G	H	I	J
1					P =	$1,000				
2										
3						INTEREST	RATES			
4		TIME		2%	3%	4%	5%	6%	7%	8%
5		IN	15	=$F$1+$F$1*$C5*D$4						
6		YEARS	30							

Once we drag and scroll across and down, all value in the chart fill in. The entire Excel chart will look as follows:

	A	B	C	D	E	F	G	H	I	J
1					P =	$1,000				
2										
3						INTEREST	RATES			
4		TIME		2%	3%	4%	5%	6%	7%	8%
5		IN	15	$1,300	$1,450	$1,600	$1,750	$1,900	$2,050	$2,200
6		YEARS	30	$1,600	$1,900	$2,200	$2,500	$2,800	$3,100	$3,400

b. According to **a.**, the future value amount at 8% and 30 years is $3400. The amount we would have to invest (P) at 2% to get this amount is shown by the following formula:

$$A = P + P \cdot r \cdot t$$
$$A = P(1 + r \cdot t)$$
$$\frac{A}{(1 + r \cdot t)} = P$$

So we put the following formula in Excel, where the ratio is referenced by the values in the chart:

	A	B	C	D	E	F	G	H	I	J
1					P =	$1,000				
2										
3						INTEREST	RATES			
4		TIME		2%	3%	4%	5%	6%	7%	8%
5		IN	15	$1,300	$1,450	$1,600	$1,750	$1,900	$2,050	$2,200
6		YEARS	30	$1,600	$1,900	$2,200	$2,500	$2,800	$3,100	$3,400
7										
8										
9										
10			Find the new P for part b:			=J6/(1+D4*C6)				

This gives us a P of $2125.00, as verified by Excel:

				INTEREST	RATES			
TIME		2%	3%	4%	5%	6%	7%	8%
IN	15	$1,300	$1,450	$1,600	$1,750	$1,900	$2,050	$2,200
YEARS	30	$1,600	$1,900	$2,200	$2,500	$2,800	$3,100	$3,400
	Find the new P for part b:			$2,125				

2.13 a. We use the continuous compound equation in Excel: $A = Pe^{rt}$

In Excel, we set up the table, placing time in years in the rows and interest rates in columns. We enter the *continuous compound formula*, referencing values for P, r, and t, respectively. We solve for A. For the principal (P), we click on the appropriate cell and fix it as an absolute reference in the formula since that value remains constant throughout the chart. We do this by inserting dollar signs in front of the column and row references. For the time in years (t) and interest rates (r), we use mixed references, placing dollar signs in appropriate locations in the formula. The initial chart and formula follows:

	A	B	C	D	E	F	G	H	I	J
1					P =	$1,000				
2										
3						INTEREST	RATES			
4		TIME		2%	3%	4%	5%	6%	7%	8%
5		IN	15	=$F$1*EXP($C5*D$4)						
6		YEARS	30							

Once we drag and scroll across and down, all value in the chart fill in. The entire Excel chart will look as follows:

	A	B	C	D	E	F	G	H	I	J
1					P =	$1,000				
2										
3						INTEREST	RATES			
4		TIME		2%	3%	4%	5%	6%	7%	8%
5		IN	15	$1,349.86	$1,568.31	$1,822.12	$2,117.00	$2,459.60	$2,857.65	$3,320.12
6		YEARS	30	$1,822.12	$2,459.60	$3,320.12	$4,481.69	$6,049.65	$8,166.17	$11,023.18

b. According to **a.**, the future value amount at 8% and 30 years is $11,023.18. The amount we would have to invest (P) at 2% to get this amount is shown by the following formula:

$$A = Pe^{rt}$$
$$\Rightarrow \frac{A}{e^{rt}} = P$$

So we put the following formula in Excel, where the ratio is referenced by the values in the chart:

	A	B	C	D	E	F	G	H	I	J
1					P =	$1,000				
2										
3						INTEREST	RATES			
4		TIME		2%	3%	4%	5%	6%	7%	8%
5		IN	15	$1,349.86	$1,568.31	$1,822.12	$2,117.00	$2,459.60	$2,857.65	$3,320.12
6		YEARS	30	$1,822.12	$2,459.60	$3,320.12	$4,481.69	$6,049.65	$8,166.17	$11,023.18
7										
8										
9										
10			Find the new P for part b:			=J6/(EXP(D4*C6))				

This gives us a P of $6049.65, as verified by Excel:

				INTEREST	RATES			
TIME		2%	3%	4%	5%	6%	7%	8%
IN	15	$1,349.86	$1,568.31	$1,822.12	$2,117.00	$2,459.60	$2,857.65	$3,320.12
YEARS	30	$1,822.12	$2,459.60	$3,320.12	$4,481.69	$6,049.65	$8,166.17	$11,023.18
	Find the new P for part b:			$6,049.65				

Asset Three

3.1 a. We find 15% of the population: $(250{,}000)(0.15) = 37{,}500$

We expect 37,500 people out of 250,000 to have a score between 650 and 699.

b. We first find 5% of the population: (250,000)(0.05) = 12,500

We then find 71% of this result: (12,500)(0.71) = 8875

Out of 250,000 people, we expect 8875 to have a score between 500 and 549 and who are also delinquent on payments.

3.3 **Method One**

The monthly payment is $442.04 in Example 3.3 and $428.18 in Example 3.4. This means that each month, the savings is $13.86. In four years, we calculate the total savings for four years or 48 months to get:

$$(13.86)(48) = 665.28$$

Method Two

The total interest paid in Example 3.3 is given by:

$$(442.04)(48) - 19{,}500 = 1717.92$$

The total interest paid in Example 3.4 is given by:

$$(428.18)(48) - 19{,}500 = 1052.64$$

The overall savings by finding the difference:

$$1717.92 - 1052.64 = 665.28$$

Using either method, we see that Tom saved a total of $665.28.

3.5 We solve for *PMT* in Equation 3.1. Note that our time is entered as $t = 1.5$:

$$2198.26 = \frac{PMT\left[1 - \left(\frac{0.1977}{12} + 1\right)^{-12(1.5)}\right]}{\frac{0.1977}{12}}$$

When we solve for *PMT*, we find that the monthly payment is $142.12.

3.7 At 4.1%, we first solve for *PMT* in:

$$329{,}800 = \frac{PMT\left[1 - \left(\frac{0.041}{12} + 1\right)^{-12(30)}\right]}{\frac{0.041}{12}}$$

The value for *PMT* is $1593.59. So, the total interest over the 360-month (30-year) period is:

$$\text{Total Interest Paid} = (1593.59)(360) - 329{,}800 = 243{,}892.40$$

At 3.66%, we solve for *PMT* in:

$$329,800 = \frac{PMT\left[1 - \left(\frac{0.0366}{12} + 1\right)^{-12(30)}\right]}{\frac{0.0366}{12}}$$

The value for *PMT* = \$1510.56. So, the total interest over the 360-month period is:

$$\text{Total Interest Paid} = (1510.56)(360) - 329,800 = 214,001.60$$

Finally, the total amount saved over the 30-year period is the difference in interest for both interest rate scenarios, or \$29,890.80

$$\text{Total Savings} = 243,892.40 - 214,001.60 = 29,890.80$$

3.9 We solve for *PMT* in the following two annuity formulas, distinguished only by the repayment time period:

20 Years

$$841,000 = \frac{PMT\left[1 - \left(\frac{0.0394}{12} + 1\right)^{-12(20)}\right]}{\frac{0.0394}{12}}$$

30 Years

$$841,000 = \frac{PMT\left[1 - \left(\frac{0.0394}{12} + 1\right)^{-12(30)}\right]}{\frac{0.0394}{12}}$$

For 20 years, *PMT* = \$5069.74. For 30 years, *PMT* = \$3986.03

After 20 years, we pay \$375,737.60 in total interest:

$$\text{Total Interest Paid} = (5069.74)(240) - 841,000 = 375,737.60$$

After 30 years, we pay \$593,970.80 in total interest:

$$\text{Total Interest Paid} = (3986.03)(360) - 841,000 = 593,970.80$$

So, our completed table looks as such:

Charlie's Home Loan	Monthly Payment	Total Interest Paid
20 years	\$5069.74	\$375,737.60
30 years	\$3986.03	\$593,970.80

3.11 a. We use the present value of an annuity equation in Excel:

$$PVA = \frac{PMT\left[1 - \left(\frac{r}{c} + 1\right)^{-ct}\right]}{\frac{r}{c}}$$

In Excel, we set up the table, placing time in years in the rows and interest rates in columns. We enter a version of the *present value of an annuity formula*, referencing values for *PVA*, *r*, *c*, and *t*, respectively. We solve for *PMT*. To do this, we enter the formula in Excel based on solving for the *PMT* variable, referenced as follows:

$$PVA = \frac{PMT\left[1 - \left(\frac{r}{c} + 1\right)^{-ct}\right]}{\frac{r}{c}}$$

$$\Rightarrow PMT = \frac{PVA\left(\frac{r}{c}\right)}{\left[1 - \left(\frac{r}{c} + 1\right)^{-ct}\right]}$$

This is the formula we enter in Excel using the cells in which the variables appear.

For the annuity value (*PVA*) and compounding period (*c*), we click on the appropriate cells and fix them as absolute references in the formula since those values remain constant throughout the chart. We do this by inserting dollar signs in front of the column and row references. For the time in years (*t*), compounding period (*c*), and interest rates (*r*), we use mixed references, placing dollar signs in appropriate locations in those cells. The initial chart and formula follows:

	A	B	C	D	E	F	G	H	I
1					PVA =	$100,000		c =	12
2									
3						INTEREST	RATES		
4				3%	4%	5%	6%	7%	8%
5			10	=($F$1*D$4/$I$1)/(1-(D$4/$I$1+1)^(-$I$1*$C5))					
6		TIME	15						
7		IN	20						
8		YEARS	25						
9			30						

Once we drag and scroll across and down, all value in the chart fill in. The entire Excel chart will look as follows:

	A	B	C	D	E	F	G	H	I	J	K
4				3%	4%	5%	6%	7%	8%	9%	10%
5			10	$ 965.61	$1,012.45	$ 1,060.66	$1,110.21	$1,161.08	$1,213.28	$1,266.76	$1,321.51
6		TIME	15	$ 690.58	$ 739.69	$ 790.79	$ 843.86	$ 898.83	$ 955.65	$1,014.27	$1,074.61
7		IN	20	$ 554.60	$ 605.98	$ 659.96	$ 716.43	$ 775.30	$ 836.44	$ 899.73	$ 965.02
8		YEARS	25	$ 474.21	$ 527.84	$ 584.59	$ 644.30	$ 706.78	$ 771.82	$ 839.20	$ 908.70
9			30	$ 421.60	$ 477.42	$ 536.82	$ 599.55	$ 665.30	$ 733.76	$ 804.62	$ 877.57

Note that monthly payments are lowest when there is a higher interest rate paid over the longest time.

b. To find the total interest paid during the life of the loan, we use the *PMT* values in **a.** as a starting point. We simply take each value of *PMT* and multiply it by how many times we make that monthly payment throughout the duration of the loan repayment. Once we compute that total repayment amount, we subtract the original amount of the loan, which is \$100,000. In general, then, we calculate the total interest paid by the following formula:

$$\text{Total Interest Paid} = (PMT)(c \cdot t) - PVA$$

Using values in **a.**, we enter this formula in Excel. The absolute references are *PVA*, the original amount of the loan, and *c*, the compounding period. These will have double dollar signs to attached to their cell references. The monthly payments (*PMT*) will have no dollar signs attached to their cell references because we wish for them to change at every stage when we drag the fill handle. The time (*t*) will only change as we scroll downward, not across. So it will have a mixed cell reference or one dollar sign attached. In Excel, the formula we enter looks as follows:

	A	B	C	D	E	F	G	H	I	J	K
1					PVA =	$100,000		c =	12		
2											
3						INTEREST	RATES				
4				3%	4%	5%	6%	7%	8%	9%	10%
5			10	$ 965.61	$1,012.45	$ 1,060.66	$ 1,110.21	$1,161.08	$1,213.28	$1,266.76	$1,321.51
6		TIME	15	$ 690.58	$ 739.69	$ 790.79	$ 843.86	$ 898.83	$ 955.65	$1,014.27	$1,074.61
7		IN	20	$ 554.60	$ 605.98	$ 659.96	$ 716.43	$ 775.30	$ 836.44	$ 899.73	$ 965.02
8		YEARS	25	$ 474.21	$ 527.84	$ 584.59	$ 644.30	$ 706.78	$ 771.82	$ 839.20	$ 908.70
9			30	$ 421.60	$ 477.42	$ 536.82	$ 599.55	$ 665.30	$ 733.76	$ 804.62	$ 877.57
10											
11											
12						TOTAL	INTEREST	PAID			
13				3%	4%	5%	6%	7%	8%	9%	10%
14			10	=D5*$I$1*$C14-$F$1							
15		TIME	15								
16		IN	20								
17		YEARS	25								
18			30								

Once we drag and scroll across and down, all value in the chart fill in. The entire Excel chart will look as follows:

	A	B	C	D	E	F	G	H	I	J	K
1					PVA =	$100,000		c =	12		
2											
3						INTEREST	RATES				
4				3%	4%	5%	6%	7%	8%	9%	10%
5			10	$ 965.61	$ 1,012.45	$ 1,060.66	$ 1,110.21	$ 1,161.08	$ 1,213.28	$ 1,266.76	$ 1,321.51
6		TIME	15	$ 690.58	$ 739.69	$ 790.79	$ 843.86	$ 898.83	$ 955.65	$ 1,014.27	$ 1,074.61
7		IN	20	$ 554.60	$ 605.98	$ 659.96	$ 716.43	$ 775.30	$ 836.44	$ 899.73	$ 965.02
8		YEARS	25	$ 474.21	$ 527.84	$ 584.59	$ 644.30	$ 706.78	$ 771.82	$ 839.20	$ 908.70
9			30	$ 421.60	$ 477.42	$ 536.82	$ 599.55	$ 665.30	$ 733.76	$ 804.62	$ 877.57
10											
11											
12						TOTAL	INTEREST	PAID			
13				3%	4%	5%	6%	7%	8%	9%	10%
14			10	$ 15,872.89	$21,494.17	$ 27,278.62	$ 33,224.60	$ 39,330.18	$ 45,593.11	$ 52,010.93	$ 58,580.88
15		TIME	15	$ 24,304.70	$33,143.83	$ 42,342.85	$ 51,894.23	$ 61,789.09	$ 72,017.38	$ 82,567.99	$ 93,428.92
16		IN	20	$ 33,103.42	$45,435.28	$ 58,389.38	$ 71,943.45	$ 86,071.74	$ 100,745.62	$115,934.25	$131,605.19
17		YEARS	25	$ 42,263.39	$58,351.05	$ 75,377.01	$ 93,290.42	$112,033.76	$ 131,544.87	$151,758.91	$172,610.22
18			30	$ 51,777.45	$71,869.51	$ 93,255.78	$ 115,838.19	$139,508.90	$ 164,155.25	$189,664.14	$215,925.77

Note that we pay back the most in interest when there is a higher interest rate paid over the longest time. So even though our monthly payments are the least (\$877.57) when financed at 10% over a 30-year period, we pay back the most in interest (a whopping \$215,925.77).

Note that the amount we pay back in interest under these parameters is more than the original $100,000 we borrowed for the home. Yikes!

Asset Four

4.1 We solve for *FVA* in Equation 4.1.

$$FVA = \frac{PMT\left[\left(\frac{r}{c}+1\right)^{ct} - 1\right]}{\frac{r}{c}}$$

$$= \frac{411\left[\left(\frac{0.0114}{12}+1\right)^{12(25)} - 1\right]}{\frac{0.0114}{12}}$$

$$= \frac{411\left[(1.00095)^{300} - 1\right]}{0.00095}$$

$$= \frac{411(0.329582138)}{0.00095}$$

$$= 142,587.64$$

Solving for *FVA*, we find that the amount in the retirement account is $142,587.64.

4.3 We solve for *PMT* in Equation 4.1.

$$189,440 = \frac{PMT\left[\left(\frac{0.0219}{12}+1\right)^{12(17)} - 1\right]}{\frac{0.0219}{12}}$$

$$189,440 = \frac{PMT\left[(1.001825)^{204} - 1\right]}{0.001825}$$

$$189,440 = \frac{PMT(0.450575957)}{0.001825}$$

$$189,440 = PMT(246.8909353)$$

$$767.302 = PMT$$

Solving for *PMT*, we see that the contributions are $767.30 per month.

4.5 **a.** We solve for *PMT* in Equation 4.1 when Denise makes monthly contributions ($c = 12$).

$$400{,}000 = \frac{PMT\left[\left(\frac{0.0352}{12}+1\right)^{12(35)}-1\right]}{\frac{0.0352}{12}}$$

$$400{,}000 = \frac{PMT\,(2.421902186)}{0.002933333}$$

$$484.46768 = PMT$$

Contributions would be \$484.47 per month.

b. We solve for *PMT* in Equation 4.1 when Denise makes quarterly contributions ($c = 4$).

$$400{,}000 = \frac{PMT\left[\left(\frac{0.0352}{4}+1\right)^{4(35)}-1\right]}{\frac{0.0352}{4}}$$

$$400{,}000 = \frac{PMT\,(2.409653911)}{0.0088}$$

$$1460.7907 = PMT$$

Contributions would be \$1460.79 per quarter (every three months).

4.7 We first solve for t in Equation 4.1.

$$500{,}000 = \frac{550\left[\left(\frac{0.0444}{12}+1\right)^{12t}-1\right]}{\frac{0.0444}{12}}$$

$$500{,}000 = \frac{550\left[(1.0037)^{12t}-1\right]}{0.0037}$$

$$4.3636363 = (1.0037)^{12t}$$

$$\log(4.3636363) = 12t\log(1.0037)$$

$$\frac{\log(4.3636363)}{12\log(1.0037)} = t$$

$$33.25 \approx t$$

It takes approximately 33 years and three months to reach \$500,000 in the retirement account. If the goal is to retire at 60, then she must start saving at 60 − 33.25 years of age, or 26.75, which is roughly 27 years old.

4.9 We first solve for *PMT* in Equation 4.1 when the retirement goal is \$315,000.

$$315{,}000 = \frac{PMT\left[\left(\frac{0.032}{12}+1\right)^{12(40)}-1\right]}{\frac{0.032}{12}}$$

$$315{,}000 = \frac{PMT\,(2.590517566)}{0.002666667}$$

$$324.2595673 = PMT$$

Solving for *PMT*, we see that the contributions should be \$324.26 per month to guarantee a retirement of \$315,000.

Then, we solve for PMT when the retirement goal is \$415,000.

$$415{,}000 = \frac{PMT\left[\left(\frac{0.032}{12}+1\right)^{12(40)}-1\right]}{\frac{0.032}{12}}$$

$$415{,}000 = \frac{PMT\,(2.590517566)}{0.002666667}$$

$$427.1991124 = PMT$$

Solving for *PMT*, we see that the contributions should be \$427.20 per month to guarantee a retirement of \$415,000.

This means we have to invest \$102.94 more per month to have a retirement of \$415,000 instead of \$315,000 (\$427.20 − \$324.26 = \$102.94).

Asset Five

5.1 a. The allotment for food is 10%. Or we have 3050(0.10) = 305. So, he should allot \$305 for food.
b. The allotment for transportation is 15%. Or we have 3050(0.15) = 457.50. So, he should allot \$457.50 for transportation.
c. The allotment for housing (and utilities) is 30%. Or we have 3050(0.30) = 915. So, he should allot \$915 for housing costs.

5.3 The annual gross salary is \$73,729, which translates into 24 payments of \$3072.04 for the year, or $\frac{73{,}729}{24} = 3072.04$. A total of 1.45% of the payment is taken for mandatory Medicare expenses (FICA Med Tax), while 6.2% is paid for mandatory social security taxes (FICA SS Tax).

Hence, for mandatory Medicare expenses, we have 3072.04(0.0145) = 44.54458. So, \$44.54 is taken out for the FICA Med Tax.

For mandatory social security taxes, we have 3072.04(0.062) = 190.46648. So, $190.47 is taken out for the FICA SS Tax.

5.5 We use Gereen's gross salary at $95,820 as a starting point in both scenarios to find the requested information.

a. First, we figure out her 2016 federal taxable income using the federal standard deduction ($6300) and federal personal exemption ($4050), which are verified at https://goo.gl/1Z2Zg4. Her taxable income is:

$95,820 *(gross salary)*
– $6,300 *(federal standard deduction)*
– $4,050 *(federal personal exemption)*

$85,470 *(federal taxable income)*

Taxable Income Between ...	2016 Tax Due Is ...
$0 and $9275	10% of taxable income
$9276 and $37,650	$927.50 + 15% of amount over $9275
$37,651 and $91,150	$5183.75 + 25% of amount over $37,650
$91,151 and $190,150	$18,558.75 + 28% of amount over $91,150
$190,151 and $413,350	$46,278.75 + 33% of amount over $190,150
$413,351 and $415,050	$119,934.75 + 35% of amount over $413,350
$415,051 +	$120,529.75 + 39.6% of amount over $415,050

Now, we figure out how much she owes in federal taxes. Her taxable income of $85,470 falls within the federal tax bracket of $37,651 and $91,150. In this bracket, she is responsible for paying a base of $5183.75 plus 25% of her salary amount that exceeds $37,650. The amount that exceeds $37,650 is $47,820 (or $85,470 – $37,650). So we have:

$$\begin{aligned}\text{Federal Taxes} &= 5183.75 + (0.25)47,820\\ &= 5183.75 + 11,955\\ &= 17,138.75\end{aligned}$$

Hence, Gereen's federal tax due for 2016 is $17,138.75.

b. We figure out her 2016 state taxable income using the standard deduction for Maine ($11,600) and personal exemption for Maine ($4050), which are verified at http://goo.gl/sSdyvm. Her taxable income is:

$95,820 *(gross salary)*
– $11,600 *(standard deduction for Maine)*
– $4,050 *(personal exemption for Maine)*

$80,170 *(taxable income for Maine)*

To find how much she owes in state taxes, we use her taxable income of $80,170 and percentages specific to Maine, also referenced at the following: http://goo.gl/sSdyvm. They are as follows:

Portion of Taxable Income ...	2016 Tax Due Is ...
From $0 to $21,049	5.80%
From $21,050 to $37,499	6.75%
Above $37,499	7.15%

Range	Amount of Taxable Income	Applied Percentage
$0–$21,049	$21,049	21,049(0.0580) = 1220.84
$21,050–$37,499	$16,450	16,450(0.0675) = 1110.38
$37500 and above	$42,671	42,671(0.0715) = 3050.98

Thus, Gereen's state tax due for 2016 is $5382.20, the sum of the values in the Applied Percentage column.

5.7 With no pre-tax deductions, our taxable income for 2016 is:

$49,355 (*income*)
– $6300 (*standard deduction*)
– $4050 (*personal exemption*)
$39,005 (*taxable income*)

With pretax deductions, our taxable income for 2016 is:

$49,355 (*income*)
– $6300 (*standard deduction*)
– $4050 (*personal exemption*)
– $5822 (*401 (k)*)
– $1725 (*FSA*)
– $2400 (*preapproved parking*)
$29,058 (*taxable income*)

Our 2016 taxable income of $39,005 falls within the range tier of $37,651 and $91,150. The amount of federal taxes owed for this tier is $5183.75 + 25% of the taxable income amount over $37,650. The amount over $37,650 is $1355 ($39,005 − $37,650). So, we have:

$$\begin{aligned}\text{Federal Taxes} &= 5183.75 + (0.25)1355\\ &= 5183.75 + 338.75\\ &= 5522.50\end{aligned}$$

Our 2016 taxable income of \$29,058 falls within the range tier of \$9276 and \$37,650. The amount of federal taxes owed for this tier is \$927.50 + 15% of the taxable income amount over \$9275. The amount over \$9275 is \$19,783 (\$29,058 − \$9275). So, we have:

$$\begin{aligned}\text{Federal Taxes} &= 927.50 + (0.15)19{,}783 \\ &= 927.50 + 2967.45 \\ &= 3894.95\end{aligned}$$

Hence, if you did not make these pretax contributions, you would have paid \$1627.55 *more* in federal taxes in 2016 (\$5522.50 − \$3894.95).

5.9 Answers shown here reflect income and deductions for 2016. Answers may vary, depending on notable changes to the Internal Revenue Service calculator for subsequent years.

Based on data provided, anticipated federal tax due for 2016 would be \$458. Such is verified from the IRS results page, shown here:

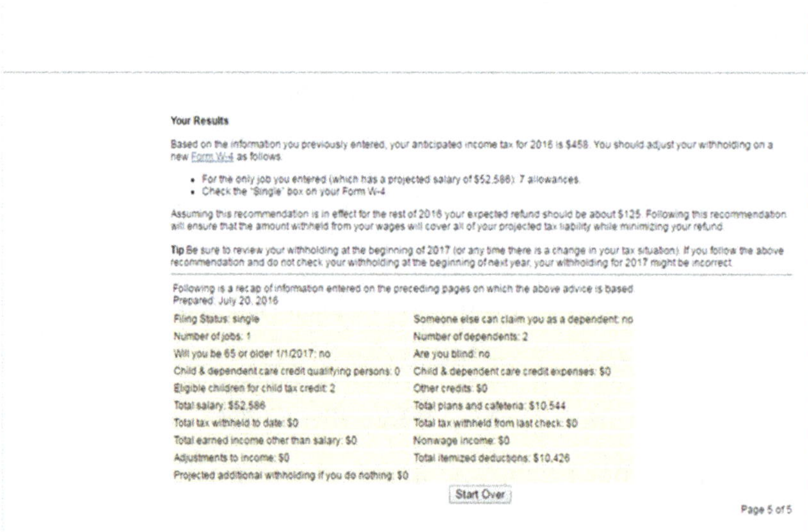

Your Results

Based on the information you previously entered, your anticipated income tax for 2016 is \$458. You should adjust your withholding on a new Form W-4 as follows.

- For the only job you entered (which has a projected salary of \$52,586): 7 allowances.
- Check the "Single" box on your Form W-4

Assuming this recommendation is in effect for the rest of 2016 your expected refund should be about \$125. Following this recommendation will ensure that the amount withheld from your wages will cover all of your projected tax liability while minimizing your refund.

Tip Be sure to review your withholding at the beginning of 2017 (or any time there is a change in your tax situation). If you follow the above recommendation and do not check your withholding at the beginning of next year, your withholding for 2017 might be incorrect.

Following is a recap of information entered on the preceding pages on which the above advice is based
Prepared: July 20, 2016

Filing Status: single	Someone else can claim you as a dependent: no
Number of jobs: 1	Number of dependents: 2
Will you be 65 or older 1/1/2017: no	Are you blind: no
Child & dependent care credit qualifying persons: 0	Child & dependent care credit expenses: \$0
Eligible children for child tax credit: 2	Other credits: \$0
Total salary: \$52,586	Total plans and cafeteria: \$10,544
Total tax withheld to date: \$0	Total tax withheld from last check: \$0
Total earned income other than salary: \$0	Nonwage income: \$0
Adjustments to income: \$0	Total itemized deductions: \$10,426
Projected additional withholding if you do nothing: \$0	

Start Over

Page 5 of 5

Asset Six

6.1 Since the number of bedrooms generally determines, explains, or justifies the asking price, then the number of bedrooms would be the *explanatory* variable. The asking price of the Chelsea loft would be the *response* variable.

6.3 **a.** The scatterplot for the data is shown:

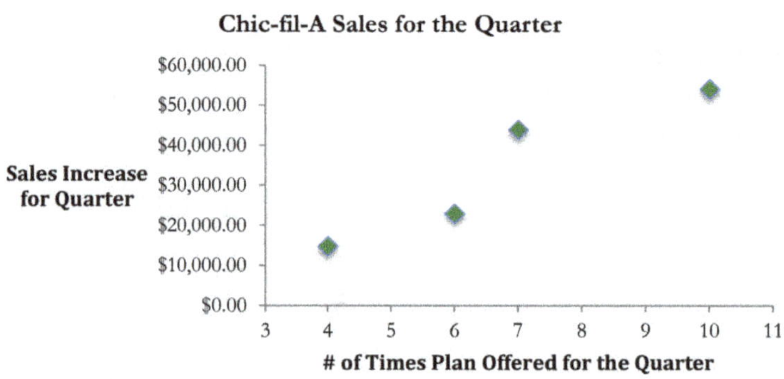

b. Using the values for the slope and y-intercept in 6.2, we have a least-squares regression equation that is given by:

$$\hat{y} = 6856.96x - 12,364.5$$

c. When $x = 5$, we have:

$$\begin{aligned}\hat{y}(5) &= 6856.96(5) - 12,364.5\\ &= 34,284.8 - 12,364.5\\ &= 21,920.3\end{aligned}$$

Hence, when the free meal plan is offered five times during the quarter, the sales increase for the quarter is predicted to be \$21,920.30.

When $x = 9$, we have:

$$\begin{aligned}\hat{y}(5) &= 6856.96(9) - 12,364.5\\ &= 61,712.64 - 12,364.5\\ &= 49,348.14\end{aligned}$$

Thus, when the free-meal plan is offered nine times during the quarter, the sales increase for the quarter is predicted to be \$49,348.14.

d. The scatterplot with regression line drawn is shown below:

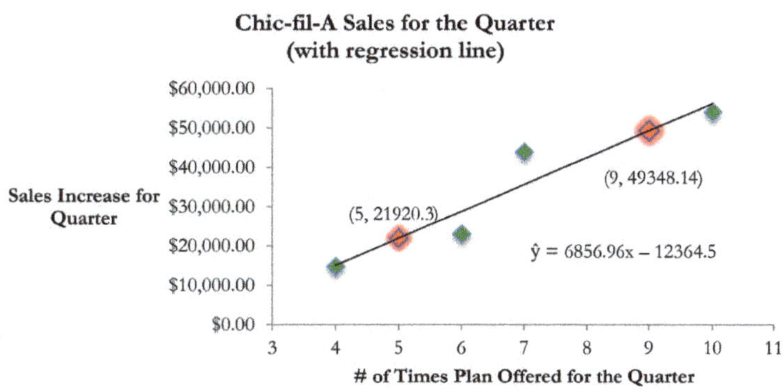

6.5 **a.** The slope in the regression equation is $-0.15\left(m = -0.15 = \dfrac{-0.15}{1}\right)$. In this scenario, the interpretation of the slope is that for every \$1 that students earn per month during the fall semester, students' grade point average (GPA) decreases by 0.15 points.

b. Since $x = 0$ is assumed to be in the range of data values, we may offer an interpretation of the y-intercept. Its proper interpretation is that when students earn no money per month during the fall semester ($x = 0$), students' GPA is predicted to be around 3.01, on average.

6.7 Excel regression results are as follows:

	A	B	C	D	E	F
1	SUMMARY OUTPUT					
2						
3	*Regression Statistics*					
4	Multiple R	0.369975076				
5	R Square	0.136881557				
6	Adjusted R Square	-0.006971517				
7	Standard Error	2117.498327				
8	Observations	8				
9						
10	ANOVA					
11		*df*	*SS*	*MS*	*F*	*Significance F*
12	Regression	1	4266501.893	4266502	0.951537	0.367000665
13	Residual	6	26902794.98	4483799		
14	Total	7	31169296.88			
15						
16		*Coefficients*	*Standard Error*	*t Stat*	*P-value*	*Lower 95%*
17	Intercept	32776.64875	5474.700836	5.98693	0.000976	19380.53839
18	Education	349.7670251	358.5634086	0.975468	0.367001	-527.6060287

a. The correlation coefficient, displayed as "Multiple R" is approximately 0.37 ($r = 0.37$). We conclude that the regression line in this problem, $\hat{y}$, is an unreliable and fairly weak predictor of one's salary given one's education level. There is a weak positive linear relationship between the two variables in this case as r is fairly close to 0.

b. The coefficient of determination, displayed as "R Square" is approximately 0.137 ($r^2 = 0.137$). This means that 13.7% (or 100×0.137) of the variation in one's salary is explained by the variation in one's education level. This means that a whopping 86.3% of the variation (or $100\% - 13.7\%$) in one's salary is explained by the variation in factors other than one's education level.

6.9 a. Regression equation is: $\hat{y} = 4887.52 - 661.09x_2 + 0.96x_3$

Scatterplot:

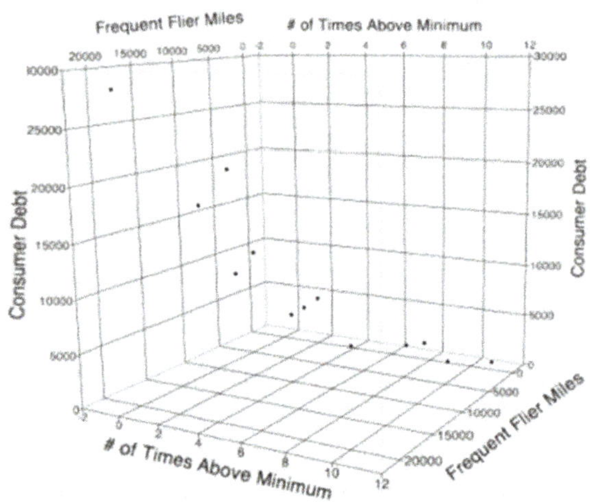

b. Regression equation is: $\hat{y} = 1020.23 + 2.27x_1 - 404.90x_2 + 0.91x_3$

c. The y-intercept occurs when $x_1 = 0$, $x_2 = 0$, and $x_3 = 0$. We verify that $x_1 = 0$, $x_2 = 0$, and $x_3 = 0$ are included in the x ranges of the original data. Since they are, our interpretation of the y-intercept here will be valid. If either of the data columns is missing this zero value, the interpretation would not be valid (because we would not be able to assume a linear association outside of that range). When we place zero in place of these x values, we have $\hat{y} = 1020.23$. So we say that when there are no increases in salary ($x_1 = 0$), no over-the-minimum payments ($x_2 = 0$), and no frequent-flier miles earned ($x_3 = 0$), the predicted credit card debt incurred is predicted to be $1020.23.

d. We perform a quick check first to be sure all three values are with the ranges for their respective columns. If even only one of the values is outside of the range for its respective column, we would not be able to offer a prediction, as we would not be able to assume a linear relationship outside of this range. Since all values fall within column ranges, we proceed to find the requested prediction:

$$\begin{aligned}\hat{y} &= 1020.23 + 2.27x_1 - 404.90x_2 + 0.91x_3 \\ &= 1020.23 + 2.27(1500) - 404.90(4) + 0.91(8500) \\ &= 1020.23 + 3405 - 1619.6 + 7735 \\ &= 10{,}540.63\end{aligned}$$

When consumers received a salary increase of $1500, paid more than minimum payments four times, and gained 8500 frequent flyer miles, the predicted credit card debt is $10,540.63.

e. Since $x_1 = \$5000$ falls outside of the data range of given x_1 values ($0–$2900), then we are not able to predict the credit card debt in this instance.

Asset Seven

7.1 At $48.03 per share, the price of 24 shares is represented by:

a. $\dfrac{\$48.03}{\text{share}} \cdot \dfrac{24 \text{ shares}}{1} = \$1152.72$

You pay a total of $1152.72 for the MSFT shares.

b. If you have $775 and shares are $39 per share, the number of shares purchased is represented by:

$$\frac{\$775}{\$39/\text{share}} = \frac{\$775}{1} \cdot \frac{1 \text{ share}}{\$39} \approx 19.87 \text{ shares}$$

You are able to secure approximately 19.87 HSY shares.

7.3 a. To find the new value, we find the amount of decrease first:

$$\begin{aligned} \frac{\text{amount of decrease}}{\text{base amount}} &= \frac{\text{percent}}{100} \\ \Rightarrow \quad \frac{x}{109{,}000} &= \frac{5.7}{100} \\ \Rightarrow \quad 621{,}300 &= 100x \\ \Rightarrow \quad x &= 6213 \end{aligned}$$

Now, we subtract this amount from the base to find the new value, or we have: \$109,000 − \$6213 = \$102,787. Hence, the new value of Melody's retirement portfolio is \$102,787.

b. The amount of increase in the stock price is \$10.15 (or \$48.27 − \$38.12). The starting or base amount is \$38.12. We use these values to find the percent increase:

$$\begin{aligned}
\frac{\text{amount of increase}}{\text{base amount}} &= \frac{\text{percent}}{100} \\
\Rightarrow \qquad \frac{10.15}{38.12} &= \frac{x}{100} \\
\Rightarrow \qquad 1015 &= 38.12x \\
\Rightarrow \qquad 26.63 &= x
\end{aligned}$$

This represents a 26.63% increase in the stock price.

7.5 a. The SMA(5) value for Wednesday is based on the five shoe sales values from Monday through Friday. In this case, we simply find the average of all five values to get:

$$\text{SMA(5) for Wednesday} = \frac{7388 + 9344 + 4887 + 7190 + 11987}{5} = 8159.2$$

Hence, Wednesday's SMA(5) value is \$8159.20.

b. Saturday's shoe sales are related to Thursday's SMA(5) value. The SMA(5) value for Thursday is based on the five values for shoe sales from Tuesday through Saturday. We solve for x, where x represents Saturday's shoe sales:

$$\begin{aligned}
\frac{9344 + 4887 + 7190 + 11987 + x}{5} &= 9921.33 \\
\Rightarrow \qquad \frac{33{,}408 + x}{5} &= 9921.33 \\
\Rightarrow \qquad 33{,}408 + x &= 49{,}606.65 \\
\Rightarrow \qquad x &= 16{,}198.65
\end{aligned}$$

Hence, shoe sales for Saturday are valued at \$16,198.65.

7.7 a. The resulting columns, divided into two sets, are as follows:

	A	B	C	D	E	F	G
1	Year	Homes Sold	EWMA(λ=0.8)		Year	Homes Sold	EWMA(λ=0.8)
2	1964	565	565.00		1990	534	558.30
3	1965	575	=0.8*B3+0.2*C2		1991	509	518.86
4	1966	461	483.40		1992	610	591.77
5	1967	487	486.28		1993	666	651.15
6	1968	490	489.26		1994	670	666.23
7	1969	448	456.25		1995	667	666.85
8	1970	485	479.25		1996	757	738.97
9	1971	656	620.65		1997	804	790.99
10	1972	718	698.53		1998	886	867.00
11	1973	634	646.91		1999	880	877.40
12	1974	519	544.58		2000	877	877.08
13	1975	549	548.12		2001	908	901.82
14	1976	646	626.42		2002	973	958.76
15	1977	819	780.48		2003	1086	1060.55
16	1978	817	809.70		2004	1203	1174.51
17	1979	709	729.14		2005	1283	1261.30
18	1980	545	581.83		2006	1051	1093.06
19	1981	436	465.17		2007	776	839.41
20	1982	412	422.63		2008	485	555.88
21	1983	623	582.93		2009	375	411.18
22	1984	639	627.79		2010	323	340.64
23	1985	688	675.96		2011	306	312.93
24	1986	750	735.19		2012	368	356.99
25	1987	671	683.84		2013	429	414.60
26	1988	676	677.57		2014	437	432.52
27	1989	650	655.51		2015	501	487.30

Values in B2 and C2 will always be the same. The formula to find exponential weighted moving average (EWMA) values is shown in cell C3.

b. Plots of the original housing data and the EWMA column are shown here:

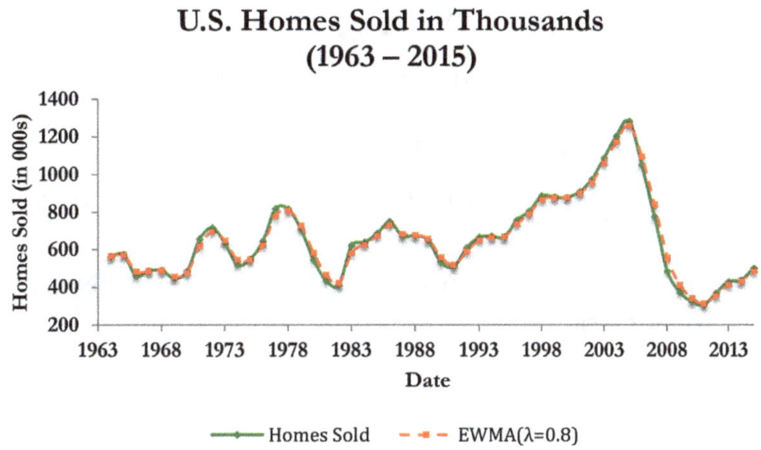

c. Although not noticeably apparent, the EWMA seems to reveal that there is an overall increasing trend, despite decreasing home sales from 2007 onward (probably as a result of the famous recession).

7.9 a. For the EWMA value for the number of museum visitors between 3:00pm and 4:00pm, we find as follows:

$$\begin{aligned} \text{EWMA}_{3:00\text{pm}-4:00\text{pm}} &= \lambda Y_{3:00\text{pm}-4:00\text{pm}} + (1-\lambda)\text{EWMA}_{2:00\text{pm}-3:00\text{pm}} \\ &= (0.4)(24) + (0.6)(25) \\ &= 24.6 \end{aligned}$$

The requested EWMA value is 24.6.

b. To find the approximate number of museum visitors from 5:00pm to 6:00pm, we find as follows:

$$\begin{aligned} \text{EWMA}_{5:00\text{pm}-6:00\text{pm}} &= \lambda Y_{5:00\text{pm}-6:00\text{pm}} + (1-\lambda)\text{EWMA}_{4:00\text{pm}-5:00\text{pm}} \\ \Rightarrow \quad 33.90 &= (0.4)Y_{5:00\text{pm}-6:00\text{pm}} + (0.6)(29.16) \\ \Rightarrow \quad 33.90 &= (0.4)Y_{5:00\text{pm}-6:00\text{pm}} + 17.496 \\ \Rightarrow \quad 16.404 &= (0.4)Y_{5:00\text{pm}-6:00\text{pm}} \\ \Rightarrow \quad 41.01 &= Y_{5:00\text{pm}-6:00\text{pm}} \end{aligned}$$

The approximate number of museum visitors during this time is 41 (rounded to the nearest visitor).

c. To forecast the approximate number of visitors during the requested time period, we have the following:

$$\hat{Y}_{t+1} = \lambda Y_t + (1-\lambda)\hat{Y}_t$$

$$\Rightarrow \hat{Y}_{(6{:}00\text{pm}-7{:}00\text{pm})+1} = \lambda Y_{6{:}00\text{pm}-7{:}00\text{pm}} + (1-\lambda)\hat{Y}_{6{:}00\text{pm}-7{:}00\text{pm}}$$

$$\Rightarrow \hat{Y}_{7{:}00\text{pm}-8{:}00\text{pm}} = (0.4)(12) + (0.6)(25.14)$$

$$\Rightarrow \hat{Y}_{7{:}00\text{pm}-8{:}00\text{pm}} = 4.8 + 15.084$$

$$\Rightarrow \hat{Y}_{7{:}00\text{pm}-8{:}00\text{pm}} = 19.884$$

There are approximately 20 visitors that are forecasted to arrive between 7:00pm and 8:00pm (rounded to the nearest visitor).

7.11 a. The resulting columns are as follows:

	A	B	C
1	Year	Closing Price	EWMA(λ=0.3)
2	2004	104.04	104.04
3	2005	127.71	=0.3*B3+0.7*C2
4	2006	199.35	137.60
5	2007	215.05	160.84
6	2008	84.39	137.90
7	2009	168.84	147.18
8	2010	168.16	153.48
9	2011	90.43	134.56
10	2012	127.56	132.46
11	2013	177.26	145.90
12	2014	193.83	160.28
13	2015	180.23	166.27
14	2016	239.45	188.22

Values in B2 and C2 will always be the same. The formula to find EWMA values is shown in cell C3.

b. To forecast the closing price for 2017, we use both the closing price and EWMA value for 2016. We show the formula used in Excel along with the chart with the actual forecasted value filled in.

	A	B	C
1	Year	Closing Price	EWMA(λ=0.3)
2	2004	104.04	104.04
3	2005	127.71	111.14
4	2006	199.35	137.60
5	2007	215.05	160.84
6	2008	84.39	137.90
7	2009	168.84	147.18
8	2010	168.16	153.48
9	2011	90.43	134.56
10	2012	127.56	132.46
11	2013	177.26	145.90
12	2014	193.83	160.28
13	2015	180.23	166.27
14	2016	239.45	188.22
15			
16	2017		=0.3*B14+0.7*C14

	A	B	C
1	Year	Closing Price	EWMA(λ=0.3)
2	2004	104.04	104.04
3	2005	127.71	111.14
4	2006	199.35	137.60
5	2007	215.05	160.84
6	2008	84.39	137.90
7	2009	168.84	147.18
8	2010	168.16	153.48
9	2011	90.43	134.56
10	2012	127.56	132.46
11	2013	177.26	145.90
12	2014	193.83	160.28
13	2015	180.23	166.27
14	2016	239.45	188.22
15			
16	2017		203.59

Using EWMA techniques, the forecasted 2017 value is $203.59.

c. To perform a regression on the data, we insert an Alias Date Counter column to properly index the data in the Year column.

	A	B	C
1	Year	Alias	Closing Price
2	2004	0	104.04
3	2005	1	127.71
4	2006	2	199.35
5	2007	3	215.05
6	2008	4	84.39
7	2009	5	168.84
8	2010	6	168.16
9	2011	7	90.43
10	2012	8	127.56
11	2013	9	177.26
12	2014	10	193.83
13	2015	11	180.23
14	2016	12	239.45

When we run a regression on columns B and C, we get the following partial results in Excel (column B is the x column while column C is the y column):

	A	B	C	D	E	F
1	SUMMARY OUTPUT					
2						
3	*Regression Statistics*					
4	Multiple R	0.41480949				
5	R Square	0.172066913				
6	Adjusted R Square	0.096800269				
7	Standard Error	46.45307327				
8	Observations	13				
9						
10	ANOVA					
11		*df*	*SS*	*MS*	*F*	*Significance F*
12	Regression	1	4933.143141	4933.143	2.2860978	0.158722479
13	Residual	11	23736.76818	2157.888		
14	Total	12	28669.91132			
15						
16		*Coefficients*	*Standard Error*	*t Stat*	*P-value*	*Lower 95%*
17	Intercept	128.4778022	24.34802617	5.276724	0.0002616	74.88815793
18	Alias	5.206263736	3.443330882	1.511985	0.1587225	-2.372456437

Excel results show that the forecasting equation (rounded) is the following:

$$\hat{y} = 5.206x + 128.478$$

d. The next value in the Alias column would be 13, which corresponds to the value for 2017. When we place $x = 13$ into the forecasting equation, we get:

$$\begin{aligned}\hat{y}(13) &= 5.206(13) + 128.478 \\ &= 196.156\end{aligned}$$

Using regression techniques, the Goldman Sachs closing price for 2017 is predicted to be \$196.16.

e. Regression results in c. show that the coefficient of determination is the value beside "R Square," which is approximately 0.172 ($r^2 = 0.172$). At 17.2%, this statistic basically provides a sense of how well the regression line predicts Goldman Sachs closing prices. In this case, this percentage is not particularly comforting since it is notably less than 100%. Hence, this forecast of \$196.16 is terribly unreliable since the percentage of variation in Goldman Sachs closing prices that is explained by the overall trend is very low.

Index

www.ingramcontent.com/pod-product-compliance
Lightning Source LLC
LaVergne TN
LVHW080651011026
849160LV00014B/1383